~ THE ~

# SUNFLOWER

# ~ THE ~
# SUNFLOWER

*On the Possibilities and Limits
of Forgiveness*

## SIMON WIESENTHAL

*with a symposium edited by
Harry James Cargas and Bonny V. Fetterman*

**REVISED AND EXPANDED EDITION**

SCHOCKEN BOOKS   NEW YORK

All rights reserved under international and Pan-American Copyright Conventions. Published in the United States by Schocken Books Inc., New York. Distributed by Pantheon Books, a division of Random House, Inc., New York.

SCHOCKEN and colophon are trademarks of Schocken Books Inc.

This work was originally published in France as *Die Sonnenblume* by Opera Mundi, Paris, in 1969. First English translation published by Opera Mundi, Paris, in 1970. First edition published by Schocken Books in 1976. Symposium contributions by Mark Goulden, Hans Habe, Abraham J. Heschel, Christopher Hollis, Primo Levi, Herbert Marcuse, Martin E. Marty, Cynthia Ozick, Terence Prittie, and Manès Sperber are reprinted here from the 1976 edition. All other symposium contributions are new to this edition.
Mr. Wiesenthal's text was translated from the German by H.A. Pichler. Symposium contributions by Jean Améry, Cardinal Franz König, and Albert Speer were translated from the German by Barbara Harshav and Marianne M. Friedrich. Smail Balić's contribution was translated from the German by Shelley Frisch. Tzvetan Todorov's contribution was translated from the French by Barbara Harshav.

Library of Congress Cataloging-in-Publication Data

Wiesenthal, Simon.
[Sonnenblume. English]
The sunflower : on the possibilities and limits of
forgiveness / Simon Wiesenthal ; edited by Harry James Cargas
and Bonny V. Fetterman.—Rev. and expanded ed.
p.    cm.
ISBN 0-8052-4145-0
1. Wiesenthal, Simon. 2. Wiesenthal, Simon. Sonnenblume.
3. World War, 1939–1945—Personal narratives, Jewish. 4. World War, 1939–1945—Concentration camps. 5. Forgiveness. I. Cargas, Harry J. II. Title.
D810.J4W5313   1997
179.7—dc21                                          96–36831
                                                        CIP

Random House Web Address: http://www.randomhouse.com/

Book design by M. Kristen Bearse

Printed in the United States of America
Second Edition
2   4   6   8   9   7   5   3   1

# CONTENTS

v
~

# CONTENTS

# CONTENTS

# PREFACE

When the first American edition of *The Sunflower* was published by Schocken Books in 1976, courses about the Holocaust had just begun to appear in the curricula of colleges, high schools, and seminaries. Because it's a book that invites discussion, *The Sunflower* soon became one of the most widely used books in teaching settings. Simon Wiesenthal tells a personal story of an incident that occurred in a concentration camp and asks, what would you have done in his place? Theologians, political and moral leaders, and writers responded to his question—a question that is at once religious, political, moral, and personal— each from their own perspective. As would be expected, a wide variety of opinions were expressed. Nevertheless, each and every respondent had to imagine him or herself in the place of a concentration camp prisoner, to face the enormity of the crime before them, and reflect on the implications of their decision. In this one isolated case, was forgiveness an option, and what would it mean for the victim as well as the perpetrator of these crimes?

The twentieth anniversary of its publication in this country is the occasion for a new edition of *The Sunflower*. This second edition presents thirty-two new responses written for this volume, ten retained from the previous edition, and one, by Edward H. Flannery, revised for this edition. Three contributions—by Jean Améry, Cardinal König, and Albert Speer—were translated from the 1981 German edition and appear here for the first time in English translation.

Why a new edition of *The Sunflower*? In light of the events of the last twenty years, we felt it would be interesting to hear the responses of a new generation. On the one hand, time blunts memory; on the other, our knowledge and awareness of the Holocaust has increased through education. Even those who do not have a living memory of the Holocaust have begun to assimilate what it means for a people to lose one-third of its members to genocide, together with their culture, language, and history. The uniqueness of this event has finally started to sink in to the popular consciousness. Moreover, we suspected that the major changes in the Catholic church's teachings about Jews in these years, as well as other interfaith events and developments, would produce responses that differed from the first generation of respondents. Finally, the world has not stopped seeing horrors that approach genocide—in Bosnia, Cambodia, China, and countless other troubled nations around the globe—as whole classes of people are targeted for extinction by criminal regimes. The issue posed by Simon Wiesenthal in this book is still with us, transcending its original context, and forcing itself upon a contemporary one.

Few people would deny the necessity of bringing criminal leaders and policymakers to justice. Wiesenthal's Dokumentationszentrum, which seeks out Nazi criminals, has helped to bring over 1,100 Nazis to justice since the end of the war. For his work, Wiesenthal has been honored by the governments of the United States, Holland, Italy, and Israel. Committed to the necessity of enforcing international law, Wiesenthal wrote to President Clinton in July of 1995, urging him to condemn the organizers of terror in the former Yugoslavia: "The events in Bosnia, as the media portray them for us today, with all their crimes against humanity—the ethnic cleansing, the slaughtering of civilians regardless of age, the rape of Muslim women— while they do not constitute a Holocaust, repeat many of its horrors. . . . I believe that the condemnation of Karadzic and Mladic—verbal, at first—and the threat to put them before a tribunal—would have an effect. The United States could, I hope, put an end to the deeds of these two men and their soldiers by publicly announcing that the crimes they committed will not remain unpunished." The importance to the world of holding such individuals responsible for their crimes is indisputable.

But the question posed in *The Sunflower* is more subtle and, in some sense, more vexing. What about the rank-and-file, the faceless individuals who carry out the crimes against other people ordered by their leaders? What about the individual responsibility of ordinary people, blinded or coerced by the reigning political ideology of their day, and of the small number who may regret their actions or repudiate them in a different climate? We laud the heroic individuals who defy and undermine the immoral actions of their governments, despite the mortal dangers such resistance entails—but what of the converse?

Moreover, when the killing has stopped, how can a people make peace with another who moments before were their mortal enemies? What are the limits of forgiveness, and is repentance—religious or secular—enough? Is it possible to forgive and not forget? How can victims come to peace with their past, and hold on to their own humanity and morals in the process?

All of these issues are raised in this simple and unpretentious book of questioning, based on a single and exceptional encounter between two individuals whose paths strangely and tragically crossed.

BONNY V. FETTERMAN
October 1996

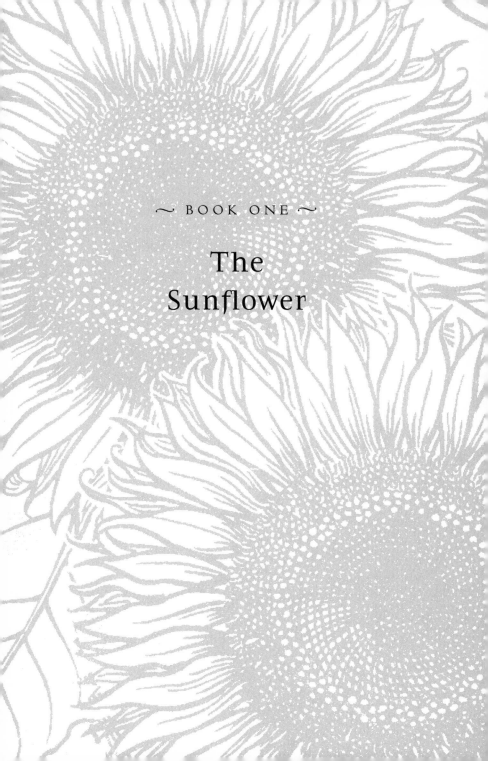

~ BOOK ONE ~

# The
# Sunflower

What was it Arthur said last night? I tried hard to remember. I knew it was very important. If only I were not so tired!

I was standing on the parade ground, where the prisoners were slowly assembling. They had just had their "breakfast"— a dark, bitter brew which the camp cooks had the nerve to call coffee. The men were still swallowing the stuff as they mustered for the roll call, anxious not to be late.

I had not fetched my coffee as I did not want to force my way through the crowd. The space in front of the kitchen was a favorite hunting-ground for the many sadists among the SS. They usually hid behind the huts and whenever they felt like it they swooped like birds of prey on to the helpless prisoners. Every day some were injured; it was part of the "program."

As we stood around silent and gloomy waiting for the order to fall in my thoughts were not concerned with the dangers which always lurked on such occasions, but were entirely centered on last night's talk.

Yes, now I remembered!

. . .

It was late at night. We lay in the dark; there were low groans, soft whispering, and an occasional ghostly creak as someone moved on his plank bed. One could hardly discern faces but could easily identify a speaker by his voice. During the day two of the men from our hut had actually been in the Ghetto. The guard officer had given them his permission. An irrational whim? Perhaps inspired by some bribe? I did not know. The likelihood was that it was a mere whim, for what did a prisoner possess to bribe an officer with?

And now the men were making their report.

Arthur huddled up close to them so as not to miss a word. They brought news from outside, war news. I listened half-asleep.

The people in the Ghetto had plenty of information and we in the camp had only a small share of their knowledge. We had to piece bits together from the scanty reports of those who worked outside during the day and overheard what the Poles and Ukrainians were talking about—facts or rumors. Sometimes even people in the street whispered a piece of news to them, from sympathy or as consolation.

Seldom was the news good, and when it was, one questioned if it was really true or merely wishful thinking. Bad news, on the other hand, we accepted unquestioningly; we were so used to it. And one piece of bad news followed another, each more alarming than the last. Today's news was worse than yesterday's, and tomorrow's would be worse still.

The stuffy atmosphere in the hut seemed to stifle thought, as week after week we slept huddled together in the same sweat-sodden clothes that we wore at work during the day. Many of us were so exhausted we did not even take off our boots. From time to time in the night a man would scream in his sleep—a nightmare perhaps, or his neighbor may have kicked him. The hut had once been a stable, and the half-open skylight did not admit enough air to provide oxygen for the hundred and fifty men who lay penned together on the tiers of bunks.

In the polyglot mass of humanity were members of varied social strata: rich and poor; highly educated and illiterate; religious men and agnostics; the kindhearted and the selfish; courageous men and the dull-witted. A common fate had made them all equal. But inevitably they splintered into small groups, close communities of men who in other circumstances would never be found together.

The group to which I belonged included my old friend Arthur and a Jew named Josek, a recent arrival. These were my closest companions. Josek was sensitive and deeply religious. His faith could be hurt by the environment of the camp and by the jeers or insinuations of others, but it could never be shaken. I, for one, could only envy him. He had an answer for everything, while we others vainly groped for explanations and fell victims to despair. His peace of mind sometimes disconcerted us; Arthur especially, whose attitude to life was ironic, was irritated by Josek's placidity and sometimes he even mocked him or was angry with him.

Jokingly I called Josek "Rabbi." He was not of course a rabbi; he was a businessman, but religion permeated his life. He knew that he was superior to us, that we were the poorer for our lack of faith but he was ever ready to share his wealth of wisdom and piety with us and give us strength.

But what consolation was it to know that we were not the first Jews to be persecuted? And what comfort was it when

Josek, rummaging among his inexhaustible treasure of anecdotes and legends, proved to us that suffering is the companion of every man from birth onward?

As soon as Josek spoke, he forgot or ignored his surroundings completely. We had the feeling that he was simply unaware of his position. On one occasion we nearly quarreled on this point.

It was a Sunday evening. We had stopped work at midday and lay in our bunks relaxing. Someone was talking about the news; it was of course sad as usual. Josek seemed not to be listening. He asked no questions as the others were doing but suddenly he sat up and his face looked radiant. Then he began to speak.

"Our scholars say that at the Creation of man four angels stood as godparents. The angels of Mercy, Truth, Peace, and Justice. For a long time they disputed as to whether God ought to create man at all. The strongest opponent was the angel of Truth. This angered God and as a punishment He sent him into banishment on earth. But the other angels begged God to pardon him and finally he listened to them and summoned the angel of Truth back to heaven. The angel brought back a clod of earth which was soaked in his tears, tears that he had shed on being banished from heaven. And from this clod of earth the Lord God created man."

Arthur the cynic was vexed and interrupted Josek's discourse.

"Josek," he said, "I am prepared to believe that God created a Jew out of this tear-soaked clod of earth, but do you expect me to believe He also made our camp commandant, Wilhaus, out of the same material?"

"You are forgetting Cain," replied Josek.

"And you are forgetting where you are. Cain slew Abel in anger, but he never tortured him. Cain had a personal attachment to his brother, but we are strangers to our murderers."

I saw at once that Josek was deeply hurt and to prevent a quarrel I joined in the conversation.

"Arthur," I said, "you are forgetting the thousands of years of evolution; what is known as progress."

But both of them merely laughed bitterly—in times like these such platitudes were meaningless.

Arthur's question wasn't altogether unjustified. Were we truly all made of the same stuff? If so, why were some murderers and other victims? Was there in fact any personal relationship between us, between the murderers and their victims, between our camp commandant, Wilhaus, and a tortured Jew?

And last night I was lying in my bunk half-asleep. My back hurt. I felt dizzy as I listened to the voices which seemed to come from far away. I heard something about a piece of news from the BBC in London—or from Radio Moscow.

Suddenly Arthur gripped my shoulder and shook me.

"Simon, do you hear?" he cried.

"Yes," I murmured, "I hear."

"I hope you are listening with your ears, for your eyes are half-closed, and you really must hear what the old woman said."

"Which old woman?" I asked. "I thought you were talking about what you had heard from the BBC?"

"That was earlier. You must have dozed off. The old woman was saying . . ."

"What could she have said? Does she know when we will get out of here? Or when they are going to slaughter us?"

"Nobody knows the answers to those questions. But she said something else, something that we should perhaps think

about in times like these. She thought that God was on leave."
Arthur paused for a moment in order to let the words sink in.
"What do you think of that, Simon?" he asked. "God is on
leave."

"Let me sleep," I replied. "Tell me when He gets back."

For the first time since we had been living in the stable I
heard my friends laughing, or had I merely dreamt it?

.

We were still waiting for the order to fall in. Apparently there
was some sort of hitch. So I had time to ask Arthur how much
of what I recalled was dream and how much real.

"Arthur," I asked, "what were we talking about last night?
About God? About 'God on leave'?"

"Josek was in the Ghetto yesterday. He asked an old
woman for news, but she only looked up to heaven and said seriously: 'Oh God Almighty, come back from your leave and
look at Thy earth again.'"

"So that's the news; we live in a world that God has abandoned?" I commented.

I had known Arthur for years, since the time when I was a
young architect and he was both my adviser and my friend. We
were like brothers, he a lawyer and writer with a perpetual
ironic smile around the corners of his mouth, while I had gradually become resigned to the idea that I would never again build
houses in which people would live in freedom and happiness.
Our thoughts in the prison camp often ran on different lines.
Arthur was already living in another world and imagined things
that would probably not happen for years. True, he did not believe that we could survive, but he was convinced that in the last
resort the Germans would not escape unpunished. They would

perhaps succeed in killing us and millions of other innocent people, but they themselves would thereby be destroyed.

I lived more in the present: savoring hunger, exhaustion, anxiety for my family, humiliations . . . most of all humiliations.

I once read somewhere that it is impossible to break a man's firm belief. If I ever thought that true, life in a concentration camp taught me differently. It is impossible to believe anything in a world that has ceased to regard man as man, which repeatedly "proves" that one is no longer a man. So one begins to doubt, one begins to cease to believe in a world order in which God has a definite place. One really begins to think that God is on leave. Otherwise the present state of things wouldn't be possible. God must be away. And He has no deputy.

What the old woman had said in no way shocked me, she had simply stated what I had long felt to be true.

We had been back in the camp again for a week. The guards at the Eastern Railway works had carried out a fresh "registration." These registrations involved new dangers that were quite unimaginable in normal life. The oftener they registered us, the fewer we became. In SS language, registering was not a mere stocktaking. It meant much more: the redistribution of labor, culling the men who were no longer essential workers and throwing them out—usually into the death chamber. From bitter personal experience we mistrusted words whose natural meaning seemed harmless. The Germans' intentions toward us had never been harmless. We were suspicious of everything and with good reason.

Until a short time ago about two hundred of us had been

employed at the Eastern Railway works. Work there was far from light, but we felt free to some extent and did not need to return to the camp each night. Our food was brought from the camp, and it tasted accordingly. But as the guards were railway police we were not continually exposed to the unpredictable whims of the SS camp patrols.

The Germans looked on many of the overseers and foremen as second-class citizens. The ethnic Germans were better treated, but the Poles and Ukrainians formed a special stratum between the self-appointed German supermen and the subhuman Jews, and already they were trembling at the thought of the day when there would be no Jews left. Then the well-oiled machinery of extermination would be turned in their direction. The ethnic Germans too did not always feel comfortable and some of them betrayed their uneasiness by behaving more "German" than the average German. A few showed sympathy toward us by slipping us pieces of bread on the quiet and seeing to it that we were not worked to death.

Among those who demanded a daily stint in cruelty was an elderly drunkard called Delosch, who, when he had nothing to drink, passed the time by beating up the prisoners. The group he guarded often bribed him with money to buy liquor, and sometimes a prisoner would try to enlist his maudlin sympathy by describing the fate of the Jews. It worked when he was sufficiently "under the influence." His bullying was as notorious in the works as his pet witticism. When he learned that some prisoner's family had been exterminated in the Ghetto Delosch's invariable response was: "There will always be a thousand Jews left to attend the funeral of the last Jew in Lemberg." We heard this several times a day and Delosch was immensely proud of this particular wisecrack.

By the time the various groups had formed up on the command to fall in, we who longed for outside work had already resigned ourselves to the prospect of remaining in the camp. In the camp construction work went on without interruption, and every day there were deaths in the camp; Jews were strung up, trampled underfoot, bitten by trained dogs, whipped and humiliated in every conceivable manner. Many who could bear it no longer voluntarily put an end to their lives. They sacrificed a number of days, weeks, or months of their lives, but they saved themselves countless brutalities and tortures.

Staying in camp meant that one was guarded not by a single SS man but by many, and often the guards amused themselves by wandering from one workshop to another, whipping prisoners indiscriminately, or reporting them to the commandant for alleged sabotage, which always led to dire punishment. If an SS man alleged that a prisoner was not working properly, his word was accepted, even if the prisoner could point to the work he had done. What an SS man said was always right.

The work assignment was almost finished and we from the Eastern Railway works stood around despondently. Apparently we were no longer wanted on the railway. Then suddenly a corporal came over to us and counted off fifty men. I was among these, but Arthur was left behind. We were formed up in threes, marched through the inner gate where six "askaris" were assigned us as guards. These were Russian deserters or prisoners who had enlisted for service under the Germans. The term "askari" was used during the First World War to describe the Negro soldier employed by the Germans in East Africa. For some reason the SS used the name for the Russian auxiliaries. They were employed in concentration camps to assist the guards and they knew only too well what the Germans expected from them. And most of them lived up to expectations. Their brutality was only mitigated by their corruptibility. The "kapos" (camp captains) and foremen kept on fairly good terms with them, providing them with liquor and cigarettes. So outside working parties were thus able to enjoy a greater degree of liberty under the guardianship of the askaris.

Strangely enough the askaris were extremely keen on singing: music in general played an important part in camp life. There was even a band. Its members included some of the best musicians in and around Lemberg. Richard Rokita, the SS lieutenant who had been a violinist in a Silesian café, was mad about "his" band. This man, who daily slaughtered prisoners from sheer lust for killing, had at the same time only one ambition—to lead a band. He arranged special accommodation for his musicians and pampered them in other ways, but they were never allowed out of camp. In the evenings they played works of Bach and Wagner and Grieg. One day Rokita brought along a songwriter called Zygmunt Schlechter and ordered him to compose a "death tango." And whenever the band played this tune, the sadistic monster Rokita had wet eyes.

In the early mornings, when the prisoners left the camp to go to work, the band played them out, the SS insisting that we march in time to the music. When we passed the gate we began to sing.

The camps songs were of a special type, a mixture of melancholy, sick humor, and vulgar words, a weird amalgam of Russian, Polish, and German. The obscenities suited the mentality of the askaris who constantly demanded one particular song. When they heard it broad grins came over their faces and their features lost some of their brutal appearance.

Once we had passed beyond the barbed wire, the air

seemed fresher; people and houses were no longer seen through wire mesh and partly hidden by the watch towers.

Pedestrians often stood and stared at us curiously and sometimes they started to wave but soon desisted, fearing the SS might notice the gestures of friendliness.

Traffic on the streets seemed uninfluenced by the war. The front line was seven hundred miles away, and the presence of a few soldiers was the only reminder that it was not peacetime.


One askari began to sing, and we joined in although few of us were in the mood for singing. Women among the gaping passersby turned their heads away shamefacedly when they heard the obscene passages in the song and naturally this delighted the askaris. One of them left the column, ran over to the pavement to accost a girl. We couldn't hear what he said, but we could well imagine it as the girl blushed and walked rapidly away.

Our gaze roamed the crowds on the pavements looking anxiously for any face we might recognize, although some kept eyes on the ground, fearing to encounter an acquaintance.

You could read on the faces of the passersby that we were written off as doomed. The people of Lemberg had become accustomed to the sight of tortured Jews and they looked at us as one looks at a herd of cattle being driven to the slaughterhouse. At such times I was consumed by a feeling that the world had conspired against us and our fate was accepted without a protest, without a trace of sympathy.

I for one no longer wanted to look at the indifferent faces of the spectators. Did any of them reflect that there were still Jews and as long as they were there, as long as the Nazis were still busy with the Jews, they would leave the citizens alone? I suddenly remembered an experience I had had a few days before, not far from here. As we were returning to camp, a man whom I had formerly known passed by, a fellow student, now a Polish engineer. Perhaps understandably he was afraid to nod to me openly, but I could see from the expression in his eyes that he was surprised to see me still alive. For him we were as good as dead; each of us was carrying around his own death certificate, from which only the date was missing.

Our column suddenly came to a halt at a crossroads.

I could see nothing that might be holding us up but I noticed on the left of the street there was a military cemetery. It was enclosed by a low barbed wire fence. The wires were threaded through sparse bushes and low shrubs, but between them you could see the graves aligned in stiff rows.

And on each grave there was planted a sunflower, as straight as a soldier on parade.

I stared spellbound. The flower heads seemed to absorb the sun's rays like mirrors and draw them down into the darkness of the ground as my gaze wandered from the sunflower to the grave. It seemed to penetrate the earth and suddenly I saw before me a periscope. It was gaily colored and butterflies fluttered from flower to flower. Were they carrying messages from grave to grave? Were they whispering something to each flower to pass on to the soldier below? Yes, this was just what they were doing; the dead were receiving light and messages.

Suddenly I envied the dead soldiers. Each had a sunflower to connect him with the living world, and butterflies to visit his grave. For me there would be no sunflower. I would be buried in a mass grave, where corpses would be piled on top of me.

No sunflower would ever bring light into my darkness, and no butterflies would dance above my dreadful tomb.

I do not know how long we stood there. The man behind gave me a push and the procession started again. As we walked on I still had my head turned toward the sunflowers. They were countless and indistinguishable one from another. But the men who were buried under them had not severed all connection with the world. Even in death they were superior to us . . .

I rarely thought of death. I knew that it was waiting for me and must come sooner or later, so gradually I had accustomed myself to its proximity. I was not even curious as to how it would come. There were too many possibilities. All I hoped was that it would be quick. Just how it would happen I left to Fate.

But for some strange reason the sight of the sunflowers had aroused new thoughts in me. I felt I would come across them again; that they were a symbol with a special meaning for me.

As we reached Janowska Street, leaving the cemetery behind us, I turned my head for a last look at the forest of sunflowers.

We still did not know where we were being taken. My neighbor whispered to me: "Perhaps they have set up new workshops in the Ghetto."

It was possible. The rumor was that new workshops were being started. More and more German businessmen were settling Lemberg. They were not so anxious for profits. It was more important for them to keep their employees and save them from military service which was comparatively easy in peaceful Lemberg, far from the front line. What most of these enterprises brought with them from Germany was writing paper, a rubber stamp, a few foremen, and some office furniture. Only a short time ago Lemberg had been in the hands of the Russians, who had nationalized most of the building firms, many of which had previously been owned by Jews. When the Russians withdrew, they were unable to take the machines and tools with them. So what they left behind was taken to a "booty depot" and was now being divided among the newly established German factories.

There was no trouble in any case about getting labor. So long as there were still Jews, one could get cheap, almost free labor. The workshop applying had merely to be recognized as important for the war, but a certain degree of protection and bribery was also necessary. Those with connections got permission to set up branches in occupied territory, they were given cheap labor in the shape of hundreds of Jews, and they also had an extensive machine depot at their disposal. The men they brought with them from Germany were exempt from active service. Homes in the German quarter of Lemberg were assigned to them—very nice houses abandoned by wealthy Poles and Jews to make room for the master race.

To the Jews it was an advantage that so many German enterprises were being started in Poland. Work was not particularly hard, and as a rule the workshop managers fought for "their" Jews, without whose cheap labor the workshops would have had to move further east nearer the front.

All around me I heard the anxious whispers: "Where are we going?"

"Going" means to carry out with the feet a decision which the brain has formed, but in our case our brains made no decisions. Our feet merely imitated what the front man did. They stopped when he stopped and they moved on when he moved on.

We turned right into Janowska Street; how often had I sauntered along it, as a student and later as an architect? For a time I had even had lodgings there with a fellow student from Przemysl.

Now we marched mechanically along the street—a column of doomed men.

It was not yet eight o'clock, but there was already plenty of traffic. Peasants were coming into the city to barter their wares; they no longer had confidence in money as is always the case in war time and in crises. The peasants paid no attention to our column.

As we moved out of the city the askaris, having sung themselves hoarse, were taking a rest. Detrained soldiers with their baggage hurried along Janowska; SS men passed, looking contemptuously at us, and at one point an army officer stopped to stare. Around his neck hung a camera, but he could not make up his mind to use it on us. Hesitatingly he passed the camera from right to left hand and then let it go again. Perhaps he was afraid of trouble with the SS.

We came in sight of the church at the end of Janowska Street, a lofty structure of red brick and squared stone. Which direction would the askari, at the head of our column, take? To the right, down to the station, or to the left along Sapiehy Street, at the end of which lay the notorious Loncki Prison?

We turned left.

I knew the way well. In Sapiehy Street stood the Technical High School. For years I had walked along this street several times a day, when I was working for the Polish diploma.

Even then for us Jewish students Sapiehy Street was a street of doom. Only a few Jewish families lived there and in times of disorder the district was avoided by Jews. Here lived Poles—regular officers, professional men, manufacturers, and officials. Their sons were known as the "gilded youth" of Lemberg and supplied most of the students in the Technical High School and in the High School of Agriculture. Many of them were rowdies, hooligans, antisemites, and Jews who fell into their hands were often beaten up and left bleeding on the ground. They fastened razor blades to the end of their sticks which they used as weapons against the Jewish students. In the evenings it was dangerous to walk through this street, even if one were merely Jewish in appearance, especially at times when the young National Democrats or Radical Nationals were turning their anti-Jewish slogans from theory into practice. It was rare for a policeman to be around to protect the victims.

What was incomprehensible was that at a time when Hitler was on Poland's western frontiers, poised to annex Polish territory, these Polish "patriots" could think of only one thing: the Jews and their hatred for them.

In Germany, at that time, they were building new factories to raise armament potential to the maximum; they were building strategic roads straight toward Poland and then were calling up more and more young Germans for military service. But the Polish parliament paid little heed to this menace; it had "more important" tasks—new regulations for kosher butchering, for instance—which might make life more difficult for the Jews.

Such parliamentary debates were always followed by street battles, for the Jewish intelligentsia was ever a thorn in the flesh of the antisemites.

Two years before the outbreak of war the Radical elements

had invented a "day without Jews," whereby they hoped to re-
duce the number of Jewish academics, to interfere with their
studies and make it impossible for them to take examinations.
On these feast days there assembled inside the gates of the
High Schools a crowd of fraternity students wearing ribbons
inscribed "the day without the Jews." It always coincided with
examination days. The "day without the Jews" was thus a mov-
able festival, and as the campus of the Technical High School
was ex-territorial, the police were not allowed to interfere except by express request of the Rector. Such requests were rarely
made. Although the Radicals formed a mere 20 percent of the
students, this minority reigned because of the cowardice and
laziness of the majority. The great mass of the students were
unconcerned about the Jews or indeed about order and justice.
They were not willing to expose themselves, they lacked
willpower, they were wrapped up in their own problems, completely indifferent to the fate of Jewish students.

The proportions were about the same among the teaching
staff. Some were confirmed antisemites, but even from those
who were not, the Jewish students had trouble getting a substi-
tute date for the examinations which they missed because of
the "day without Jews" outbreaks. For Jews who came from
poor families the loss of a term meant inevitably an end to
their studies. So they had to go to the High School even on the
antisemitic feast days and this led to grotesque situations. In
the side streets ambulances waited patiently and they had
plenty to do on examination days. The police too waited to
prevent violence from spreading outside the campus. From
time to time a few of the most brutal students were arrested
and tried but they emerged from prison as heroes and on their
lapels they proudly wore a badge designed as a prison gate.

They had suffered for their country's cause! Honored by their comrades, they were given special privileges by some of the professors, and never was there any question of expelling them.

Such memories crowded into my mind as, under the guard of the askaris, I marched past the familiar houses. I looked into the faces of the passersby. Perhaps I would see a former fellow student. I would spot him at once because he would visibly show the hatred and contempt which they always evinced at the mere sight of a Jew. I had seen this expression too often during my time as a student ever to forget it.

Where are they now, these super-patriots who dreamt of a "Poland without Jews"? Perhaps the day when there would be no more Jews was not far off, and their dreams would be realized. Only there wouldn't be a Poland either!

We halted in front of the Technical High School. It looked unaltered. The main building, a neoclassic structure in terra-cotta and yellow, stood some distance back from the street, from which it was separated by a low stone wall with a high iron fence. At examination time I had often walked along this fence and gazed through the railings at the Radical students waiting for their victims. Over the broad entrance gates would be a banner inscribed "the day without Jews." From the gate to the door of the building armed students forming a cordon would scrutinize everybody who wanted to enter the building.

So here I was, once again standing outside this gateway. This time there were no banners, no students to make the Jews run the gauntlet, only a few German guards and, above the entrance, a board inscribed "Reserve Hospital." An SS man from the camp had a few words with a sentry, and then the gate opened. We marched past the well-kept lawns, turned left from the main entrance and were led round the building into the courtyard. It lay in deep shadow. Ambulances drove in and out, and once or twice we had to stand aside to let them pass. Then we were handed over to a sergeant of the medical corps, who assigned us our duties. I had a curious feeling of strangeness in these surroundings although I had spent several years here. I tried to remember whether I had ever been in this back court-yard. What would have brought me here? We were usually content to be able to get into the building and out again without being molested, or without explaining the topography.

Large concrete containers were arranged around the court-yard and they seemed to be filled with bloodstained bandages. The ground was covered with empty boxes, sacks, and packing material which a group of prisoners was busy loading into trucks. The air stank with a mixture of strong-smelling medicaments, disinfectants, and putrefaction.

Red Cross sisters and medical orderlies were hurrying to and fro. The askaris had left the shady smelly courtyard and were sunning themselves on the grass a short distance away. Some were rolling cigarettes of newspaper stuffed with to-bacco—just as they were wont to do in Russia.

Some lightly wounded and convalescent soldiers sat on the benches, watching the askaris, whom they recognized at once as Russians in spite of the German uniforms they wore. We could hear them inquiring about us too.

One soldier got up from the bench and came over toward us. He looked at us in an impersonal way as if we were animals in a zoo. Probably he was wondering how long we had to live. Then he pointed to his arm, which was in a sling, and called out: "You Jewish swine, that's what your brothers the damned

Communists have done for me. But you'll soon kick the bucket, all of you."

The other soldiers didn't seem to share his views. They looked at us sympathetically and one of them shook his head doubtfully; but none dared to say a word. The soldier who had approached us uttered a few more curses and then sat down again in the sunshine.

I thought to myself that this vile creature would one day have a sunflower planted on his grave to watch over him. I looked at him closely and all at once I saw only the sunflower. My stare seemed to upset him, for he picked up a stone and threw it at me. The stone missed and the sunflower vanished. At that moment I felt desperately alone and wished Arthur had been included in my group.

The orderly in charge of us finally led us away. Our job was to carry cartons filled with rubbish out of the building. Their contents apparently came from the operating theaters and the stench made one's throat contract.

As I stepped aside to get a few breaths of clean air, I noticed a small, plump nurse who wore the gray-blue uniform with white facings and the regulation white cap. She looked at me curiously and then came straight over to me.

"Are you a Jew?" she asked.

I looked at her wonderingly. Why did she ask, could not she see it for herself from my clothes and my features? Was she trying to be insulting? What was the object of her question?

A sympathetic soul perhaps, I thought. Maybe she wanted to slip me some bread, and was afraid to do it here with the others looking on.

Two months previously when I was working on the Eastern Railway, loading oxygen cylinders, a soldier had climbed out of a truck on a siding close by and come over to me. He said he had been watching us for some time, and we looked as if we did not get enough to eat.

"In my knapsack over there you'll find a piece of bread; go and fetch it."

I asked. "Why don't you give it to me yourself?"

"It is forbidden to give anything to a Jew."

"I know," I said. "All the same if you want me to have it you give it to me."

He smiled. "No, you take it. Then I can swear with a clear conscience that I didn't give it to you."

I thought of this incident as I followed the Red Cross nurse into the building, in accordance with her instructions.

The thick walls made the inside of the building refreshingly cool. The nurse walked rather fast. Where was she taking me? If her purpose was to give me something, then she could have done it here and now in front of the staircase, since nobody was in sight. But the nurse just turned round once, to confirm that I was still following her.

We climbed the staircase, and, strange to relate, I could not remember ever having seen it before. At the next story I saw nurses were coming toward us and a doctor looked at me sharply as if to say: What is that fellow doing here?

We reached the upper hall, where, not so long ago, my diploma had been handed to me.

The nurse stopped and exchanged a few words with another nurse. I asked myself whether I had better bolt. I was on well-known ground. I knew where each corridor led to and could easily escape. Let her look for somebody else, whatever it was she needed.

Suddenly I forgot why I was there. I forgot the nurse and

even the camp. There on the right was the way to Professor Bagierski's office and there on the left the way to Professor Derdacki's. Both were notorious for their dislike of Jewish students. I had done my diploma work with Derdacki—a design for a sanatorium. And Bagierski had corrected many of my essays. When he had to deal with a Jewish student he seemed to lose his breath and stuttered more than usual. I could still see his hand making lines across my drawings with a thick pencil, a hand with a large signet ring.

Then the nurse signaled me to wait, and I came back to earth. I leaned over the balustrade and looked down at the busy throng in the lower hall. Wounded were being brought in on stretchers. There was a constant coming and going. Soldiers limped past on crutches and one soldier on a stretcher looked up at me, his features distorted with pain.

Then another fragment from the past recurred to my memory. It was during the student riots of 1936. The antisemitic bands had hurled a Jewish student over the balustrade into the lower hall and he lay there just like this soldier, possibly on the very same spot.

Just past the balustrade was a door which had led to the office of the Dean of Architecture and it was here we handed in our exercise books to the professors to be marked. The Dean in my time was a quiet man, very polite, very correct. We had never known whether he was for or against the Jews. He always responded to our greetings with distant politeness. One could almost physically feel his aloofness. Or was it merely an excess of sensitiveness that made us divide people into two groups: those that liked Jews and those who disliked them. Constant Jew-baiting gave rise to such thoughts.

The nurse came back and dragged me once again out of

the past. I could see from the look in her eyes that she was pleased to find me still there.

She walked quickly along the balustrade around the hall and stopped in front of the door of the Dean's room.

"Wait here till I call you."

I nodded and looked up the staircase. Orderlies were bringing down a motionless figure on a stretcher. There had never been a lift in the building and the Germans had not installed one. After a few moments the nurse came out of the Dean's room, caught me by the arm, and pushed me through the door.

I looked for the familiar objects, the writing desk, the cupboards in which our papers were kept, but those relics of the past had vanished. There was now only a white bed with a night table beside it. Something white was looking at me out of the blankets. At first I could not grasp the situation.

Then the nurse bent over the bed and whispered and I heard a somewhat deeper whisper, apparently in answer. Although the place was in semidarkness I could now see a figure wrapped in white, motionless on the bed. I tried to trace the outlines of the body under the sheets and looked for its head.

The nurse straightened up and said quietly: "Stay here." Then she went out of the room.

From the bed I heard a weak, broken voice exclaim: "Please come nearer, I can't speak loudly."

Now I could see the figure in the bed far more clearly. White, bloodless hands on the counterpane, head completely bandaged with openings only for mouth, nose, and ears. The feeling of unreality persisted. It was an uncanny situation: those corpse-like hands, the bandages, and the place in which this strange encounter was taking place.

I did not know who this wounded man was, but obviously he was a German.

Hesitatingly, I sat down on the edge of the bed. The sick man, perceiving this, said softly: "Please come a little nearer, to talk loudly is exhausting."

I obeyed. His almost bloodless hand groped for mine as he tried to raise himself slightly in the bed.

My bewilderment was intense. I did not know whether this unreal scene was actuality or dream. Here was I in the ragged clothes of a concentration camp prisoner in the room of the former Dean of Lemberg High School—now a military hospital—in a sickroom which must be in reality a death chamber.

As my eyes became accustomed to the semidarkness I could see that the white bandages were mottled with yellow stains. Perhaps ointment, or was it pus? The bandaged head was spectral.

I sat on the bed spellbound. I could not take my eyes off the stricken man and the gray-yellow stains on the bandages seemed to me to be moving, taking new shapes before my eyes.

"I have not much longer to live," whispered the sick man in a barely audible voice. "I know the end is near."

Then he fell silent. Was he thinking what next to say, or had his premonition of death scared him? I looked more closely. He was very thin, and under his shirt his bones were clearly visible, almost bursting through his parched skin.

I was unmoved by his words. The way I had been forced to exist in the prison camps had destroyed in me any feeling or fear about death.

Sickness, suffering, and doom were the constant companions of us Jews. Such things no longer frightened us.

Nearly a fortnight before this confrontation with the dying man I had had occasion to visit a store in which cement sacks were kept. I heard groans and going to investigate, I saw one of the prisoners lying among the sacks. I asked him what was the matter.

"I am dying," he muttered in a choked voice, "I shall die; there is nobody in the world to help me and nobody to mourn my death." Then he added casually, "I am twenty-two."

I ran out of the shed and found the prison doctor. He shrugged his shoulders and turned away. "There are a couple of hundred men working here today. Six of them are dying." He did not even ask where the dying man was.

"You ought to at least go and look at him," I protested.

"I couldn't do anything for him," he answered.

"But you as a doctor have more liberty to move about, you could explain your absence to the guards better than I could. It is frightful for a man to die lonely and abandoned. Help him at least in his dying hour."

"Good, good," he said. But I knew that he would not go. He too had lost all feeling for death.

At the evening roll call there were six corpses. They were included without comment. The doctor's estimate was correct.

"I know," muttered the sick man, "that at this moment thousands of men are dying. Death is everywhere. It is neither infrequent nor extraordinary. I am resigned to dying soon, but before that I want to talk about an experience which is torturing me. Otherwise I cannot die in peace."

He was breathing heavily. I had the feeling that he was staring at me through his head bandage. Perhaps he could see through the yellow stains, although they were nowhere near his eyes. I could not look at him.

"I heard from one of the sisters that there were Jewish prisoners working in the courtyard. Previously she had brought me a letter from my mother . . . She read it out to me and then went away. I have been here for three months. Then I came to a decision. After thinking it over for a long time . . .

"When the sister came back I asked her to help me. I wanted her to fetch a Jewish prisoner to me, but I warned she must be careful, that nobody must see her. The nurse, who had no idea why I had made this request, didn't reply and went away. I gave up all hope of her taking such a risk for my sake. But when she came in a little while ago she bent over me and whispered that there was a Jew outside. She said it as if complying with the last wish of a dying man. She knows how it is with me. I am in a death chamber, that I know. They let the hopeless cases die alone. Perhaps they don't want the others to be upset."

Who was this man to whom I was listening? What was he trying to say to me? Was he a Jew who had camouflaged himself as a German and now, on his deathbed, wanted to look at a Jew again? According to gossip in the Ghetto and later in the camp there were Jews in Germany who were "Aryan" in appearance and had enlisted in the army with false papers. They had even got into the SS. That was their method of survival. Was this man such a Jew? Or perhaps a half-Jew, son of a mixed marriage? When he made a slight movement I noticed that his other hand rested on a letter but which now slipped to the floor. I bent down and put it back on the counterpane.

I didn't touch his hand and he could not have seen my movement—nevertheless he reacted.

"Thank you—that is my mother's letter," the words came softly from his lips.

And again I had the feeling he was staring at me.

His hand groped for the letter and drew it toward him, as if he hoped to derive a little strength and courage from contact with the paper. I thought of my own mother who would never write me another letter. Five weeks previously she had been dragged out of the Ghetto in a raid. The only article of value which we still possessed, after all the looting, was a gold watch which I had given to my mother so that she might be able to buy herself off when they came to fetch her. A neighbor who had valid papers told me later what had happened to the watch. My mother gave it to the Ukrainian policeman who came to arrest her. He went away, but soon came back and bundled my mother and others into a truck that carried them away to a place from which no letters ever emerged . . .

Time seemed to stand still as I listened to the croaking of the dying man.

"My name is Karl . . . I joined the SS as a volunteer. Of course—when you hear the word SS . . ."

He stopped. His throat seemed to be dry and he tried hard to swallow a lump in it.

Now I knew he couldn't be a Jew or half-Jew who had hidden inside a German uniform. How could I have imagined such a thing? But in those days anything was possible.

"I must tell you something dreadful . . . Something inhuman. It happened a year ago . . . has a year already gone by?" These last words he spoke almost to himself.

"Yes, it is a year," he continued, "a year since the crime I

29

committed. I have to talk to someone about it, perhaps that will help."

Then his hand grasped mine. His fingers clutched mine tightly, as though he sensed I was trying unconsciously to withdraw my hand when I heard the word "crime." Whence had he derived the strength? Or was it that I was so weak that I could not take my hand away?

"I must tell you of this horrible deed—tell you because . . . you are a Jew."

Could there be some kind of horror unknown to us?

All the atrocities and tortures that a sick brain can invent are familiar to me. I have felt them on my own body and I have seen them happen in the camp. Any story that this sick man had to tell couldn't surpass the horror stories which my comrades in the camp exchanged with each other at night.

I wasn't really curious about his story, and inwardly I only hoped the nurse had remembered to tell an askari where I was. Otherwise they would be looking for me. Perhaps they would think I had escaped . . .

I was uneasy. I could hear voices outside the door, but I recognized one as the nurse's voice and that reassured me. The strangled voice went on: "Some time elapsed before I realized what guilt I had incurred."

I stared at the bandaged head. I didn't know what he wanted to confess, but I knew for sure that after his death a sunflower would grow on his grave. Already a sunflower was turning toward the window, the window through which the sun was sending its rays into this death chamber. Why was the sunflower already making its appearance? Because it would accompany him to the cemetery, stand on his grave, and sustain his connection with life. And this I envied him. I envied him also because in his last moments he was able to think of a live mother who would be grieving for him.

"I was not born a murderer . . ." he wheezed.

He breathed heavily and was silent.

"I come from Stuttgart and I am now twenty-one. That is too soon to die. I have had very little out of life."

Of course it is too soon to die I thought. But did the Nazis ask whether our children whom they were about to gas had ever had anything out of life? Did they ask whether it was too soon for them to die? Certainly nobody had ever asked me the question.

As if he had guessed my mental reaction he said: "I know what you are thinking and I understand. But may I not still say that I am too young . . . ?"

Then in a burst of calm coherency he went on: "My father, who was manager of a factory, was a convinced Social Democrat. After 1933 he got into difficulties, but that happened to many. My mother brought me up as a Catholic, I was actually a server in the church and a special favorite of our priest who hoped I would one day study theology. But it turned out differently; I joined the Hitler Youth, and that of course was the end of the Church for me. My mother was very sad, but finally stopped reproaching me. I was her only child. My father never uttered a word on the subject . . .

"He was afraid lest I should talk in the Hitler Youth about what I had heard at home . . . Our leader demanded that we should champion our cause everywhere . . . Even at home . . . He told us that if we heard anyone abuse it we must report to him. There were many who did so, but not I. My parents nevertheless were afraid and they stopped talking when I was near. Their mistrust annoyed me, but, unfortunately, there was no time for reflection in those days.

"In the Hitler Youth, I found friends and comrades. My days were full. After school most of our class hurried to the clubhouse or sports ground. My father rarely spoke to me, and when he had something to say he spoke cautiously and with reserve. I know now what depressed him—often I watched him sitting in his armchair for hours, brooding, without saying a word . . .

"When the war broke out I volunteered, naturally in the SS. I was far from being the only one in my troop to do so; almost half of them joined the forces voluntarily—without a thought, as if they were going to a dance or on an outing. My mother wept when I left. As I closed the door behind me I heard my father say: 'They are taking our son away from us. No good will come of it.'

"His words made me indignant. I wanted to go back and argue with him. I wanted to tell him that he simply did not understand modern times. But I let it be, so as not to make my departure worse for all of us by an ugly scene.

"Those words were the last I ever heard my father speak . . . Occasionally he would add a few lines to my mother's letter but my mother usually made excuses by saying he was not back from work and she was anxious to catch the post."

He paused, and groped with his hand for the glass on the night table. Although he could not see it he knew where it was. He drank a mouthful of water and put the glass back safely in its place before I could do it for him. Was he really in such a bad way as he had said?

"We were first sent to a training camp at an army base

where we listened feverishly to the radio messages about the Polish campaign. We devoured the reports in the newspapers and dreaded that our services might not after all be needed. I was longing for experience, to see the world, to be able to recount my adventures . . . My uncle had had such exciting tales to tell of the war in Russia, how they had driven Ivan into the Masurian Lakes. I wanted to play my part in that sort of thing . . ."

I sat there like a cat on hot bricks and tried to release my hand from his. I wanted to go away, but he seemed to be trying to talk to me with his hands as well as his voice. His grip grew tighter . . . as if pleading with me not to desert him. Perhaps his hand was a replacement for his eyes.

I looked around the room and glancing at the window, I saw a part of the sun-drenched courtyard, with the shadow of the roof crossing it obliquely—a boundary between light and dark, a defined boundary without any transition.

Then the dying man told of his time in occupied Poland, mentioning a place. Was it Reichshof? I didn't ask.

Why the long prelude? Why didn't he say what he wanted from me? There was no necessity to break it so gently.

Now his hand began to tremble and I took the opportunity to withdraw mine, but he clutched it again and whispered: "Please." Did he want to fortify himself—or me?—for what was to come?

"And then—then came the terrible thing . . . But first I must tell you a little more about myself."

He seemed to detect my uneasiness. Had he noticed I was watching the door, for suddenly he said:

"No one will come in. The nurse promised to keep watch out there . . .

"Heinz, my schoolmate, who was with me in Poland too, always called me a dreamer. I didn't really know why, perhaps because I was always merry and happy—at least until that day came and it happened . . . It's a good thing that Heinz cannot hear me now. My mother must never know what I did. She must not lose her image of a good son. That is what she always called me. She must always see me as she wanted to see me.

"She used to read my letters out to all the neighbors . . . and the neighbors said that they were proud I got my wound fighting for the Führer and the Fatherland . . . you know the usual phrase . . ."

His voice grew bitter as if he wanted to hurt himself, give himself pain.

"In my mother's memory I am still a happy boy without a care in the world . . . Full of high spirits. Oh, the jokes we used to play . . ."

As he recalled his youth and comrades, I too thought back on the years when practical jokes were a hobby of mine. I thought of my old friends . . . my schoolmates in Prague. We had had many a joke together, we who were young with life stretching before us.

But what had my youth in common with his? Were we not from different worlds? Where were the friends from my world? Still in camp or already in a nameless mass grave . . . And where are his friends? They are alive, or at least they have a sunflower on their graves and a cross with their name on it.

And now I began to ask myself why a Jew must listen to the confession of a dying Nazi soldier. If he had really redis-covered his faith in Christianity, then a priest should have been sent for, a priest who could help him die in peace. If I were dy-ing to whom should I make my confession if indeed I had anything to confess? And anyway I would not have as much time as this man had. My end would be violent, as had happened to millions before me. Perhaps it would be an unexpected surprise, perhaps I would have no time to prepare for the bullet. He was still talking about his youth as if he were reading aloud and the only effect was that it made me think of my youth too. But it was so far away that it seemed unreal. It seemed as if I had always been in prison camps, as though I were born merely to be maltreated by beasts in human shape who wanted to work off their frustrations and racial hatreds on defenseless victims. Remembrance of time past only made me feel weak, and I badly needed to remain strong, for only the strong in these dire times had a hope of survival. I still clung to the belief that the world one day would revenge itself on these brutes—in spite of their victories, their jubilation at the battles they had won, and their boundless arrogance. The day would surely come when the Nazis would hang their heads as the Jews did now . . .

All my instincts were against continuing to listen to this deathbed disavowal. I wanted to get away. The dying man must have felt this, for he dropped the letter and groped for my arm. The movement was so pathetically helpless that all of a sudden I felt sorry for him. I would stay, although I wanted to go. Quietly he continued talking.

"Last spring we saw that something was afoot. We were told time after time we must be prepared for great doings. Each of us must show himself a man . . . He must be tough. There was no place for humanitarian nonsense. The Führer needed real men. That made a great impression on us at the time.

"When the war with Russia began, we listened over the radio to a speech by Himmler before we marched out. He spoke of the final victory of the Führer's mission . . . On smoking out subhumans . . . We were given piles of literature about the Jews and the Bolsheviks, we devoured the 'Sturmer,' and many cut caricatures from it and pinned them above our beds. But that was not the sort of thing I cared for . . . In the evenings, in the canteen we grew heated with beer and talk about Germany's future. As in Poland, the war with Russia would be a lightning campaign, thanks to the genius of our leader. Our frontiers would be pushed further and further eastward. The German people needed room to live."

For a moment he stopped as though exhausted.

"You can see for yourself on what sort of career my life was launched."

He was sorry for himself. His words were bitter and resigned.

I again looked through the window and perceived that the boundary between light and shadow was now above the other windows of the inner façade. The sun had climbed higher. One of the windows caught the sun's rays and reflected them as it was closed again. For a moment the flash of light looked like a heliographic signal. At that time we were ready to see symbols in everything. It was a time rife for mysticism and superstition. Often my fellow prisoners in the camp told ghost stories. Everything for us was unreal and insubstantial: the earth was peopled with mystical shapes; God was on leave, and in His absence others had taken over, to give us signs and hints. In normal times we would have laughed at anybody who believed in supernatural powers. But nowadays we expected them to intervene in the course of events. We devoured every word spoken by alleged soothsayers and fortune-tellers. We often clung to completely nonsensical interpretations if only they gave us a ray of hope for better times. The eternal optimism of the Jew surpassed all reason, but now even reason was out of place. What in this Nazi world was reasonable and logical? You lost yourself in fantasy merely in order to escape from the appalling truth. And in such circumstances reason would have been a barrier. We escaped into dreams and we didn't want to awake from those dreams.

I forgot for a moment where I was and then I heard a buzzing sound. A bluebottle, probably attracted by the smell, flew round the head of the dying man, who could not see it nor could he see me wave it away.

"Thanks," he nevertheless whispered. And for the first time I realized that I, a defenseless subhuman, had contrived to lighten the lot of an equally defenseless superman, without thinking, simply as a matter of course.

The narration proceeded: "At the end of June we joined a unit of storm troops and were taken to the front in trucks. We drove past vast fields of wheat which stretched as far as the eye could see. Our platoon leader said that Hitler had intentionally started the campaign against Russia at a time which would enable us to bring in the harvest. We thought that clever. On our endless journey we saw by the wayside dead Russians, burnt-out tanks, broken-down trucks, dead horses. And there were wounded Russians too, lying there helpless, with nobody to care for them; all the way we could hear their screams and groans.

"One of my comrades spat at them and I protested. He simply replied with a phrase that our officer had used: 'No pity for Ivan . . .'

"His words sounded like a sober military command. He

spoke in the style of a war correspondent. His words were parrotlike, unthinking. His conversation was full of stupid phrases which he had taken from newspapers.

"Finally we came to a Ukrainian village and here I had my first contact with the enemy. We shot up a deserted farmhouse in which Russians had barricaded themselves. When we stormed in we found only a few wounded men lying about with whom we did not bother. That is, I did not bother. But our platoon leader . . . gave them the coup de grâce . . .

"Since I have been in hospital here these details constantly recur to me. I live it all over again, but much more precisely and vividly . . . Now I have plenty of time.

"The fighting was inhuman. Many of us could hardly stand it. When our major saw this he shouted at us: 'Believe you me, do you think the Russians act differently toward our men? You need only see how they treat their own people. The prisons we come across are full of murdered men. They simply mow down their prisoners when they cannot take them away. He who has been selected to make history cannot be bothered with such trifles.'

"One evening a comrade took me aside in order to express his horror, but after the very first sentence he stopped. He did not trust me.

"We continued to make history. Day after day we heard victory reports and constantly we were told that the war would soon be over. Hitler said so and Himmler . . . For me it is now really over . . ."

He took a deep breath. Then a sip of water. Behind me I heard a noise and looked around. I had not noticed that the door was open. But he had heard it.

"Sister, please . . ."

"All right, I only wanted to look round . . ."

She shut the door again.

"One hot summer day we came to Dnepropetrovsk. Everywhere there were abandoned cars and guns. Many of them still intact. Obviously the Russians had left in great haste. Houses were burning and the streets were blocked by hastily erected barricades, but there was nobody left to defend them. There were deaths among the civilians. On the pavement I saw the body of a woman and over her crouched two weeping children . . .

"When the order came to fall out we leaned our rifles against the house walls, sat down, and smoked. Suddenly we heard an explosion and looked up, but there was no plane in sight. Then we saw a whole block of houses had blown up.

"Many house blocks had been mined by the Russians before they retreated and as soon as our troops entered, the buildings blew up. One comrade declared that the Russians had learned such tactics from the Finns. I was glad we had been resting. We had escaped again.

"Suddenly a staff car stopped near us. A major climbed out and sent for our captain. Then came a number of trucks which took us to another part of the town. There the same miserable picture presented itself.

"In a large square we got out and looked around us. On the other side of the square there was a group of people under close guard. I assumed they were civilians who were to be taken out of the town, in which fighting was still going on. And then the word ran through our group like wildfire: 'They're Jews' . . . In my young life I had never seen many Jews. No doubt there had formerly been some, but for the most part they had emigrated when Hitler came to power. The few who remained simply disappeared later. It was said they had been sent to the Ghetto. Then they were forgotten. My mother sometimes mentioned our family doctor, who was a Jew and for whom she mourned deeply. She carefully preserved all his prescriptions, for she had complete trust in his medical knowledge. But one day the chemist told her that she must get her medicines prescribed by a different doctor, he was not allowed to make up the prescriptions of a Jewish doctor. My mother was furious but my father just looked at me and held his tongue.

"I need not tell you what the newspapers said about the Jews. Later in Poland I saw Jews who were quite different from ours in Stuttgart. At the army base at Debicka some Jews were still working and I often gave them something to eat. But I stopped when the platoon leader caught me doing it. The Jews had to clean out our quarters and I often deliberately left behind on the table some food which I knew they would find.

"Otherwise all I knew about the Jews was what came out of the loudspeaker or what was given us to read. We were told they were the cause of all our misfortunes . . . They were trying to get on top of us, they were the cause of war, poverty, hunger, unemployment . . ."

I noticed that the dying man had a warm undertone in his voice as he spoke about the Jews. I had never heard such a tone in the voice of an SS man. Was he better than the others—or did the voices of SS men change when they were dying?

"An order was given," he continued, "and we marched toward the huddled mass of Jews. There were a hundred and fifty of them or perhaps two hundred, including many children who stared at us with anxious eyes. A few were quietly crying. There were infants in their mothers' arms, but hardly any young men; mostly women and graybeards.

"As we approached I could see the expression in their eyes—fear, indescribable fear . . . apparently they knew what was awaiting them . . .

"A truck arrived with cans of petrol which we unloaded and took into a house. The strong men among the Jews were ordered to carry the cans to the upper stories. They obeyed—apathetically, without a will of their own, like automatons.

"Then we began to drive the Jews into the house. A sergeant with a whip in his hand helped any of the Jews who were not quick enough. There was a hail of curses and kicks. The house was not very large, it had only three stories. I would not have believed it possible to crowd them all into it. But after a few minutes there was no Jew left on the street."

He was silent and my heart started to beat violently. I could well imagine the scene. It was all too familiar. I might have been among those who were forced into that house with the petrol cans. I could feel how they must have pressed against each other; I could hear their frantic cries as they realized what was to be done to them.

The dying Nazi went on: "Then another truck came up full of more Jews and they too were crammed into the house with the others. Then the door was locked and a machine gun was posted opposite."

I knew how this story would end. My own country had been occupied by the Germans for over a year and we had heard of similar happenings in Bialystok, Brody, and Gródek. The method was always the same. He could spare me the rest of his gruesome account.

So I stood up ready to leave but he pleaded with me: "Please stay. I must tell you the rest."

I really do not know what kept me. But there was something in his voice that prevented me from obeying my instinct to end the interview. Perhaps I wanted to hear from his own mouth, in his own words, the full horror of the Nazis' inhumanity.

"When we were told that everything was ready, we went back a few yards, and then received the command to remove safety pins from hand grenades and throw them through the windows of the house. Detonations followed one after another . . . My God!"

Now he was silent, and he raised himself slightly from the bed: his whole body was shivering.

But he continued: "We heard screams and saw the flames eat their way from floor to floor . . . We had our rifles ready to shoot down anyone who tried to escape from that blazing hell . . .

"The screams from the house were horrible. Dense smoke poured out and choked us . . ."

His hand felt damp. He was so shattered by his recollection that he broke into a sweat and I loosened my hand from his grip. But at once he groped for it again and held it tight.

"Please, please," he stammered, "don't go away, I have more to say."

I no longer had any doubts as to the ending. I saw that he was summoning his strength for one last effort to tell me the rest of the story to its bitter end.

". . . Behind the windows of the second floor, I saw a man with a small child in his arms. His clothes were alight. By his side stood a woman, doubtless the mother of the child. With his free hand the man covered the child's eyes . . . then he jumped into the street. Seconds later the mother followed.

Then from the other windows fell burning bodies ... We shot ... Oh God!"

The dying man held his hand in front of his bandaged eyes as if he wanted to banish the picture from his mind.

"I don't know how many tried to jump out of the windows but that one family I shall never forget—least of all the child. It had black hair and dark eyes ..."

He fell silent, completely exhausted.

The child with the dark eyes he had described reminded me of Eli, a boy from the Lemberg Ghetto, six years old with large, questioning eyes—eyes that could not understand— accusing eyes—eyes that one never forgets.

The children in the Ghetto grew up quickly, they seemed to realize how short their existence would be. For them days were months, and months were years. When I saw them with toys in their hands, they looked unfamiliar, uncanny, like old men playing with childish things.

When had I first seen Eli? When did I talk to him for the first time? I could not remember. He lived in a house near the Ghetto gate. Sometimes he wandered right up to the gate. On one occasion I heard a Jewish policeman talking to him and that is how I knew his name—Eli. It was rare that a child dared to approach the Ghetto gate. Eli knew that. He knew it from instinct without understanding why.

"Eli" is a pet name for Elijah—Eliyahu Hanavi, the prophet.

Recalling the very name awoke memories in me of the time when I too was a child. At the Passover Seder, there stood on the table among the dishes a large, ornate bowl of wine which nobody was allowed to touch. The wine was meant for Eliyahu Hanavi. After a special prayer one of us children was sent to open the door: the Prophet was supposed to come into the room and drink the wine reserved for him. We children watched the door with eyes large with wonder. But, of course, nobody came. But my grandmother always assured me that the Prophet actually drank from the cup and when I looked into the cup and found that it was still full, she said: "He doesn't drink more than a tear!"

Why did she say that? Was a tear all that we could offer the Prophet Elijah? For countless generations since the exodus from Egypt we had been celebrating the Passover in its memory. And from the great event arose the custom of reserving a cup of wine for Eliyahu Hanavi.

We children looked on Eliyahu as our protector, and in our fancy he took every possible form. My grandmother told us that he was rarely recognizable; he might appear in the form of a village peasant, a shopkeeper, a beggar, or even as a child. And in gratitude for the protection that he afforded us he was given the finest cup in the house at the Seder service filled with the best wine—but he drank no more than a single tear from it.

Little Eli in the Ghetto survived miraculously the many raids on the children, who were looked upon as "nonworking, useless mouths." The adults worked all day outside the Ghetto, and it was during their absence that the SS usually rounded up the children and took them away. A few always escaped the body snatchers, for the children learned how to hide themselves. Their parents built hiding holes under the floors, in the stoves, or in cupboards with false walls, and in time they developed a sort of sixth sense for danger, no matter how small they were.

But gradually the SS discovered the cleverest hiding places and they came out the winner in this game of hide-and-seek with death.

Eli was one of the last children that I saw in the Ghetto. Each time I left the camp for the Ghetto—for a period I had an entry permit for it—I looked for Eli. If I saw him I could be sure that for the moment there was no danger. There was already famine at that time in the Ghetto, and the streets were littered with people dying of hunger. The Jewish policemen constantly warned Eli's parents to keep him away from the gate, but in vain. The German policeman at the Ghetto gate often gave him something to eat.

One day when I entered the Ghetto Eli was not by the gate but I saw him later. He was standing by a window and his tiny hand was sweeping up something from the sill. Then his fingers went to his mouth. As I came closer I realized what he was doing, and my eyes filled with tears: he was collecting the crumbs which somebody had put out for the birds. No doubt he figured that the birds would find some nourishment outside the Ghetto, from friendly people in the city who dare not give a hungry Jewish child a piece of bread.

Outside the Ghetto gate there were often women with sacks of bread or flour trying to barter with the inmates of the Ghetto, food for clothes, silver plate, or carpets. But there were few Jews left who possessed anything they could barter with.

Eli's parents certainly had nothing to offer in exchange for even a loaf of bread.

SS Group Leader Katzmann—the notorious Katzmann—

knew that there must still be children in the Ghetto in spite of repeated searches, so his brutish brain conceived a devilish plan: he would start a kindergarten! He told the Jewish Council that he would set up a kindergarten if they could find accommodation for it and a woman to run it. Then the children would be looked after while the grown-ups were out at work. The Jews, eternal and incorrigible optimists, took this as a sign of a more humane attitude. They even told each other that there was now a regulation against shooting. Somebody said that he had heard on the American radio that Roosevelt had threatened the Germans with reprisals if any more Jews were killed. That was why the Germans were going to be more humane in the future.

Others talked of an International Commission which was going to visit the Ghetto. The Germans wanted to show them a kindergarten—as proof of their considerate treatment of the Jews.

An official from the Gestapo named Engels, a grayhaired man, came with a member of the Jewish Council to see for himself that the kindergarten was actually set up in suitable rooms. He said he was sure there were still enough children in the Ghetto who would like to use the kindergarten, and he promised an extra ration of food. And the Gestapo did actually send tins of cocoa and milk.

Thus the parents of the hungry children still left were gradually persuaded to send them to the kindergarten. A committee from the Red Cross was anxiously awaited. But it never came. Instead, one morning three SS trucks arrived and took all the children away to the gas chambers. And that night, when the parents came back from work, there were heart-rending scenes in the deserted kindergarten.

Nevertheless, a few weeks later I saw Eli again. His instinct had made him stay at home on that particular morning.

For me the dark-eyed child of whom the man in the bed had spoken was Eli. His little face would be stamped on my memory forever. He was the last Jewish child that I had seen.

Up to this moment my feelings toward the dying man had tended toward sympathy: now all that was past. The touch of his hand caused me almost physical pain and I drew away.

But I still didn't think of leaving. There was something more to come: of that I was sure. His story must go on . . .

He murmured something which I did not understand. My thoughts were far away, although I was here only to listen to what he was so anxious to tell me. It seemed to me that he was forgetting my presence, just as for a time I had forgotten his. He was talking to himself in a monotone. Sick people when they are alone often talk to themselves. Was he continuing the story that he wanted to tell me? Or was it something that he would like to tell me but which he dare not express in comprehensible words? Who knows what he still had to say? Unimaginable. One thing I had learned: no deed was so awful that its wickedness could not be surpassed.

"Yes. I see them plain before my eyes . . ." he muttered.

What was he saying? How could he see them? His head and eyes were swathed in bandages.

"I can see the child and his father and his mother," he went on.

He groaned and his breath came gasping from his lungs.

"Perhaps they were already dead when they struck the pavement. It was frightful. Screams mixed with volleys of shots. The volleys were probably intended to drown the shrieks. I can never forget—it haunts me. I have had plenty of time to think, but yet perhaps not enough . . ."

Did I now hear shots? We were so used to shooting that nobody took any notice. But I could hear them quite plainly. There was constant shooting in the camp. I shut my eyes and in my memory I heard and saw all the shocking details.

During his narration, which often consisted of short, broken phrases, I could see and hear everything as clearly as if I had been there. I saw the wretches being driven into the house, I heard their screams, I heard them praying for their children and then I saw them leaping in flames to earth.

"Shortly afterwards we moved on. On the way we were told that the massacre of the Jews was in revenge for the Russian time bombs which had cost us about thirty men. We had killed three hundred Jews in exchange. Nobody asked what the murdered Jews had to do with the Russian time bombs.

"In the evening there was a ration of brandy. Brandy helps one forget . . . Over the radio came reports from the front, the numbers of torpedoed ships, of prisoners taken, or planes shot down, and the area of the newly conquered territories . . . It was getting dark . . .

"Fired by the brandy we sat down and began to sing. I too sang. Today I ask myself how I could have done that. Perhaps I wanted to anesthetize myself. For a time I was successful. The events seemed to recede further and further away. But during the night they came back . . .

"A comrade who slept next to me was Peter and he too came from Stuttgart. He was restless in his sleep, tossing to and fro and muttering. I sat up and stared at him. But it was too dark to see his face and I could only hear him saying, 'No, no,' and 'I won't.' In the morning I could see by the faces of some of my comrades that they too had had a restless night. But nobody would talk about it. They avoided each other. Even our platoon leader noticed it.

"'You and your sensitive feelings! Men, you cannot go on like this. This is war! One must be hard! They are not our people. The Jew is not a human being! The Jews are the cause of all our misfortunes! And when you shoot one of them it is not the same thing as shooting one of us—it doesn't matter whether it is a man, woman, or child, they are different from us. Without question one must get rid of them. If we had been soft we should still be other people's slaves, but the Führer . . .'

"Yes, you see," he began but did not continue.

What had he been going to say? Something perhaps that might be of comfort to himself. Something that might explain why he was telling me his life story? But he did not return to the subject.

"Our rest period did not last long. Toward midday we resumed the advance, we were now part of the storm troops. We mounted the trucks and were transported to the firing line, but here too there was not much to be seen of the enemy. He had evacuated villages and small towns, giving them up without a fight. There were only occasional skirmishes as the enemy retreated. Peter was wounded, Karlheinz killed. Then we had another rest, with time to wash up and to write letters. Talk centered on different subjects, but there was hardly a word said about the happenings in Dnepropetrovsk.

"I went to see Peter. He had been shot in the abdomen but was still conscious. He recognized me and looked at me with tears in his eyes. I sat down by him and he told me he was soon to be taken away to hospital. He said, 'The people in that house, you know what I mean . . .' Then he lost consciousness. Poor Peter. He died with the memory of the most dreadful experience of his life."

I now heard footsteps in the corridor. I looked toward the door which might open at any moment, and stood up. He stopped me.

"Do stay, the nurse is waiting outside. Nobody will come in. I won't keep you much longer, but I still have something important to say . . ."

I sat down again unwillingly but made up my mind to depart as soon as the nurse returned.

What could this man still have to tell me? That he was not the only person who had murdered Jews, that he was simply a murderer among murderers?

He resumed his soul-searching: "In the following weeks we advanced toward the Crimea. Rumor had it that there was hard fighting in front of us, the Russians were well entrenched; it wasn't going to be a walkover any more, but close fighting, man to man . . ."

He paused for breath. The pauses were becoming more frequent. Obviously he was overtaxing his strength. His breathing was irregular; his throat seemed to dry up: his hand groped for the glass of water.

I did not move. He appeared content as long as he was aware of my presence.

He found the glass and gulped down some water.

Then he sighed and whispered: "My God, my God."

Was he talking about God? But God was absent . . . on leave, as the woman in the Ghetto had said. Yet we all needed Him; we all longed to see signs of His omnipresence.

For this dying man, however, and for his like there could be no God. The Führer had taken His place. And the fact that their atrocities remained unpunished merely strengthened their belief that God was a fiction, a hateful Jewish invention. They never tired of trying to "prove" it. But now this man, who was dying here in his bed, was asking for God!

He went on: "The fighting in the Crimea lasted for weeks. We had severe losses. Everywhere military cemeteries sprang up. I heard they were well tended and on every grave were growing flowers. I like flowers. There are many in my uncle's garden. I used to lie on the grass for hours and admire the flowers . . ."

Did he know already that he would get a sunflower when he was buried? The murderer would own something even when he was dead . . . And I?

"We were approaching Taganrog, which was strongly held by Russians. We lay among the hills, barely a hundred yards from them. Their artillery fire was incessant. We cowered in our trenches and tried to conquer our fear by drinking from brandy flasks passed from hand to hand. We waited for the order to attack. It came at last and we climbed out of the trenches and charged, but suddenly I stopped as though rooted to the ground. Something seized me. My hands, which held my rifle with fixed bayonet, began to tremble.

"In that moment I saw the burning family, the father with the child and behind them the mother—and they came to meet me. 'No, I cannot shoot at them a second time.' The thought flashed through my mind . . . And then a shell exploded by my side. I lost consciousness.

"When I woke in hospital I knew that I had lost my eyesight. My face and the upper part of my body were torn to ribbons. The nurse told me that the surgeon had taken a whole basinful of shell splinters out of my body. It was a miracle that I was still alive—even now I am as good as dead . . ."

He sighed. His thoughts were once again centered on himself and he was filled with self-pity.

"The pain became more and more unbearable. My whole body is covered with marks from pain-killing injections . . . I was taken from one field hospital to another, but they never sent me home . . . That was the real punishment for me. I wanted to go home to my mother. I knew what my father would say in his inflexible severity. But my mother . . . She would look at me with other eyes."

I saw that he was torturing himself. He was determined to gloss over nothing.

Once again he groped for my hand, but I had withdrawn it sometime before and was sitting on it, out of his reach. I did not want to be touched by the hand of death. He sought my pity, but had he any right to pity? Did a man of his kind deserve anybody's pity? Did he think he would find pity if he pitied himself . . .

"Look," he said, "those Jews died quickly, they did not suffer as I do—though they were not as guilty as I am."

At this I stood up to go—I, the last Jew in his life. But he held me fast with his white, bloodless hand. Whence could a man drained of blood derive such strength?

"I was taken from one hospital to another, they never sent me home. But I told you that before . . . I am well aware of my condition and all the time I have been lying here I have never stopped thinking of the horrible deed at Dnepropetrovsk. If only I had not survived that shell—but I can't die yet, although I have often longed to die . . . Sometimes I hoped that the doctor would give me an injection to put me out of my misery. I have indeed asked him to put me to sleep. But he has no pity for me although I know he has released other dying men from their sufferings by means of injections. Perhaps he is deterred by my youth. On the board at the foot of my bed is not only my name but also my date of birth, perhaps that keeps him back. So I lie here waiting for death. The pains in my body are terrible, but worse still is my conscience. It never ceases to remind me of the burning house and the family that jumped from the window."

He lapsed into silence, seeking for words. He wants something from me, I thought, for I could not imagine that he had brought me here merely as an audience.

"When I was still a boy I believed with my mind and soul in God and in the commandments of the Church. Then everything was easier. If I still had that faith I am sure death would not be so hard.

"I cannot die . . . without coming clean. This must be my confession. But what sort of confession is this? A letter without an answer . . ."

No doubt he was referring to my silence. But what could I say? Here was a dying man—a murderer who did not want to be a murderer but who had been made into a murderer by a murderous ideology. He was confessing his crime to a man who perhaps tomorrow must die at the hands of these same murderers. In his confession there was true repentance, even though he did not admit it in so many words. Nor was it necessary, for the way he spoke and the fact that he spoke to *me* was a proof of his repentance.

"Believe me, I would be ready to suffer worse and longer pains if by that means I could bring back the dead, at Dnepropetrovsk. Many young Germans of my age die daily on the battlefields. They have fought against an armed enemy and have fallen in the fight, but I . . . I am left here with my guilt. In the last hours of my life you are with me. I do not know who you are, I only know that you are a Jew and that is enough."

I said nothing. The truth was that on his battlefield he had also "fought" against defenseless men, women, children, and the aged. I could imagine them enveloped in flames jumping from the windows to certain death.

He sat up and put his hands together as if to pray.

"I want to die in peace, and so I need . . ."

I saw that he could not get the words past his lips. But I was in no mood to help him. I kept silent.

"I know that what I have told you is terrible. In the long nights while I have been waiting for death, time and time again I have longed to talk about it to a Jew and beg forgiveness from him. Only I didn't know whether there were any Jews left . . .

"I know that what I am asking is almost too much for you, but without your answer I cannot die in peace."

Now, there was an uncanny silence in the room. I looked through the window. The front of the buildings opposite was flooded with sunshine. The sun was high in the heavens. There was only a small triangular shadow in the courtyard.

What a contrast between the glorious sunshine outside and the shadow of this bestial age here in the death chamber! Here lay a man in bed who wished to die in peace—but he could not, because the memory of his terrible crime gave him no rest. And by him sat a man also doomed to die—but who did not want to die because he yearned to see the end of all the horror that blighted the world.

Two men who had never known each other had been

brought together for a few hours by Fate. One asks the other for help. But the other was himself helpless and able to do nothing for him.

I stood up and looked in his direction, at his folded hands. Between them there seemed to rest a sunflower.

At last I made up my mind and without a word I left the room.

The nurse was not outside the door. I forgot where I was and did not go back down the staircase up which the nurse had brought me. As I used to do in student days, I went downstairs to the main entrance and it was not until I saw surprised looks from the nurses and doctors that I realized I was taking the wrong way down. But I did not retreat. Nobody stopped me and I walked through the main door into the open air and returned to my comrades . . . The sun at its zenith was blazing down.

My comrades were sitting on the grass spooning soup out of their mess tins. I too was hungry, and just in time to get the last of the soup. The hospital had made us all a present of a meal.

But my thoughts were still with the dying SS man. The encounter with him was a heavy burden on me, his confession had profoundly disturbed me.

"Where have you been all this time?" asked somebody. I did not know his name. He had been marching beside me the whole way from the camp to the hospital.

"I was beginning to think you had made a bolt for it which would have meant a nice reception for us back in the camp."

I did not reply.

"Did you get anything?" he asked as he peered into the

empty bread sack, which, like every other prisoner, I carried over my shoulder. He looked at me suspiciously, as to imply: you've got something, but won't admit it for fear of having to share it with us.

I let him think what he liked and said nothing.

"Are you annoyed with me?" he questioned.

"No," said I. I didn't want to talk to him—not at that moment.

After a short pause we resumed work. There seemed to be no end to the containers which we had to empty. The trucks which carried the rubbish to be burnt somewhere in the open kept coming back incessantly. Where did they take all this refuse? But really I did not care. The only thing I desired was to get away from this place.

At long last we were told to stop work, and to come back the next day to cart away more rubbish. I went cold when I heard this.

On the way back to the camp our guards, the askaris, didn't seem to be in a singing mood. They marched along beside us in silence and did not even urge us on. We were all tired, even I, who had spent most of the day in a sickroom. Had it really lasted several hours? Again and again my thoughts returned to that macabre encounter.

On the footpaths, past which we were marching, people were staring at us. I could not distinguish one face from another, they all seemed to be exactly alike—probably because they were all so utterly indifferent to us in spite of their stares.

Anyhow, why should they behave otherwise? They were long since used to the sight of us. Of what concern were we to them? A few might later on suffer the pangs of conscience for gawking at doomed men so callously.

We were not walking fast, because a horse and cart in front impeded us. I had time to conjecture that among these people must be many who had once been amused at the "day without the Jews" in the High School, and I asked myself if it was only the Nazis who had persecuted us. Was it not just as wicked for people to look on quietly and without protest at human beings enduring such shocking humiliation? But in their eyes were we human beings at all?

Two days before, some newcomers at the camp had told us a very sad but also a very characteristic story. Three Jews had been hanged in public. They were left swinging on the gallows, and a witty fellow had fastened to each body a piece of paper bearing the words "kosher meat." The bystanders had split their sides with laughter at this brilliant joke, and there was a constant stream of spectators to share in the merriment. A woman who disapproved of the vile obscenity was promptly beaten up.

We all knew that at public executions the Nazis were at pains to encourage large audiences. They hoped thus to terrify the populace and so stifle any further resistance. Of course they were well aware of the anti-Jewish feeling of most on-lookers. These executions corresponded to the "bread and circuses" of ancient Rome, and the ghastly scenes staged by the Nazis were by no means generally resented. All of us in camp were tireless in describing every detail of the horrors we had witnessed. Some talked as if they had just got home after a circus performance. Perhaps some of those who were now standing on the pavement and gaping at us were people who would gape at gibbeted Jews. I heard laughter—perhaps the show they were witnessing, a march past of kosher meat, tickled their fancy.

At the end of Grodezka Street we turned left into Janowska Street and we were brought to a halt to let a string of crowded tramcars go past. People clung to the doors like bunches of grapes, tired but happy people struggling to get home to their families, where they would spend the evening together, playing cards, discussing politics, listening to the radio—perhaps even listening to forbidden foreign transmissions. They all had one thing in common: they had dreams and hopes. We, on the other hand, had to attend the evening roll call and perform gymnastic exercises laid down according to the mood of the officer in charge. Often doing interminable knee bends until the officer tired of his joke. Or there awaited us the "vitamin B" exercise in which hour after hour we had to carry planks through a lane of SS men. Evening work was dubbed "vitamins," but unlike the real vitamins, these killed not cured.

If a man was missing at roll call, they would count us over and over again, and then in place of the missing man they would take any ten of his comrades out of the ranks and execute them as a deterrent to the other would-be absentees.

And the same thing would happen tomorrow, and perhaps the day after tomorrow, until we were all gone.

Thoughts of tomorrow . . . made me think of the dying SS man with his bandaged head. Tomorrow or perhaps the day after tomorrow he would get his sunflower. For me, tomorrow or the day after tomorrow, perhaps a mass grave waited. Indeed at any moment the order might come to clear the hut in which I and my comrades slept—or I might be one of the ten to be selected as a deterrent.

One day a rumor ran round the camp that fresh prisoners

were arriving from the provinces. If so, there would be no room in our existing huts, and if the camp authorities couldn't raise any new ones, they would make room in another way. Quite a simple matter, they simply liquidated the original prisoners—hut by hut, to make room for the newcomers. It happened every two months. It accelerated the natural decrease in our numbers, and the goal of making Galicia and Lemberg "Jew-free" grew ever nearer.

The narrow-fronted houses in Janowska Street were a dirty gray and showed traces of war damage: bullet marks on the house fronts and windows boarded up, sometimes merely with cardboard. Janowska Street was one of the most important arteries in Lemberg, and violent fighting had taken place there when the Germans had captured the city.

At the end of the rows of houses we passed once again the military cemetery with its long lines of graves, but somehow the sunflowers looked different now. They were facing in another direction. The evening sunshine gave them a reddish tinge, and they trembled gently in the breeze. They seemed to be whispering to each other. Were they horrified by the ragged men who were marching past on tired feet? The colors of the sunflowers—orange and yellow, gold and brown—danced before my eyes. They grew in a fertile brown soil, from carefully tended mounds—and behind them grew gnarled trees forming a dark background, and above everything the deep-blue clear sky.

As we neared camp, the askaris gave the order to sing, and to march in step and proper formation. The commandant might be watching the return of his prisoners and he insisted they must always march out singing and (apparently) happy, and return in the same way. The askaris had to help him to keep up the pretense. We must radiate contentment—and singing was part of it.

Woe to us if our performance did not satisfy the commandant! We suffered for it. The askaris too would have nothing to laugh at—after all they were only Russians.

Luckily the commandant was nowhere to be seen so we marched into camp behind another working party unobserved and fell in on the parade ground for roll call.

I saw Arthur in another column and waved to him furtively. I was dying to tell him about my experience in the hospital, and also to tell Josek.

I wondered what these two men so different from each other would have to say. I also wanted to talk to them about the sunflowers. Why had we never noticed them before? They had been in flower for weeks. Had nobody noticed them? Or was I the only person for whom they had any significance?

We were lucky, roll call was over sooner than usual and I touched Arthur on the shoulder.

"Well, how was it? Hard work?" He smiled at me in a friendly way.

"Not so bad. Do you know where I was?"

"No. How should I know?"

"At the Technical High School."

"Really? But in a different capacity than formerly!"

"You may well say that."

"You look rather depressed," Arthur remarked.

I did not reply. The men were crowding toward the kitchen and soon we were standing in a queue waiting for the food issue.

Josek came past us with his mess tin full. He nodded to us. We sat on the steps in front of the hut door eating our food and on the parade ground stood groups of prisoners telling each other of the day's happenings. Some of them perhaps had succeeded in scrounging oddments during their work outside the camp and they were now exchanging these among each other.

My gaze wandered to the "pipe," a narrow, fenced passage running round the inner camp and ending at the sandhills where the executions usually took place.

Sometimes men waited for two or three days in the "pipe" before they were murdered. The SS fetched them out of the huts or arrested them in the city, where they had been in hiding. They operated a "rational" system of shooting a number of men together, so several days would sometimes pass before the number was large enough to warrant the SS executioner's effort to make his way to the sandhills.

On that particular evening there was nothing to be seen in the "pipe." Arthur told me why. "There were five today but they had not long to wait. Kauzor fetched them. A fellow in our hut knew them and said they had been unearthed in a good hiding place in the city."

Arthur spoke calmly and quietly as if he was recounting something very commonplace.

"There was a boy among them," he continued after a while, and now his voice was a little more emotional. "He had lovely fair hair. He didn't look the slightest bit Jewish. If his parents had put him into an Aryan family, he would never have been noticed."

I thought of Eli.

"Arthur, I must talk to you. In the High School, which they are now using as a military hospital, I had an experience today which I am not finished with. You might laugh at me when you hear it, but I want to know just what you think about it. I have faith in your judgment."

"Go on," he said.

"No, not now. We will talk about it later. I want Josek to be there to hear it."

Was I right after all to tell them what had happened? I thought of the five men in the "pipe" who had been shot that day. Was this SS man more to me than they were? Perhaps it was better to keep my mouth shut about what I had heard in the hospital death chamber.

I feared that Arthur, the cynic, might say: "Just look at him; he can't forget a dying SS man while countless Jews are tortured and killed every hour." He might add: "You have let yourself be infected by the Nazis. You are beginning to think that the Germans are in some way superior, and that's why you are worrying about your dying SS man."

This would hurt me and then no doubt Arthur would tell me about the unspeakable crimes that the Nazis had committed. I would be ashamed of myself. So perhaps it was better to keep to myself what had happened in the hospital.

I strolled over to the parade ground and chatted to some acquaintances.

Suddenly one of them hissed: "Six!" That was the agreed warning that SS men were approaching, I hurried back to Arthur and sat down by him as the two SS men walked to the bandsmen's hut.

"What were you going to tell us?" asked Arthur.

"I have been thinking it over and I don't want to talk about it. You might not understand or . . ."

"Or what? Tell us," Arthur insisted.

I was silent.

"All right, as you like." Arthur stood up. He seemed annoyed.

But two hours later I told them the story. We were sitting in our stuffy hut on our bunks. I told them about our march through the city and about the sunflowers.

"Have either of you ever noticed them?"

"Of course I have," said Josek. "What is so special about them?"

I was reluctant to tell him the impression the sunflowers had made on me. I could not say I had envied the dead Germans their sunflowers or that I had been seized with a childish longing to have a sunflower of my own.

Arthur joined in: "Well, sunflowers are something to please the eye. The Germans after all are great romantics. But flowers aren't much use to those rotting under the earth. The sunflowers will rot away like them; next year there won't be a trace unless someone plants new ones. But who knows what's going to happen next year?" he added scornfully.

I continued my story. I described how the nurse had fetched me and taken me to the Dean's room, and then I told them in detail of the dying SS man by whose bed I had sat for hours, and of his confession. To the child who had leaped to death with his father I gave the name of Eli.

"How did the man know the child's name?" asked one of them.

"He didn't. I gave him the name because it reminded me of a boy in the Lemberg Ghetto."

They all seemed grimly fascinated by my story and once when I paused to gather my thoughts they urged me to go on.

When I finally described how the dying man had pleaded with me to pardon his crime and how I had left him without saying a word, I noticed a slight smile appear on Josek's face. I was sure it signified his agreement with my action and I nodded to him.

It was Arthur who first broke the silence: "One less!" he exclaimed.

The two words expressed exactly what we all felt in those days but Arthur's reaction somehow disturbed me. One of the men, Adam—he seldom wasted words—said thoughtfully: "So you saw a murderer dying . . . I would like to do that ten times a day. I couldn't have enough such hospital visits."

I understood his cynicism. Adam had studied architecture, but had had to abandon his career when the war broke out. During the Russian occupation he worked on building sites. All his family possessions had been nationalized by the Russians. When in the summer of 1940 the great wave of deportations to Siberia began, embracing all of "bad social origin" (i.e., especially members of the well-to-do classes), he and his family had hidden for weeks.

At our first meeting after his arrival in the camp he had said: "You see it was worthwhile hiding from the Russians. If they had caught me I should now be in Siberia. As it is I am still in Lemberg. Whether this may be an advantage . . ."

He was completely indifferent to his surroundings. His fiancée was in the Ghetto but he rarely had news from her. She must have been working in some army formation.

His parents, to whom he was deeply devoted, had perished in the very first days after the German occupation. Sometimes in his disregard for his surroundings he seemed to me like a sleepwalker. He grew more and more remote, and at first we could not rightly understand why. But gradually we all came to resemble him. We too had lost most of our relatives.

My story had apparently roused Arthur a little from his apathy, but for a long time nothing more was said by any of my listeners.

Then Arthur got up and went to a bunk where a friend of his was retailing the radio news. And the others went about their own business.

Only Josek stayed with me.

"Do you know," he began, "when you were telling us about your meeting with the SS man, I feared at first, that you had really forgiven him. You would have had no right to do this in the name of people who had not authorized you to do so. What people have done to you yourself, you can, if you like, forgive and forget. That is your own affair. But it would have been a terrible sin to burden your conscience with other people's sufferings."

"But aren't we a single community with the same destiny, and one must answer for the other," I interrupted.

"Be careful, my friend," continued Josek. "In each person's life there are historic moments which rarely occur—and today you have experienced one such. It is not a simple problem for you . . . I can see you are not entirely pleased with yourself. But I assure you that I would have done the same as you did. The only difference perhaps is that I would have refused my pardon quite deliberately and openly and yet with a clear conscience. You act more unconsciously. And now you don't know whether it was right or wrong. But believe me it was right. You have suffered nothing because of him, and it follows that what he has done to other people you are in no position to forgive."

Josek's face was transfigured.

"I believe in Haolam Emes—in life after death, in another, better world, where we will all meet again after we are dead.

How would it seem then if you had forgiven him? Would not the dead people from Dnepropetrovsk come to you and ask: 'Who gave you the right to forgive our murderer?' "

I shook my head thoughtfully. "Josek," I said, "you make it all sound so simple, probably because your faith is strong. I could argue with you for hours, although I would not want to alter my actions—even if I could. I will only say one thing, and I am anxious to know what you think: the fellow showed a deep and genuine repentance, he did not once try to excuse what he had done. I saw that he was really in torment . . ."

Josek interrupted: "Such torment is only a small part of his punishment."

"But," I continued, "he has no time left to repent or atone for his crimes."

"What do you mean by 'atone for'?"

He now had me where he wanted me: I had no reply. I dropped the argument and tried another gambit.

"This dying man looked on me as a representative, as a symbol of the other Jews whom he could no longer reach or talk to. And moreover he showed his repentance entirely of his own accord. Obviously he was not born a murderer nor did he want to be a murderer. It was the Nazis who made him kill defenseless people."

"So you mean you ought to have forgiven him after all?"

At this juncture Arthur came back. He had heard only Josek's last sentence and in his quiet voice he said: "A superman has asked a subhuman to do something which is superhuman. If you had forgiven him, you would never have forgiven yourself all your life."

"Arthur," I said, "I have failed to carry out the last wish of a dying man. I gave him no answer to his final question!"

"But surely you must know there are requests that one cannot and dare not grant. He ought to have sent for a priest of his own church. They would soon have come to an agreement."

Arthur's words were delicately, almost imperceptibly ironical.

"Why," I asked, "is there no general law of guilt and expiation? Has every religion its own ethics, its own answers?"

"Probably, yes."

There was nothing more to say. What in those circumstances, in those terrible times, could be said, had been said. The subject dropped.

To distract our thoughts, Arthur told us about the news that he had heard but his words met with only half my attention.

In thought I was still in the death chamber of the German hospital.

Perhaps Arthur was wrong. Perhaps his idea of the superman asking a subhuman for something superhuman was not more than a phrase which sounded very enlightened, but was no real answer. The SS man's attitude toward me was not that of an arrogant superman. Probably I hadn't successfully conveyed all my feelings: a subhuman condemned to death at the bedside of an SS man condemned to death . . . Perhaps I hadn't communicated the atmosphere and the despair at his crime so clearly expressed in his words.

And suddenly I was assailed by a doubt as to the reality of all this. Had I actually been in the Dean's room that day?

It all seemed to me doubtful and unreal as our whole existence in those days . . . it could not have been all true; it was a dream induced by hunger and despair . . . it was too illogical—like the whole of our lives.

The prisoner in the camp was driven, and he had to learn to let himself be driven without a will of his own. In our world, nothing any longer obeyed the laws of normal everyday life, here everything had its own logic. What laws were still valid in captivity? The only law that was left as a reliable basis for judgment was the law of death. That law alone was logical, certain and irrefutable. All other laws paled into insignificance, the result was a general passivity. We constantly reminded ourselves that this was the one law that was inevitable, that one could do nothing to change it. The effect on us was a mental paralysis, and the inconsolable attitude in which we were enveloped was the clear expression of the hopelessness of our lot.

During the night I saw Eli. His face seemed paler than ever and his eyes expressed the dumb, eternally unanswered question: Why?

His father brought him to me in his arms. As he approached he covered his eyes with his hands. Behind the two figures raged a sea of flames from which they were fleeing. I wanted to take Eli, but all that existed was a bloody mess . . .

"What are you shouting about? You will bring the guards in."

Arthur shook me by the shoulders. I could see his face by the weak light bulb high above on the ceiling.

I was not yet fully awake. Before my eyes danced something resembling a bandaged head with yellow stains. Was that too a dream? I saw everything as if through frosted glass.

"I will bring you a glass of water; perhaps you are feverish," said Arthur as he shook me again. And then I looked him full in the face.

"Arthur," I stammered, "Arthur, I don't want to go on that working party to the hospital tomorrow."

"First of all," he replied "it is already today, and secondly you could perhaps get attached to another party. I will go to the hospital in your place."

Arthur was trying to calm me. He talked as if I were a child.

"Are you suddenly frightened to look death in the eye, just because you have seen an SS man dying? How many Jews have you seen killed; did that make you shout out in the night? Death is our constant companion, have you forgotten that? It doesn't even spare the SS."

"You had just gone to sleep when the guards came in and fetched one of us away—the man sleeping right at the back in the corner. They took him only as far as the door of the hut, and then he collapsed. He was dead. Wake up properly and come with me. Look at him and then you will understand that you are making too much fuss about your SS man."

Why did Arthur stress "your SS man"? Did he mean to hurt me?

He noticed the way I flinched. "Fine feelings nowadays are a luxury we can't afford. Neither you nor I."

"Arthur," I repeated, "I don't want to go back to the hospital."

"If they send you there, you'll have to go: there's nothing you can do. Many will be only too pleased not to stay in the camp all day." Arthur still seemed unable to understand me.

"I haven't told you about the people in the streets. I don't want to see any of them any more. And they mustn't see me either. I don't want their sympathy."

Arthur gave up. He turned round in his bunk and went to

sleep. I tried to keep awake. I feared the dream would return. But then I suddenly saw the men in the street. And I realized that the break with the world around us was now complete. They did not like us Jews—and that was no new thing. Our fathers had crept out of the confines of the ghetto into the open world. They had worked hard and done all they could to be recognized by their fellow creatures. But it was all in vain. If the Jews shut themselves away from the rest of the world they were foreign bodies. If they left their own world and conformed, then they were undesirable immigrants to be hated and rejected. Even in my youth I realized that I had been born a second-class citizen.

A wise man once said that the Jews were the salt of the earth. But the Poles thought that their land had been ruined by over-salting. Compared with Jews in other countries, therefore, we were perhaps better prepared for what the Nazis had in store for us. And perhaps we were thereby made more resistant.

From birth onward we had lived with the Poles, grown up with them, gone to school with them, but nevertheless to them we were always foreigners. A bridge of mutual understanding between a Jew and a non-Jew was a rarity. And nothing had changed in that respect, even though the Poles were now themselves subjugated. Even in our common misery there were still barriers between us.

I no longer wanted even to look at Poles; in spite of everything, I preferred to stay in camp.

Next morning we assembled again for roll call. I was hoping that Arthur would accompany me if I had to go back to the hospital, and if the nurse came to fetch me again I would ask her to take Arthur in my place.

The commandant arrived. He was not always present at the

roll call; yesterday, for instance, he had not been there. He brought with him a large black Doberman on a lead. By him stood the officer (who was calling the roll) and other SS men.

First of all the prisoners were counted. Luckily the figure was correct.

Then the commandant ordered: "Working parties fall in: as yesterday."

There was considerable confusion. The prisoners were supposed to fall in according to huts, not working parties. The re-arrangement into working parties was not quick enough for the commandant. He began to bellow.

The dog became restless and strained on its lead. Any moment the commandant would let it loose. But again we were lucky. An officer came over from the commandant's office with a message. Whatever it was he marched off with the dog, which saved us the usual gruesome scenes, and the aftermath of wounded and perhaps a few dead.

The band at the inner gate played a lively march as we moved off. SS men watched our ranks intently. From time to time they made a man fall out because he was conspicuous in some way or other. Perhaps he was not in step. Or perhaps he looked weaker than the others. He was then sent to the "pipe."

We were escorted by the same askaris as on the previous day. An SS man from the guard room placed himself at the head of our column. On the way I wondered where I could hide if the nurse came to look for me.

The cemetery with the sunflowers came into view again on our left. Soon the dying SS man in the hospital would join his comrades there. I tried to picture the spot reserved for him.

Yesterday my comrades had stared at the sunflowers as if spellbound, but today they seemed to disregard them. Only a few glanced at them. But my gaze traversed row after row, and I nearly stumbled over the heels of the man in front of me.

In Grodeska Street children were playing unconcernedly. They at least did not need to hide when a man in uniform appeared. How lucky they were.

My neighbor drew my attention to a passerby.

"Do you see that fellow with the Tyrolean hat? The one with the feather."

"Certainly a German," said I.

"Sort of. He is now a racial German, but three years ago he was a fanatical Pole. I know him well. I lived near him. When the Jewish shops were looted, he was there, and when they beat up the Jews in the University he was there too. Moreover he is sure to have volunteered when the Russians were looking for collaborators. He is the type who is always on the side of the people in power. Probably he has raked up a German ancestor from somewhere or other. But I am prepared to bet that he could not speak a word of German until a short time ago. The Nazis need people like him. They would be helpless without them."

In fact one constantly heard of ethnic Germans striving to make themselves 150 percent German. On working parties one had to be careful to avoid them. They were always anxious to prove they were earning their special ration cards. Many of them tried to cover their imperfect knowledge of German by being particularly beastly to Poles and Jews. The existence of Poles and Jews to be victimized was very welcome to them.

When we entered the courtyard of the Technical High School, the askaris at once lay down on the grass and rolled their fat cigarettes. Two lorries were already waiting for us prisoners. The refuse containers were again full to overflowing. There were shovels against a wall and each of us took one.

I tried to get a job on the trucks where the nurse would be unlikely to find me. But an orderly had already chosen four other men for the job.

Then I saw the nurse walking from one prisoner to another, glancing at each of them. Was it going to be a repetition of yesterday? Had the dying Nazi forgotten something? Suddenly she was standing in front of me.

"Please," she said, "come with me."

"I have to go on working here," I protested.

She turned to the orderly who was in charge of us and said a few words to him. Then she pointed to me and came back.

"Put down your shovel," she said curtly, "and come with me."

I followed her with fear in my heart. I could not bear to listen to another confession. It was beyond my powers. Most of all I feared that the dying man would renew his plea for forgiveness. Perhaps this time I would be weak enough to give in and so finish with the painful business.

But to my surprise the nurse took a different route from yesterday's. I had no idea where she was taking me. Perhaps to the mortuary? She searched among a bunch of keys and unlocked a door. We entered a room which looked as if it were used for storage. On wooden stands which stretched nearly to the ceiling, bundles and boxes were piled.

"Wait here," she ordered, "I will be back in a moment."

I stood still.

After a few moments she came back. In her hand she had a bundle tied up in a green ground sheet. Sewn to it was a piece of linen with an address.

Somebody passed along in the corridor. She looked around nervously and drew me into the storeroom. Then she gazed at

me searchingly and said: "The man with whom you spoke yesterday died in the night. I had to promise to give you all his
possessions. Except for his confirmation watch, which I am to
send to his mother."

"I don't want anything, Sister. Send the lot to his mother."

Without a word she thrust the bundle at me but I refused
to touch it.

"Please send it all to his mother, the address is on it."

The nurse looked at me uncertainly. I turned away and left
her there. She did not try to hold me back. Apparently she had
no inkling of what the SS man had told me on the previous
day.

I went back to work in the courtyard. A hearse drove past.
Were they taking away the SS man already?

"Hi you over there, you're asleep," shouted the orderly.

An askari heard him and came over flourishing a whip. In
his eyes there was a sadistic gleam. But the orderly sent him
away.

This time our midday meal was not provided by the hospital. The ordinary prisoners' food was brought to us from the
camp—an evil-smelling, gray brew misnamed soup. We swal-
lowed it ravenously. Soldiers stood around watching us as if
we were animals being fed.

For the rest of the day I worked in a trance. When I was
back again on the parade ground in the evening I could hardly
remember the return march. I had not even glanced at the sunflowers.

Later I told my friends about the death of the SS man, but
they were not interested. The whole incident was closed in their
minds after the tale I had told them the day before. But they all
agreed with me that I had done well to refuse the dead man's

possessions. Josek said: "In the story you told us yesterday there were points that seemed to need further thought. I should have liked to discuss them with Reb Schlomo, but he alas is no more. He could easily have proved to you that you acted rightly . . . But even so I am afraid that you will continue to worry about this business. But don't cudgel your brains over it. You had no right to forgive him, you could not forgive him, and it was quite right not to accept his things."

After a while he added: "The Talmud tells us . . ."

Arthur lost something of his otherwise unshakable self-possession. He said to Josek, "Don't make him any madder; he is already dreaming about it and shouting out in his sleep. Next time it may bring us misfortune. It only needs one of the guards to hear him shouting and he will put a bullet through him. It's happened before.

"And you," said Arthur, turning to me, "do stop talking about it. All this moaning and groaning leads to nothing. If we survive this camp—and I don't think we will—and if the world comes to its senses again, inhabited by people who look on each other as human beings, then there will be plenty of time to discuss the question of forgiveness. There will be votes for and against, there will be people who will never forgive you for not forgiving him . . . But anyhow nobody who has not had our experience will be able to understand fully. When we here argue about the problem, we are indulging in a luxury which we in our position simply cannot afford."

Arthur was right, I could see that. That night I slept soundly without dreaming of Eli.

At the morning roll call the inspector from the Eastern Railway was waiting for us. We could return to our former work.

• • •

Over two years passed. Years filled with suffering and constant specter of death. Once I myself was about to be shot but I was saved by a miracle. And so I know the thoughts which a man has in the moments before death.

Arthur was no longer alive. He died in my arms during an epidemic of typhus. I held him fast as he lay in the death struggle and I wiped the foam from his lips with a cloth. In his last hours fever made him unconscious, mercifully for him.

Then one day Adam sprained his ankle at work. As he was marching out with his working party, the guard noticed he was limping. He was sent off at once to the "pipe," and there he waited two days before he and others were shot.

Josek too is dead. But I only heard about this much later. Our group had been posted to the Eastern Railway and quartered there, and one day some extra labor was sent over from the camp. Among them was Josek. I could look after him a bit now. We had some contact with the outside world and we got more food. I begged our "head Jew" to arrange for Josek to stay with us, but it was almost impossible to arrange that for an individual. We tried to persuade one of the overseers to ask for more permanent labor on the railway. But that too failed.

Then one day the extra labor from the camp came without Josek. He was ill and had been put on a working party within the camp. He had a high temperature, and from time to time when his strength failed him he had to rest. His comrades warned him when the SS man was approaching, but Josek was too weak even to stand up. He was finished off with a bullet— as punishment for being "work-shy."

Of all the men whom I knew in those years, hardly one was

still alive. My time had apparently not yet come or death did not want me.

When the Germans withdrew before the advancing Red Army, the camp was evacuated and a column of prisoners and SS guards moved westward to other camps. I went through the terrors of Plaszow; I got to know Gross-Rosen and Buchenwald, and finally after countless detours via auxiliary camps I landed at Mauthausen.

I was allocated straightaway to Block 6, the death block. Although the gas chamber was working at full pressure, it could not keep up with the enormous number of candidates. Day and night above the crematoria there hung a great cloud of smoke, evidence that the death industry was in full swing.

It was unnecessary to hasten the "natural" process of death. Why provide so many corpses in so many batches? Undernourishment, exhaustion, and diseases which were often harmless in themselves but which nevertheless carried off the weak prisoners, could provide a slower and steadier, but just as certain stream of corpses for the crematoria.

We prisoners in Block 6 no longer had to work. And we hardly saw any SS men, only the dead bodies, which were carried away at regular intervals by those comrades who still had a little strength left. And we saw the newcomers who took their places.

Our hunger was almost unbearable: we were given practically nothing to eat. Each day when we were allowed a short time outside the huts we threw ourselves on the ground, tore up the scanty grass, and ate it like cattle. After such "outings" the corpse carriers had their hands full, for few could digest this "food." The corpses were piled on to the handcarts, which formed an endless procession.

In this camp I had time for thought. It was obvious that the Germans were nearing their end. But so were we. The well-oiled machinery of murder was now running by itself, liquidating the last witnesses of the unspeakable crimes. I already surmised what was later to be confirmed: there were complete plans in existence for our final destruction as soon as the Americans approached the camp.

"Only another half hour till freedom, but only a quarter of an hour till death," as one of us said.

I lay on my bunk, wasted away to a skeleton. I looked at everything as through a thin curtain, which, I supposed, was the effect of hunger. Then I would fall into a restless doze. One night when I was neither awake nor asleep the SS man from the Lemberg Hospital reappeared to me. I had forgotten all about him, there were more important things and in any case hunger dulled the thinking processes. I realized that I only had a few days to live, or at best a few weeks and yet I remembered the SS man again and his confession. His eyes were no longer completely hidden; they looked at me through small holes in the bandages. There was an angry expression in them. He was holding something in front of me—the bundle that I had refused to accept from the nurse. I must have screamed. A doctor, a young Jew from Cracow with whom I had sometimes conversed, was on watch that night.

To this day I do not know why there was a doctor in Block 6. He couldn't help us, for his whole stock of drugs consisted of indefinable red pastilles and a little paper wadding. But this was enough for the authorities to pretend that there was a physician to look after the 1,500 condemned men in Block 6.

"What's the matter with you?" asked the doctor whom I

found standing by my bunk. Four of us had to sleep on a single bunk and naturally the other three had been roused.

"What's the matter?" he repeated.

"I was only dreaming."

"Dreaming? I only wish I were able to dream again," he consoled. "When I go to sleep I wish for a dream that would take me away from here. It is never fulfilled. I sleep well but I never dream. Was yours a nice dream?"

"I dreamt of a dead SS man," I said.

I knew that he could not understand the few words I had spoken, and I was much too weak to tell him the whole story. What would have been the sense of it anyway? Not one of us was going to escape from this death hut.

So I held my peace.


During the same night one of the men in our bunk died. He had once been a judge in Budapest . . . Since his death meant we would have more room in our cramped bunk we pondered whether to report his "departure"; but in the end the fact that there was a free place could not be hidden.

Two days later, when a new consignment of prisoners arrived, a young Pole was allocated to our bunk. His name was Bolek and he had come from Auschwitz, which had been evacuated in face of the Russian advance.

Bolek was a strong character and nothing could shake him. Little disturbed him, and he retained his sangfroid in the worst situations. In some ways he reminded me of Josek, although physically he hadn't the slightest resemblance to him. At first I took him to be an intelligent country lad.

At Mauthausen nobody asked a fellow prisoner where he came from or what his profession had been. We accepted whatever he chose to tell us about himself. The past was no longer important. There were no class differences, we were all equals— except for one thing: the times of our appointments with death.

Bolek told us about the men who perished on the transportation from Auschwitz to Mauthausen. They died of starvation during the endless days of railway traveling, or they collapsed from fatigue during the all-day marches. Those who could no longer walk were shot.

One morning I heard Bolek murmuring his prayers in Polish, which was a very unusual occurrence. Very few of us still prayed. He who is incessantly tortured in spite of his innocence soon loses his faith . . .

Gradually I learned that Bolek, who had studied theology, had been arrested outside the seminary in Warsaw. In Auschwitz he endured the most inhuman treatment, for the SS knew that he was a priest in training and never tired of inventing new humiliations for him. But his faith was unbroken.

One night as he lay awake beside me in the bunk, I told him about my experience in the Lemberg hospital.

"After all, they are not all exactly alike," he said when I had finished. Then he sat up and stared straight in front of him in silence.

"Bolek," I insisted, "you who would have been a priest by now if the Nazis had not attacked Poland, what do you think I ought to have done? Should I have forgiven him? Had I in any case the right to forgive him? What does your religion say? What would you have done in my position?"

"Stop. Wait a minute," he protested. "You are overwhelm-

ing me with questions. Take it easy. I realize that this business
sticks in your memory although we have been through so much,
but I take it that your subconscious is not completely satisfied
with your attitude at the time. I think I gathered that from
what you said."

Was this true? Did my unrest come from my subcon-
sciousness? Was this what drove me again and again to think
about the encounter in the hospital? Why had I never been able
to put it behind me? Why was the business not finished and
done with? That seemed to me the most important question.

Some minutes passed in silence, although Bolek's eyes
never left mine. He too seemed to have forgotten time and
place.

"I don't think that the attitude of the great religions to the
question of forgiveness differs to any great extent. If there is
any difference, then it is more in practice than in principle. One
thing is certain: you can only forgive a wrong that has been
done to yourself. Yet on the other hand: Whom had the SS man
to turn to? None of those he had wronged were still alive."

"So he asked something from me that was impossible to
grant?"

"Probably he turned to you because he regarded Jews as a
single condemned community. For him you were a member of
this community and thus his last chance."

What Bolek was saying reminded me of the feeling I experienced during the dying man's confession: at that time I really
was his last chance of receiving absolution.

I had tried to express this view when discussing the affair
with Josek but he managed to convince me otherwise at the
time. Or was it illusion?

But Bolek continued: "I don't think he was lying to you.

When one is face to face with death one doesn't lie. On his deathbed he apparently returned to the faith of his childhood, and he died in peace because you listened to his confession. It was a real confession for him—even without a priest . . .

"Through his confession, as you surely know—though it was not a formal confession—his conscience was liberated and he died in peace because you had listened to him. He had regained his faith. He had become once again the boy who, as you said, was in close relation with his church."

"You seem to be all on his side," I protested. "Very few SS men were brought up as atheists, but none retained any teaching of their church."

"That's not the question. I thought a lot about this problem when I was in Auschwitz. I argued with the Jews there. And if I survive this camp and ever get ordained a priest, then I must reconsider what I have said about the Jews. You are aware that the Polish church in particular was always very antisemitic . . . But let us stick to your problem. So this Lemberg fellow showed signs of repentance, genuine, sincere repentance for his misdeeds—that at least is how you described it."

"Yes," I answered, "I am still convinced of that."

"Then," Bolek pronounced solemnly, "then he deserved the mercy of forgiveness."

"But who was to forgive him? I? Nobody had empowered me to do so."

"You forget one thing: this man had not enough time left to atone for his crime; he had no opportunity to expiate the sins which he had committed."

"Maybe. But had he come to the right person? I had no power to forgive him in the name of other people. What was he hoping to get from me?"

Without hesitation Bolek replied, "In our religion repentance is the most important element in seeking forgiveness . . . And he certainly repented. You ought to have thought of something: here was a dying man and you failed to grant his last request."

"That's what is worrying me. But there are requests that one simply cannot grant. I admit that I had some pity for the fellow."

We talked for a long time, but came to no conclusion. On the contrary, Bolek began to falter in his original opinion that I ought to have forgiven the dying man, and for my part I became less and less certain as to whether I had acted rightly.

Nevertheless the talk was rewarding for both of us. He, a candidate for the Catholic priesthood, and I, a Jew, had exposed our arguments to each other, and each had a better understanding of the other's views.


When at last the hour of freedom struck, it was too late for so many of us. But the survivors made their way homeward in groups. Bolek too went home and two years later I heard that he had been ill, but I never learned what happened to him eventually.

For me there was no home to return to. Poland was a cemetery and if I were to make a new life I couldn't start it in a cemetery, where every tree, every stone, reminded me of the tragedy which I had barely survived. Nor did I want to meet those who bore the guilt for our sufferings.

So soon after the liberation I joined a commission for the investigation of Nazi crimes. Years of suffering had inflicted deep wounds on my faith that justice existed in the world. It was impossible for me simply to restart my life from the point at which it had been so ruthlessly disrupted. I thought the work of the commission might help me regain my faith in humanity and in the things which mankind needs in life besides the material.

In the summer of 1946 I went on a journey with my wife and a few friends to the neighborhood of Linz. We spread a rug on the hillside and looked out on the sunny landscape. I borrowed a pair of binoculars and studied nature through them. Thus at least I could reach with my eyes objects to which my weak legs could no longer carry me.

As I looked around I suddenly saw behind me a bush and behind the bush a sunflower. I stood up and went slowly toward it. As I approached I saw other sunflowers were growing there and at once I became lost in thought. I remembered the soldiers' cemetery at Lemberg, the hospital and the dead SS man on whose grave a sunflower would now be growing . . .

When I returned, my friends looked at me anxiously. "Why are you so pale?" they asked.

I didn't want to tell them about the haunting episode of the hospital in Lemberg. It was a long time since I had thought about it, yet a sunflower had come to remind me. Remind me of what? Had I anything to reproach myself for?

As I recalled once more the details of the strange encounter I thought how lovingly he had spoken of his mother. I even remembered her name and address which appeared on the bundle containing his possessions.

A fortnight later on my way to Munich, I took the opportunity to pay a visit to Stuttgart. I wanted to see the SS man's mother. If I talked with her, perhaps it would give me a clearer picture of his personality. It was not curiosity that inspired me

but a vague feeling of duty . . . and perhaps the hope of exor-
cizing forever one of the most unpleasant experiences of my
life.

At that time the world was seeking for a more precise understanding of the Nazi atrocities. What at first nobody could
believe, chiefly because the mind could not comprehend the
enormity of it, slowly became authenticated by fresh evidence.
It gradually dawned that the Nazis committed crimes which
were so monstrous as to be incredible.

But ere long priests, philanthropists, and philosophers im-
plored the world to forgive the Nazis. Most of these altruists
had probably never even had their ears boxed, but nevertheless
found compassion for the murderers of innocent millions. The
priests said indeed that the criminals would have to appear
before the Divine Judge and that we could therefore dispense
with earthly verdicts against them, which eminently suited the
Nazis' book. Since they did not believe in God they were not
afraid of Divine Judgment. It was only earthly justice that they
feared.

Stuttgart, I found, was one great ruin. Rubble was everywhere and people were living in the cellars of bombed houses
merely to have a roof over their heads. I remembered the
"Crystal Night" when they were burning the synagogues, and
somebody had said: "Today they burn down the synagogues,
but one day their own homes will be reduced to rubble and
ashes."

On columns and walls I saw notices posted by families
who had been torn apart and were seeking to find each other
again. Parents were looking for their children; children their
parents.

I inquired for the street in which the SS man's mother was

supposed to be living. I was told that this part of the city had been devastated by the bombs and the inhabitants had been evacuated. As there was no public transport, I set out on foot to pursue my quest. Finally I stood outside an almost completely destroyed house, in which only the lower floors seemed partly inhabitable.

I climbed the decrepit, dusty stairs and knocked on the shattered wooden door. There was no immediate response and I prepared myself for the disappointment of an unfulfilled mission. Suddenly the door opened gratingly, and a small, frail old lady appeared on the threshold.

"Are you Frau Maria S——?" I asked.

"Yes," she answered.

"May I speak to you and your husband?"

"I am a widow."

She bade me come in and I looked around the room, the walls of which were cracked and the plaster on the ceiling was loose. Over the sideboard hung, not quite straight, a photograph of a good-looking, bright-eyed boy. Around one corner of the picture there was a black band. I had no doubt this was the photograph of the man who had sought my forgiveness. He was an only son. I went over to the photo and looked at the eyes that I had never seen.

"That is my son, Karl," said the woman in a broken voice. "He was killed in the war."

"I know," I murmured.

I had not yet told her why I had come, indeed I had not yet made up my mind what I wanted to say. On the way to Stuttgart many thoughts had run through my head. Originally I had wanted to talk to the mother to check the truth of the story he had told me. But was I not secretly hoping that I might hear something that contradicted it? It would certainly make things easier for me. The feeling of sympathy which I could not reject would then perhaps disappear. I reproached myself for not having planned to open the conversation. Now that I confronted the mother I did not know how to begin.

I stood in front of Karl's portrait in silence: I could not take my eyes off him. His mother noticed it. "He was my only son, a dear good boy. So many young men of his age are dead. What can one do? There is so much pain and suffering today, and I am left all alone."

Many other mothers had also been left all alone, I thought. She invited me to sit down. I looked at her grief-stricken face and said: "I am bringing you greetings from your son."

"Is this really true? Did you know him? It is almost four years since he died. I got the news from the hospital. They sent his things back to me."

She stood up and opened an old chest from which she took the very same bundle the hospital nurse had tried to give me.

"I have kept his things here, his watch, his notebook, and a few other trifles . . . Tell me, when did you see him?"

I hesitated. I did not want to destroy the woman's memory of her "good" son.

"Four years ago I was working on the Eastern Railway at Lemberg," I began. "One day, while we were working there, a hospital train drew up bringing wounded from the east. We talked to some of them through the windows. One of them handed me a note with your address on it and asked me to convey to you greetings from one of his comrades, if ever I had the opportunity to do so."

I was rather pleased with this quick improvisation.

"So actually you never saw him?" she asked.

"No," I answered. "He was probably so badly wounded that he could not come to the window."

"How then was he able to write?" she questioned. "His eyes were injured, and all the letters he sent to me must have been dictated to one of the nurses."

"Perhaps he had asked one of his comrades to write down your address," I said hesitatingly.

"Yes," she reflected, "it must have been like that. My son was so devoted to me. He was not on specially good terms with his father, although he too loved our son as much as I did."

She broke off for a moment and looked around the room.

"Forgive me, please, for not offering you anything," she apologized. "I should very much like to do so, but you know how things are today. I have nothing in the house and there is very little in the shops."

I stood up and went over to her son's photograph again. I did not know how to bring the conversation round again to him.

"Take the photograph down if you like," she suggested. I took it carefully down from the wall and put it on the table.

"Is that a uniform he is wearing?" I asked.

"Yes, he was sixteen at the time and in the Hitler Youth," she replied. "My husband did not like it at all: he was a convinced Social Democrat, and he had many difficulties because he would not join the Party. Now I am glad he didn't. In all those years he never got any promotion; he was always passed over. It was only during the war that he was at last made manager, because all the younger men were called up. Only a few weeks later, almost exactly a year from the day on which we received news of our son's death, the factory was bombed. Many lost their lives—including my husband."

In a helpless, despairing gesture she folded her hands together.

"So I am left all alone. I live only for the memories of my husband and my son. I might move to my sister's, but I don't want to give up this house. My parents lived here and my son was born here. Everything reminds me of the happy times, and if I went away I feel I should be denying the past."

As my eyes came to rest on a crucifix which hung on the wall, the old lady noticed my glance.

"I found that cross in the ruins of a house. It was buried in the rubble, except that one arm was showing, pointing up accusingly to the sky. As nobody seemed to want it I took it away. I feel a little less abandoned."

Had this woman too perhaps thought God was on leave and had returned to the world only when He saw all the ruins? Before I could pursue this train of thought, she went on: "What happened to us was a punishment from God. My husband said at the time of Hitler's coming to power that it would end in disaster. Those were prophetic words: I am always thinking about them . . .

"One day our boy surprised us with the news that he had joined the Hitler Youth, although I had brought him up on strictly religious lines. You may have noticed the saints' pictures in the room. Most of them I had to take down after 1933—my son asked me to do so. His comrades used to rag him for being crazy about the Church. He told me about it reproachfully as if it were my fault. You know how in those days they set our children against God and their parents. My husband was not a very religious man. He rarely went to church because he did not like the priests, but he would allow nothing to be said against our parish priest, for Karl was his favorite. It always made my husband happy to hear the priest's praise . . ."

The old lady's eyes filled with tears. She took the photograph in her hand and gazed at it. Her tears fell on the glass . . .

I once saw in a gallery an old painting of a mother holding a picture of her missing son. Here, it had come to life.

"Ah," she sighed, "if you only knew what a fine young fellow our son was. He was always ready to help without being asked. At school he was really a model pupil—till he joined the Hitler Youth, and that completely altered him. From then on he refused to go to church."

She was silent for a while as she recalled the past. "The result was a sort of split in the family. My husband did not talk much, as was his habit, but I could feel how upset he was. For instance, if he wanted to talk about somebody who had been arrested by the Gestapo, he first looked round to be sure that his own son was not listening . . . I stood helplessly between my man and my child."

Again she sank into a reverie. "Then the war began and my son came home with the news that he had volunteered. For the SS, of course. My husband was horrified. He did not reproach Karl—but he practically stopped talking to him . . . right up to the day of his departure. Karl went to war without a single word from his father.

"During his training he sent us snapshots but my husband always pushed the photos aside. He did not want to look at his son in SS uniform. Once I told him, 'We have to live with

Hitler, like millions of others. You know what the neighbors think of us. You will have difficulties at the factory.'

"He only answered: 'I simply can't pretend. They have even taken our son away from us.' He said the same thing when Karl left us. He seemed to have written Karl off as his son.'"

I listened intently to the woman and I nodded occasionally, to encourage her to continue. She could not tell me enough.

I had previously talked to many Germans and Austrians, and learned from them how National Socialism had affected them. Most said they had been against it, but were frightened of their neighbors. And their neighbors had likewise been frightened of them. When one added together all these fears, the result was a frightful accumulation of mistrust.

There were many people like Karl's parents, but what about the people who did not need to knuckle under because they had readily accepted the new regime? National Socialism was for them the fulfillment of their dearest wishes. It lifted them out of their insignificance. That it should come to power at the expense of innocent victims did not worry them. They were in the winners' camp and they severed relations with the losers. They expressed the contempt of the strong for the weak, the superman's scorn for the subhuman.

I looked at the old lady who was clearly kindhearted, a good mother and a good wife. Without doubt she must often have shown sympathy for the oppressed, but the happiness of her own family was of paramount importance to her. There were millions of such families anxious only for peace and quiet in their own little nests. These were the mounting blocks by which the criminals climbed to power and kept it.

Should I now tell the old lady the naked truth? Should

I tell her what her "good" boy had done in the name of his leaders?

What link was there between me, who might have been among her son's victims, and her, a lonely woman grieving for the ruin of her family amid the ruins of her people?

I saw her grief and I knew my own grief. Was sorrow our common link? Was it possible for grief to be an affinity?

I did not know the answers to these questionings.

Suddenly the woman resumed her recollections.

"One day they fetched the Jews away. Among them was our family doctor. According to the propaganda, the Jews were to be resettled. It was said that Hitler was giving them a whole province in which they could live undisturbed among their own people. But later I heard of the brutality with which the SS treated them. My son was in Poland at the time and people talked of the awful things that were happening there. One day my husband said: 'Karl is with the SS over there. Perhaps the positions are reversed and he is now treating our doctor, who formerly treated him—'

"My husband would not say what he meant by that. But I knew he was upset. I was very depressed."

Suddenly the old lady looked at me intently.

"You are not a German?" she ventured.

"No," I replied. "I am a Jew."

She became a little embarrassed. At that time all Germans were embarrassed when they met Jews.

She hastened to tell me:

"In this district we always lived with the Jews in a very peaceful fashion. We are not responsible for their fate."

"Yes," said I, "that is what they all say now. And I can well believe it of you, but there are others from whom I won't take it. The question of Germany's guilt may never be settled. But one thing is certain: no German can shrug off the responsibility. Even if he has no personal guilt, he must share the shame of it. As a member of a guilty nation he cannot simply walk away like a passenger leaving a tramcar, whenever he chooses. It is the duty of Germans to find out who was guilty. And the non-guilty must dissociate themselves publicly from the guilty."

I felt I had spoken sharply. The lonely widow looked at me sadly. She was not the person with whom one could debate about the sins and the guilt of the Germans.

This broken woman, so deeply immersed in grief, was no recipient for my reproaches. I was sorry for her. Perhaps I should not have raised the issue of guilt.

"I can't really believe the stories that they tell," she went on. "I can't believe what they say happened to the Jews. During the war there were so many different stories. My husband was the only person who seemed to have known the truth. Some of his workmen had been out east setting up machinery, and when they came back they told of things even my husband would not believe, although he knew that the Party was capable of anything. He did not tell me much of what he had heard. Probably he was afraid I might gossip unthinkingly, and then we get into trouble with the Gestapo, who were already ill-disposed toward us and kept a watchful eye on my husband. But as our Karl was with the SS they did not molest us. Some of our friends and acquaintances got into trouble—they had been denounced by their best friends.

"My husband told me once that a Gestapo official had been to see him at the works, where foreigners were employed.

He was inquiring into a case of sabotage. He talked to my husband for a long time, and finally said, 'You are above suspicion, for your son is with the SS.'

"When Father came home and told me what had happened, he said bitterly: 'They have turned the world upside down. The one thing that has hurt me more than anything else in my life is now my protection.' He simply could not understand it."

I gazed at the lonely woman sitting sadly with her memories. I formed a picture of how she lived. I knew that from time to time she would take in her arms her son's bundle, his last present, as if it were her son himself.

"I can well believe what people said—so many dreadful things happened. But one thing is certain, Karl never did any wrong. He was always a decent young man. I miss him so much now that my husband is dead . . ." I thought of the many mothers who were also bereft of their sons.

But her son had not lied to me; his home was just as he had described it. Yet the solution of my problem was not a single step nearer . . .

I took my leave without diminishing in any way the poor woman's last surviving consolation—faith in the goodness of her son.

Perhaps it was a mistake not to have told her the truth. Perhaps her tears might help to wash away some of the misery of the world.


That was not the only thought that occurred to me. I knew there was little I could say to this mother, and whatever I might have told her about her son's crime she would not have believed.

She would prefer to think me a slanderer than acknowledge Karl's crime.

She kept repeating the words "He was such a good boy," as if she wished me to confirm it. But that I could not do. Would she still have the same opinion of him if she knew all?

In his boyhood Karl had certainly been a "good boy." But a graceless period of his life had turned him into a murderer.

My picture of Karl was almost complete. His physical likeness was now established, for in his mother's home I had at last seen his face.

I knew all about his childhood and I knew all about the crime he had committed. And was pleased with myself for not having told his mother of his wicked deed. I convinced myself that I had acted rightly. In her present circumstances, to take from her her last possession would probably have also been a crime.

Today, I sometimes think of the young SS man. Every time I enter a hospital, every time I see a nurse, or a man with his head bandaged, I recall him.

Or when I see a sunflower . . .

And I reflect that people like him are still being born, people who can be indoctrinated with evil. Mankind is ostensibly striving to avert catastrophes; medical progress gives us hope that one day disease can be conquered, but will we ever be able to prevent the creation of mass murderers?

The work in which I am engaged brings me into contact with many known murderers. I hunt them out, I hear witnesses, I give evidence in courts—and I see how murderers behave when accused.

At the trial of Nazis in Stuttgart only one of the accused showed remorse. He actually confessed to deeds of which there were not witnesses. All the others bitterly disputed the truth. Many of them regretted only one thing—that witnesses had survived to tell the truth.

I have often tried to imagine how that young SS man would have behaved if he had been put on trial twenty-five years later.

Would he have spoken in court as he did to me before he died in the Dean's room? Would he openly admit what he had confessed to me on his deathbed?

Perhaps the picture that I had formed of him in my mind was kinder than the reality. I never saw him in the camp with a whip in his hand, I saw him only on his deathbed—a man who wanted absolution for his crime.

Was he thus an exception?

I could find no answer to that question. How could I know if he would have committed further crimes had he survived?

I have a fairly detailed knowledge of the life story of many Nazi murderers. Few of them were born murderers. They had mostly been peasants, manual laborers, clerks, or officials, such as one meets in normal everyday life. In their youth they had received religious instruction; and none had a previous criminal record. Yet they became murderers, expert murderers by conviction. It was as if they had taken down their SS uniforms from the wardrobe and replaced them with their consciences as well as with their civilian clothes.

I couldn't possibly know their reactions to their first crimes, but I do know that every one of them had subsequently murdered on a wholesale scale.

When I recall the insolent replies and the mocking grins of many of these accused, it is difficult for me to believe that my repentant young SS man would also have behaved in that way . . . Yet ought I to have forgiven him? Today the world demands that we forgive and forget the heinous crimes committed against us. It urges that we draw a line, and close the account as if nothing had ever happened.

We who suffered in those dreadful days, we who cannot obliterate the hell we endured, are forever being advised to keep silent.

Well, I kept silent when a young Nazi, on his deathbed, begged me to be his confessor. And later when I met his mother I again kept silent rather than shatter her illusions about her dead son's inherent goodness. And how many bystanders kept silent as they watched Jewish men, women, and children being led to the slaughterhouses of Europe?

There are many kinds of silence. Indeed it can be more eloquent than words, and it can be interpreted in many ways.

Was my silence at the bedside of the dying Nazi right or wrong? This is a profound moral question that challenges the conscience of the reader of this episode, just as much as it once challenged my heart and my mind. There are those who can appreciate my dilemma, and so endorse my attitude, and there are others who will be ready to condemn me for refusing to ease the last moment of a repentant murderer.

The crux of the matter is, of course, the question of forgiveness. Forgetting is something that time alone takes care of, but forgiveness is an act of volition, and only the sufferer is qualified to make the decision.

You, who have just read this sad and tragic episode in my life, can mentally change places with me and ask yourself the crucial question, "What would I have done?"

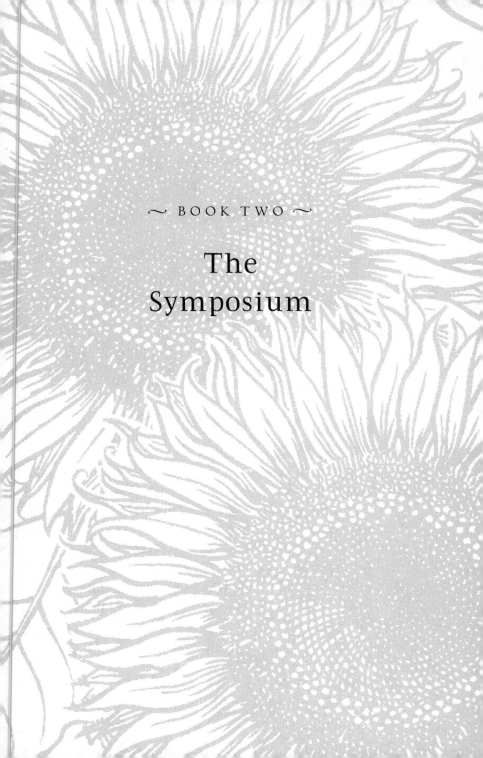

~ BOOK TWO ~

# The Symposium

# SVEN ALKALAJ

On reading *The Sunflower*, I was greatly interested in and also moved by the events described in the book. Writing as a Bosnian and a Jew, I can state that I now find myself confronted with the same question and dilemma posed by *The Sunflower.*

After World War II and the Nuremberg Trials, we assumed that what happened to the Jews of Europe would not happen ever again. "Never again." Again has happened in the very heart of Europe. Events in Bosnia and Herzegovina during the last three-and-a-half years, which have some parallels with the Holocaust, can inform the search for an answer to the question of forgiveness. I do not in any way wish to compare the genocide in Bosnia and Herzegovina with the Holocaust or to suggest that they are identical. I do wish to state, however, that clear parallels exist in regard to the worth of human life. In Sarajevo, we were forced to live like rats, scavenging for food. Our only access to the outside world ran through a dark and muddy 160-by-180-centimeter tunnel. Even our president had to endure this life-threatening trek. We were forced to live in fear that we would not see tomorrow, knowing that we could be the next victims of the best-planned "indiscriminate" shelling campaign in history. We were forced to endure this hell of a life for almost four years—and now we take pride in having survived the longest siege in the history of modern warfare.

We saw the slaughter of Srebrenica where 8,000 innocents were killed while under the protection of the United Nations. In Bosnia and Herzegovina we've seen entire families perish—children deliberately killed, tortured, and raped—and we've seen rape become a tool of war. Over 10,000 individuals, including 1,700 children, were killed in Sarajevo alone, over 200,000 people throughout the country. Now their final resting places can be found throughout the city—in its former parks, playgrounds, and backyards.

This Bosnian generation, as well as the generation that lived through the Holocaust, are among the only ones who have the right to give an answer to the question of forgiveness. Indeed, to paraphrase a colleague of Simon's: Nobody who hasn't bodily gone through what we went through will ever be able to understand fully.

If this may seem tangential to the theme of forgiveness, I can assure you that it is not. Although Simon was unsure whether his response to the dying SS man was correct, there was no question as to whether or not he should forget the crimes. It was the images of Eli and the figure of the repentant murderer that remained with Simon. Forgetting the crimes would be worse than forgiving the criminal who seeks forgiveness, because forgetting the crimes devalues the humanity that perished in these atrocities. And, as is correctly pointed out by Simon's colleagues, he had no right to forgive on behalf of the victims. This is where the issues of collective or individual guilt and victimhood must come into play.

Can we, ought we, forgive murderers who are still alive? It is also a question of how much, how quickly, how easily can any individual forgive a mass murderer. Who is entitled to speak on the behalf of the victims? And must one forget before one can forgive? Can I forgive a Serb nationalist gunner who, his breath reeking of plum brandy, lobbed shells into queues of people waiting for bread and water? Or can I forgive the thug who smoked cigarettes and drank alcohol while waiting for a mother or a father, a brother, a sister, a son, or a daughter to enter into his sniper's sight? The simple answer in this context is no.

But that is not the dilemma faced by Simon. His dilemma comes not only because the dying SS man asks for forgiveness, but also because he genuinely seems to recognize his crime and guilt. This recognition, if nothing else, is an important first step.

The question of forgiveness must be defined in individual or collective terms, just as guilt must be defined in individual or collective terms. In Bosnia and Herzegovina, the Serb fanatical leadership has fed its population such venomous propaganda that some innocent Serbs do not know what happened in the past four years. Others do know, but like the father of Karl, felt that they could not act outside the bounds of the mob mentality that swept over much of the victimizer population, both in Nazi Germany and in Serb-occupied Bosnia and Herzegovina. Therefore, at this time, there is no general accounting of what actually happened among some Serb and even Croat people, as was the case with Karl's mother. But without recognition of what happened, there can never be forgiveness. That is exactly why today's war crimes tribunal is so important. Not only will it dispense justice by punishing the guilty, but also it will show what happened during the past four years and would even eventually absolve the innocent. That way, the groundwork for reconciliation would be possible.

Simon's question is not about reconciliation, but rather forgiveness. Nevertheless, you cannot have forgiveness without reconciliation and you cannot have reconciliation without at least a shred of forgiveness. This forgiveness is not for those who killed or who orchestrated mass murder and on their deathbed seek to put their minds at ease, but for those who truly feel a collective guilt for the heinous crimes their ethnic/political/religious "brothers" committed in the name of that "brotherhood." As Simon told the mother of the dying SS man, even if a member of a society did not take part in the crimes, he or she must at least share the shame of the crimes.

I explicitly and emphatically reject the idea of collective guilt, but I do believe that there is such a thing as national or state responsibility for genocide, for mass murder, and for drumming up an artificial hatred among the ordinary people, by various means, to make that genocide easier to carry out. It cannot be stressed enough that the punishment of the guilty and some measure of justice is absolutely necessary to even consider forgiveness or reconciliation. If genocide goes unpunished, it will set a precedent for tomorrow's genocide. Without justice, there can never be reconciliation and real peace.

But when speaking of crimes against international humanitarian law, the Geneva conventions and the Genocide Convention—the very instruments of international law based on and built upon the ashes of the Holocaust—we must remember that each crime against international law is a crime against humanity and not only against the person or society targeted for extinction. That is the whole point of international law. And we must also remember that each and every victim is one of the collective *us*, whether they be Jews in Europe of the 1940s or Muslims in Europe of the 1990s.

As to the original question, I myself and the other readers will have to answer for themselves. I can say, however, that an argument can be made to forgive if there is a genuine recognition of guilt. But I cannot stress enough that to forget is unthinkable, both when discussing the Holocaust and Bosnia. In the end, reconciliation must be the end goal for a return to the inherent beauty of living.

Thus at the threshold of the twenty-first century, what have we gained from our experiences with man's inhumanity toward man? Apparently not that much. After knowing what we knew about the Holocaust, the genocide of Bosnia and Herzegovina should shame us all. Of course that shame would not bring back life to the dead of Auschwitz or Treblinka, Sarajevo or Srebrenica, but that shame does make it incumbent upon us to hold accountable those who arrogantly and immorally valued their lives so much more over those of their fellow men and women.

# JEAN AMÉRY

My high regard for your activities over the past two decades, activities that you pursued irrespective of the dangers they entailed for you personally, obliges me to comply immediately with your request to comment on the problems raised in your story, *The Sunflower.* An SS man who took part in the extermination was dying. On his deathbed, he was plagued by his Christian conscience which had persisted through the SS train-

ing, and with his final breaths, he asks for "absolution," forgiveness by a Jew. You yourself—a concentration camp inmate
at the time, surrounded by the thousand faces of death that
assailed your brothers and continually threatened you—did
not want to grant the dying man the words of forgiveness he
sought so ardently, with clasped hands even. You left him without absolution. He died without consolation. That seems to
haunt you. In any case, it preoccupies you. Quite rightly, you
challenge the opinions of your contemporaries: those who have
suffered with you, and those whom you regard, for various reasons, as moral authorities.

As for me, I am one of those who, like yourself, escaped
that giant dragnet only by chance. A survivor. Not a moral authority, to be sure. My opinion is a private one, concerning
only myself, and is of no public importance whatsoever. That
allows me a great deal of freedom. I can speak without fear that
my words could become behavioral maxims for anyone else, regardless of the small extent to which this may apply.

Dear Mr. Wiesenthal, you will inevitably be disappointed
by my comments. Your problem is not a problem for me. Let
me explain. You did not give the dying SS man absolution from
a Jew. If I had been in such a situation, perhaps I would have
been more yielding. Both your intransigence and my magna-
nimity (which is possible, but by no means certain) mean nothing to me, or rather, would mean nothing to me. As I see it, the
issue of forgiving or not-forgiving in such a case has only two
aspects: a psychological one and a political one. Psychologically,
forgiving or not-forgiving in this specific case is nothing more
than a question of temperament or feeling. I do not want to
impute any other possible behavior to you, but I can easily
imagine that, under only slightly different circumstances, you

might have forgiven the dying man. Suppose you had seen his pleading and imploring eyes, which may have had more of an effect on you than his rasping voice and folded hands. Or suppose that just before that encounter, you had been in contact with one of those "decent" SS men, whom we all knew, who had treated you with a little bit of kindness, putting you in a more tolerant mood. Or suppose you learned that some German had helped a close relative to escape. As you know better than I, such things really did happen. So, then you might have forgiven: in my view, it would have meant just as little as your (or possibly my) refusal. So much for the psychological perspective.

Now the political: Here too, in such a dramatically critical but certainly unique case—and therefore without any general implications—forgiving or not-forgiving is quite irrelevant. Whether you are an agnostic or a believer, I do not know, but your problem belongs to the realm of guilt and atonement; so even if we cast it in an agnostic form, the problem is a *theological* one, and as such, it does not exist for me, an atheist who is indifferent to and rejecting of any metaphysics of morality. I think that this does not concern individual forgiveness or individual intransigence. One can say: Your dying SS man took part in the extermination, he knew very well what he was doing. He may come to terms with his God, if he believes in one, and may just as well die unconsoled. One can also say: What difference does it make? Let him rest in peace, in the name of God or of the Devil, and if my forgiveness matters to him, I'll give it. *Politically, it does not make any difference.*

Since I see the whole question only in political terms and can deal with the problem of forgiveness from this perspective only, I must abstain from approving or condemning your behavior. (The axiomatic theory of my political thought may be rooted in morality, but this is not at issue here and would lead us too far astray.) Don't think, however, that I wish to make light of the issue or avoid painful questions by shifting to the political terrain and necessarily leaving the problematic base of your story behind. Politically, I do not want to hear anything of forgiveness! I believe that you, who have devoted your life to investigating the political realm of Nazi crimes, will understand my position. Why does it matter to me? For one simple reason: what you and I went through must *not happen again, never, nowhere.* Therefore—and I have said and written this over and over—I refuse any reconciliation with the criminals, and with those who only by accident did not happen to commit atrocities, and finally, all those who helped prepare the unspeakable acts with their words. Only if Nazi crimes like the genocide of European Jewry are not subject to a statute of limitations now or in the future, only if everyone who committed atrocities is hunted down and finally caught, will the potential murderers of tomorrow and the day after tomorrow be prevented from realizing their criminal potential. I agree with your point in your remarkable article in *Le Monde,* that too many criminals are spared by the letter of the law, that too many of the murderers in uniform, too many bloody judges of yesterday, are spending their last years in peace. Your cause, if I understand you correctly, was always a political one. Just as I leave the angels and sparrows to heaven, so I leave the moral-theological, moral-philosophical question of the answer (and, just between us, there will never be one) in the hands of the licensed professionals, that is, the speculation of tenured university professors.

Don't trouble yourself, Mr. Wiesenthal. You didn't forgive and it was certainly your right, and if you had said words of forgiveness in a fit of emotion, that would have been legitimate too. Your SS man was a devil, perhaps a *poor* devil. He and his death don't matter, just as the response of inmate Wiesenthal doesn't matter. What does matter is the activity of the director and founder of the Documentation Center. He has nothing to do with that criminal who died in the field hospital, but with others who live here among us—and live better than many of our old companions. The director of the Documentation Center should not allow them to live this sweet life but rather make sure that the arm of worldly justice, weak and ineffectual as it is, still reaches them. This is what I'm hoping for. Thankful for your work and with friendly greetings . . .

# SMAIL BALIĆ

Now that nearly thirty years have passed since *The Sunflower* was written, we can regard the horrifying events of this autobiographical story with some degree of detachment. This detachment allows for a more sober assessment of the issues the story raises concerning remorse and forgiveness. At the time of those dramatic events, the author was himself persecuted, his very existence threatened by the destructive machinery of a gruesome regime. When an SS man plagued by a bad conscience begged him for forgiveness, he saw no choice but to refuse. Most likely I would have done the same in his situation. However, many people would argue that the dying man's sincere remorse and fervent desire invited the opposite reaction, especially if one had not suffered any direct personal harm from the pleading man. The author, Simon Wiesenthal, would not have cheapened himself by granting formal forgiveness, although it would have cost him a great deal of effort. In this situation, forgiveness would have been only on his personal behalf, thus ruling out the notion of general absolution anyway. Still, it would have accomplished its purpose.

I personally feel bound by tradition to summon up some compassion (*merhamet*, as Bosnians call it) for every sufferer. This desire is of course purely theoretical. Nonetheless, in order to understand a person who has carried the burden of so much injustice and suffering, we have to imagine ourselves in his position. In the words of an oriental fable, "No doctor should go to a person who has fallen from a minaret if he has not experienced this type of fall himself." A great deal of circumspection would be required before pronouncing judgment here.

In any case, we may view the belated remorse of the young SS man of this story as a sign of hope and a signal of a new democratic beginning for Germany. Shortly after this time, Germany evolved into a stalwart supporter and friend of the Jews. By confessing and showing his remorse, the dying man testifies to his awareness of the gravity of his crimes. Thus, for whatever time might remain to him, he would be a changed man. In religious terms this decisive change in his life would be called a conversion.

Of course every person is responsible for his or her actions, and no one is able to absolve the guilt that one person bears toward others. No soul carries the burden of another. There is no such thing as collective guilt, since collective guilt would point fingers at the innocent as well as the guilty. We may only properly speak of general culpability if a society tolerates the development of a fundamentally perverted image of man.

Rectifying a misdeed is a matter to be settled between the perpetrator and the victim. A third party has no proper role other than mediator. Evil cannot be offset by good when there is no genuine remorse.

There are crimes whose enormity cannot be measured. In the view of believers, only God in His infinite mercy can cleanse the sins of the perpetrators of these crimes.

*The Sunflower* broaches many other questions of crime and punishment. One of the story's central concerns is the impassive societal reaction to the transgression. Those who might appear uninvolved in the actual crimes, but who tolerate acts of torture, humiliation, and murder, are certainly also guilty. Looking away may be a comfortable but ultimately disastrous path, the effects of which are incalculable.

The story also examines historically embedded prejudices, clichés, and stereotypes that shape the views of the masses. One of the imperative tasks of education is to come to terms with this legacy. By pinpointing mankind's failings and woes, Wiesenthal's *The Sunflower* proves a good guide.

# MOSHE BEJSKI

The subject which I was asked to relate to is complex and complicated, not only because it involves issues of conscience, morality, psychology, religion, and belief, but also because the dilemma focuses on two individuals who met under abnormal circumstances and conditions, and who ostensibly behaved and reacted in a quasi-rational manner based on the appropriate ethical considerations of human beings created in the image of God.

What is more, I was asked to relate to these events fifty years after they took place. Can considerations and behaviors be analyzed after so many years and under conditions of peace and well-being, which include the ability to overcome the spontaneous emotions caused by unexpected events? Or perhaps the distance of time and different conditions makes it difficult, if not impossible, to examine what the appropriate behavior should have been given the emotional state, the severe mental pressure, and the circumstances, which cannot be reproduced because they have never existed before and because the human mind has never invented anything like them.

Indeed, the Nazi, the SS man Karl, is a human being who was severely injured and in the throes of death. As such, and according to rational criteria, he may be worthy not only of sympathy and understanding for his suffering and his condition, but also of pardon and forgiveness for past crimes because he had confessed to them, assuming that the confession was not just formal, but based on true remorse emanating from pangs of conscience.

Yet, for Wiesenthal and others who lived under the same circumstances, Karl was a representative of German Nazism, or at least typical of the hundreds of thousands of SS troops and Sonderkommando who had joined up voluntarily and were fully aware of what they were doing. Together with others they not only routinely committed the most abominable crimes of oppression, starvation, humiliation, and forced hard labor to the point of death against the Jewish population, but were also involved in mass exterminations using methods that no human mind had thought of up to that time. Only the awareness of imminent and certain death induced Karl to think that his actions had been crimes against both humanity and God. Had he not been mortally wounded, he would almost certainly have continued to commit these crimes, along with his comrades, who had volunteered for these assignments of their own free will and in large numbers, never regretting their actions, but rather justifying them by claiming that they had only been carrying out orders.

At the time of this incident Wiesenthal is only an individual, a prisoner in a camp where he is being terrorized, worked to death, starved, and humiliated. His entire family has already been annihilated in Belzec or Treblinka and he knows that his death is certain, in another hour, another day, or another week. He, Wiesenthal, was also a witness. With his own eyes he had seen the mass shootings of naked people beside the death pits, the public hangings on the gallows. He had watched so many people die; he had seen all his relatives and fellow townspeople murdered. In this respect he is a representative witness for all those who lived or were no longer alive then and as long as the atrocities continued he certainly could not free himself of the revulsion and deep anguish he felt toward the actions of the SS man, Karl, and all his comrades who continued to commit these crimes. In his confession Karl described a mother and father who jumped together with their children from a building which had been set on fire by the Nazi troops and Wiesenthal was reminded of the child, Eli, from the Lvov Ghetto, who he had known well and cared for until he disappeared.

There are only two people in the death chamber, but each one represents an entirely different world: One—all the evil, and the horrible crimes that, up till the moment he was wounded, he himself perpetrated, and his comrades and the regime he is a part of continue to perpetrate, against human beings; and the other—the emotionally and physically broken victim of those crimes, whose pain is too much to bear because of what they have done to him, his family, and his people. Whose forgiveness was being sought—that of a Jew whose fate had already been sealed by the dying man's comrades, who did not then feel, and most likely never felt, remorse.

I never had an encounter with a dying SS man as Wiesenthal unwittingly did, but I shared his experiences in all other respects. My family was also deported to Belzec along with all the other residents of my town. I endured all the hellish nightmare of the war years in forced labor camps, in concentration and extermination camps. I saw so much death, so many executions. I was starved to death, I was degraded, made to feel subhuman; and I have forgotten none of the atrocities carried out against the Jews by the Nazi regime.

I am afraid that anyone who has been there and experienced it all would not have behaved any differently than Wiesenthal did then, and not only because the circumstances prevented him from thinking and reacting in a rational and deliberate manner, based on moral, religious, humanitarian, or philosophical considerations. But how can forgiveness be asked of someone whose death sentence will soon be carried out by the dying man's partners in crime, who are part of the same regime, when the dying person himself admits that he too has been committing these same crimes against the Jewish people and was only stopped when the hand of God overtook him.

Even if Wiesenthal believed that he was empowered to grant a pardon in the name of the murdered masses, such an act of mercy would have been a kind of betrayal and repudiation of the memory of millions of innocent victims who were unjustly murdered, among them, the members of his family.

Although Wiesenthal's reaction was instinctive and dictated by the deep suffering he was feeling for what he, his family, and an entire people had undergone, I doubt whether religious ethics (Jewish or Christian) or an altruistic conscience could lead to a level of self-sacrificing mercy beyond the ability of a human being, with the exception of saints and clergymen who act in the name of God.

In fact, religious belief had declined a great deal in the face of God's silence. A very observant relative of mine who had been preparing himself for the rabbinate before the war was with me in the Plaszow camp. On the day of the selection in May 1944 when the last two hundred eighty children remaining in the camp were deported to Auschwitz together with the old people and the sick my cousin said: "I don't believe in God anymore." Till the day he died he never regained his faith. Forgiveness could not be granted in the name of God either.

At a certain point during my testimony at the Eichmann trial in Jerusalem, when I stood face to face with the embodiment of evil, I told the judges that I doubted whether the fear, pain, helplessness, depression, and hopelessness which we felt then could be reproduced now at a distance of so many years. This is certainly true with respect to the dilemma in question. Nevertheless, I exhorted myself to be faithful only to considerations, feelings, and behaviors that relate to the circumstances and conditions that existed then. In this way I was able to arrive at the above conclusion.

We can only be thankful that the passage of time dulls the pain somewhat and heals the open wounds to a certain extent, so that we can look at the issues in a broader perspective. Yet the crimes committed by the Nazi regime were so barbarous and so destructive to the victims that those who somehow managed to survive have never been able to free themselves of the horrors they had to endure. Moreover, the few survivors found themselves with no families, and their children grew up without grandparents. Thus, in addition to all their other injustices the Nazis themselves have prevented their crimes from being forgotten. The survivors have been sentenced to bear their pain and sadness to the grave. Without forgetting there can be no forgiving.

It is indeed true that not only the German people are interested in consigning the crimes of the Nazi regime to oblivion, the world has also begun to forget too soon. Even in the countries that suffered under the occupation of that sadistic regime, the number of Nazi criminals who have been found, brought to trial, and punished, even as a deterrent for potential criminals, is dwindling. Thus thousands and perhaps hundreds of thousands of Germans who participated in and committed genocide and crimes against humanity returned to their homes and to quiet, peaceful lives, without their consciences ever bothering them, without ever feeling any remorse. Certainly these people do not need to be forgiven by anyone, not by the victims and not by God.

Does repentance alone justify and bring about forgiveness and allow crimes to be forgotten?

Even in normal criminology and penology only true regret accompanied by reformed behavior can be considered a justification for lightening a sentence, and even then not necessarily in the case of serious crimes. No matter what, regret never pardons crimes, except when the state declares an amnesty for certain crimes, generally for political reasons.

We all remember the heated debate during the 1960s over the issue of establishing a statute of limitations for prosecuting Nazi criminals for the crime of genocide and crimes against humanity. At the time the opinion was that, since the crimes in question were so terrible that humanity has never known anything like them before, there was no justification for putting a time limit on their prosecution, allowing the passage of time to atone for crimes which cannot be forgiven.

Another point about Wiesenthal's behavior, also in hindsight: I have already said that, by leaving the room after hearing Karl's confession, or more correctly, statement, Wiesenthal behaved in the only way he could have behaved, according to the reasonable feelings of an individual in his situation. He had no desire for revenge toward the person who had injured him and his people so cruelly nor did he feel any satisfaction about the circumstances. He went out of his way to visit Karl's mother, but refrained from telling her the truth about the crimes her son committed while he served in the SS, if only to help her preserve her image of a son she remembered as a good boy.

It seems to me that this restraint goes beyond what a human being could be expected to do.

Even considering the distance in time and the use of hindsight, I am certain that Wiesenthal's conscience should not be troubled by the manner in which he behaved during that macabre encounter.

# ALAN L. BERGER

I have been teaching Simon Wiesenthal's book *The Sunflower* for many years. The issues remain seemingly intractable. Students are struck by the notion of forgiveness. Was Simon right? What about the meaning of his silence? Was Karl's repentance genuine? Further, if the Holocaust was unique, how can traditional responses—including forgiveness—be applied to monstrous evil? We are engaged at the most profound levels of meaning and response.

In literary terms, silence is the principal character of this morality tale. And Simon was twice silent: once in the death chamber of the dying Nazi, and once in the presence of the dead man's mother. Are the silences the same? Do they convey different meaning? The first silence is one of confusion. Stunned, frightened, overwhelmed, Simon does not know which way to turn. He is torn between the ethical teachings of Judaism and the harsh reality of the Holocaust whose only goal was the extermination of Jews. By way of contrast, the second silence is a conscious decision. It is taken out of kindness to the mother. What, it might be argued, would there be to gain by telling the mother the truth about her son? Preserving his memory was a true gift of grace, the only such gift to have a proper place in this story. To have forgiven her son would have been a desecration both of the memory of the Jewish victims and of the sanctity of forgiveness.

In Simon's place, what would I do? This question raises a prior query. Am I entitled to forgive on behalf of the murdered? My response is, do not forgive someone for whom forgiveness is forbidden. Judaism teaches that there are two types of sins. One is that committed by humans against God, *beyn adam le-makom.* The second type consists of sin committed by humans against other humans, *beyn adam le-adam.* I may forgive one who has sinned against me. I may not forgive one who has taken the life of another.

My own thoughts are firm. Simon should, and could, not forgive on behalf of those so cruelly murdered. Further, in asking for a Jew to hear his confession Karl perpetuated the Nazi stereotype. Jews were not individuals with souls, feelings, aspirations, and emotions. Rather, they were perceived as an amorphous, undifferentiated mass. Bring me a Jew, was the dying Nazi's request. Any Jew will do. Karl has learned nothing. His desire is to "cleanse" his own soul at the expense of the Jew.

Was Karl's repentance sincere? Repentance in Hebrew comes from the word *teshuvah,* meaning a turning away from evil, a turning toward Torah. It is a process rather than a single act. When it mattered, when he shot Jews jumping from a burning house, Karl displayed no moral courage. Recent studies have demonstrated that there were those who disobeyed orders, took a moral stance, and were not punished. It is far more difficult to act morally than immorally. Repentance is formulaic: a learned ritual which soothes the troubled soul of the murderer, but does nothing for those who were murdered. Is it morally possible to say, "I am sorry for the Holocaust"? Or to apologize for individual acts of murder whose great aggregate yielded the murder of millions of Jews?

The entire issue of cheap grace, forgive and forget, is raised here. Presumably, Karl, achieving forgiveness, would go to heaven.

Whereas Simon and other Jews, including and especially the victims of the slaughter in the Polish town, would not. If the teachings of the Catholic Church were so radically deficient as to be unable to hold Karl to moral accountability, then shame on the Church. Shame on the murderers. And shame on those who ask forgiveness thereby requiring from others the moral integrity which they themselves so sorely lack.

Let us assume for a moment that Karl either was not wounded or did not die. Would he then have had pangs of conscience? After the war, would he be among the penitents? Or would he not have been among those Nazis who either gathered to reminisce about the "good old days" or simply resume his life: marrying, raising a family, prospering, and shaking his head over all the fuss Jews made over the Holocaust?

A last reflection. Simon's Jewish conscience was deeply disturbed by the event. He spoke about it to his fellow prisoners, and clearly the matter still weighs heavily upon him. In reminding himself of the foul deeds of murder committed by the Nazis, and the indifference to Jewish suffering displayed by the Poles, it seems as though Simon must present this evidence before the courtroom of his own conscience which has become the scene of this titanic struggle. Is this not what Karl depended on? After all, Hitler blamed the Jews for bringing conscience to bear in history. Granting the murderer forgiveness would have been the final victory of Nazism. Had he spoken to Karl, Simon would have sealed his own guilt.

# ROBERT McAFEE BROWN

Warsaw, 1979. We are standing in front of the memorial to those Jews who lost their lives defending the Warsaw Ghetto. It is raining. A personal friend who survived that battle is giving an impassioned address. It is in Polish. Several days later he gives me a copy of the translation. The passion carries over into English. The theme is clear: *Never forget, never forgive.*

That we must *never forget* is perhaps the clearest lesson of the Holocaust. For if we forget, a time will come when even worse atrocities will be committed against Jews, and any others whom those with power wish to destroy.

That we must *never forgive* would seem to follow from the same stern logic. For if we forgive, it will be a sign to those in the future that they can act without fear of punishment, and that the universe has a moral escape valve labeled "forgiveness" that permits evil not only to survive but to thrive. On this reading, forgiveness becomes a "weak" virtue, one that Christians seem particularly prone to champion, and one that always carries the possibility of condoning, rather than constricting, the spread of evil.

And yet, I remain uneasy with the second conviction.

Consider the absolutely worst-case scenario. It is in Auschwitz on a day when the gas chambers are falling behind their quotas. To accelerate the pace, children are lined up and thrown upon the open flames. Those toward the back of the line know full well that in a matter of moments the fate of those up front will be their fate as well. And there is nothing they can do about it.

This strikes resonating chords with the scene Simon Wiesenthal has created for us, in which Jews of all ages are locked in a house that is then set on fire.

Both episodes strain to the breaking point any contention that forgiveness would be appropriate within such circumstances. If God forgives such deeds, does not that likewise strain to the breaking point any contention that the universe of God's creation is a moral universe? A malevolent deity might be placed in charge of such arrangements but surely not a god of mercy and compassion.

And if God is not entitled to forgive, surely the same moral boundary is placed around God's children. To forgive the Nazis who threw children on the fire and locked them in houses to be incinerated is to become one with the Nazis, endorsing evil deeds rather than combatting evil deeds, and thereby becoming complicit in their actions.

Jews and Christians usually cope with the dilemma by affirming that God, rather than being removed from evil, is found *in the midst of the evil,* identifying with the victims rather than the perpetrators. So the Jewish imagery of the "Suffering Servant" in the Book of Isaiah avers, and so the Christian imagery of Christ suffering on the cross likewise avers. But, as Elie Wiesel suggests in *Ani Maamin,* such a deliverance comes too late—six million deaths too late—and such a God seems powerless to be more than a remorseful deity who can endure but cannot enable.

But perhaps there are situations where sacrificial love, with forgiveness at the heart of it, *can* make a difference, and can even empower. One thinks of Nelson Mandela, released after twenty-seven years in jail, patently entitled to wreak vengeance on his tormentors, and who responds by forgiving his jailers. Or one thinks of Tomas Borge, a Nicaraguan Sandinista fighter, captured by the contras and brutally tortured, confronting his torturer after the war had ended. The court entitled him to name the punishment appropriate for his torturer. Borge responded, "My punishment is to forgive you."

Such instances build up a moral capital on which the rest of us can draw: supposing, just supposing, that an act of forgiveness on our part could tip the scales toward compassion rather than brutality . . .

We can propound these and other examples that might mitigate some of the harshness of the imperative *Never forgive*, but in all instances we are exploring only exceptions to the rule. One cannot allow, as a human axiom, a position such as that of the philosopher-poet Heinrich Heine, "God will forgive, that's what He's here for."

So, had I been in Simon Wiesenthal's position, fearful of denying too much or of promising too little, I think I would have urged the young man to address his plea directly to God, and throw himself on the possibility of Divine Mercy, something I am not permitted to adjudicate one way or the other.

How could I justify such a response, refusing to grant either sentimentalized mercy or hard-nosed judgment? I return to Elie Wiesel, to offer two responses in the form of questions:

1. I do not believe we can supply an answer to the first question, *"Where is God in all this?"*—a question on the lips of character after character in Wiesel's novels. The closer I come to

what might be called an "answer," the more circumspect I must become, although I must keep trying, keep trying to do so. I will always come up short.

2. What we can do on the far side of such an impasse is to respond to another question and truly make it our own. In Wiesel's *The Gates of the Forest*, a rebbe, confronted with evil and God's transparent involvement in it, asks out of deep anguish, *"What is there left for us to do?"*

This is what we must exhume from the debris of our inadequate "answers." What "answers" there are will finally come not from the region of our minds, but from the precincts of our hearts. It will be in doing rather than in speculating that we will learn whatever it is permitted us to learn.

"What is there left for us to do?" Only everything from doing justly, loving-kindness, and walking humbly with God, to standing with the victims and the oppressed. And if we do so, perhaps, just perhaps, a world will begin to emerge in which we do not have to ask unanswerable questions any longer.

# HARRY JAMES CARGAS

I am afraid not to forgive because I fear not to be forgiven. At the time of Judgment, I pray for mercy rather than justice. Some theologians have it that in the last analysis, mercy and justice must exist side by side but who among us is so confident as to say "I can withstand the scrutiny of justice"?

As we consider Simon Wiesenthal's dilemma let us carry it out to a kind of logical end—almost a reductio ad absurdum problem: Should Adolf Hitler be forgiven? Recall that for years, in Spain, an annual Catholic mass was celebrated (that's the word!) for the repose of the Führer's soul. One cannot help asking if this was done from the principle of charity or if this was a continuing act of antisemitism (oddly, in a nation whose fascist leader did *not* turn Jews over for deportation to the death camps).

Forgiveness, like any apparently virtuous act, can be misunderstood, including by the forgiver. My act of charity might well turn out to be an act of arrogance if examined very closely. Perhaps when I forgive I raise myself above the other. I make that person beholden to me. It is appropriate to ask myself, "Who am I to forgive?"

Yet forgiveness is a virtue, that cannot be denied. And it is necessary to spiritual wholeness. But is it required of us in all cases? In Christian Scripture there is a reference to an unforgivable sin. There have been various interpretations of this mystery, many of them unsatisfying or unclarifying.

For me the question is not can we forgive Karl or should we forgive Karl, but *dare* we do so? If there are crimes in my lifetime which are unforgivable, certainly those of Hitler and his henchmen have committed them. I tremble with all of my being when I hold them fully responsible for their actions—but I do. Forgiveness is not something we may depend on others for. We must somehow earn it. Deathbed conversions are dramatic but in many instances they are *too easy.*

If God chooses to forgive Karl, that's God's affair. Simon Wiesenthal could not, I cannot. For me, Karl dies unforgiven. God have mercy on my soul.

# ROBERT COLES

We are told at the end of this powerfully provocative moral fable (dare I say the author's extended fantasy that became an *apologia pro sua vita?*) that the heart of the matter is "the question of forgiveness." But forgiveness by whom?—so the reader is challenged: "Forgetting is something that time alone takes care of, but forgiveness is an act of volition, and only the sufferer is qualified to make the decision."

With that observation, of course, most of us who come upon *The Sunflower* will feel the obligation of a necessary, stunned silence—of a kind, one hopes and prays, that is not incompatible with ethical reflection. Yet, we are asked a question after being told the above; we are asked to put ourselves in the author's shoes: "What would I have done?" This request, that we exercise all the moral imagination we can summon, that we try to take a huge leap in the interest of a shared contemplation (as in Conrad's *Heart of Darkness*) of "the horror, the horror," gives us sanction, encourages us to try, at least, for some sense of what, after all (and after all that took place in those unspeakable years that in their sum became the Holocaust) might be a fitting response to the moral challenge posed in this story.

Surely the critical matter posed by that concluding question has to do with the word "I"—what each of us brings to it: a particular life's experiences, with their shaping influence on what is believed and upheld, what is doubted or denied. When Wiesenthal asks "Was my silence at the bedside of the dying Nazi right or wrong?" he is, presumably, putting the question to himself, not us—challenging his moral life as he asks us to do so with that further last question mentioned above. He obviously believes his silence to have been "right"—the only decent and honorable reply his particular life allowed him to make. For us today it becomes quite another matter, the contemplation of that question: we bring to it not the life described in the story, but lives lived at a far remove from what is described, evoked with such telling, unnerving detail and power, and alas, authority—that of the one who was, unforgettably, *there.* Still, we can attempt to make our individual effort—a gesture of human solidarity with those who, like the author, survived to render an account of that worst time in the history of humankind.

With great unease and with no conviction that I would have had a ghost of a chance at surviving (either morally or physically) the sustained, moment-to-moment terror and ignominy chronicled in *The Sunflower,* I gird myself, and leap with this quite mixed, even contradictory speculation: were I to have survived, as the author did, to experience the "moment" offered in this moral drama (the call for forgiveness by the Nazi at death's door), I would have turned away in a tearful rage— even as I (that is, the person I was brought up to be) would pray for the Lord's forgiveness of that apparently repentant Nazi; pray for him as I was taught to pray for the forgiveness of any of us who somehow, some way come to realize the evil of our ways.

Not that I (foolishly, outrageously) would compare any of us ordinary "sinners" to the Nazi monsters, the leaders or their minions. The point, rather, is the limitations of our lives—we can only bring ourselves, in all our finiteness, to this table, this symposium that is, really, the merest footnote to an enor-

mously tragic and melancholy twentieth-century saga: our talk
(as in Shakespeare's "words, words, words") about how others
might have behaved under circumstances all too dreadfully familiar to them, and one has to say it, all too inconceivable to us.
Still, with caveats galore, I proceed to tell of my mother's wish
for my brother and me, that we learn how to understand, and
too, that we learn how to forgive: understand the mistakes and
errors of our ways, in the hope that we can do (can *be*) better;
and forgive ourselves, lest we give our errant or evil side the
continuing hold over us that such a refusal of forgiveness all
too commonly, readily ensures. To sustain that moral conviction is not easy even in this comfortable, this privileged life that
fate has given me—how often many of us who profess the
Christian ethic of forgiveness succumb to smugness, arrogance,
pretentiousness, a cocky self-importance that is utterly incompatible with the kind of absolution and reconciliation implied
in the act of forgiveness: no exculpation for wrong, but an ac-
knowledgment that a long, tenaciously critical look inward
justifies a wholehearted response of merciful grace, for which
one prays.

I would, then, pray to God for the forgiveness of that
Nazi, who claimed to be repentant—I, the present-day son of
my parents, the one who inhabits this life. I say the above,
though, with no conviction of righteousness, never mind (Lord,
spare us) a temptation to self-righteousness. Who am I (the
rhetorical question *must* be asked!) to tell even myself, let alone
this author who has generously taken public moral pause on
behalf of all of us, what ought have been done under circumstances, let's face it, wherein the conscience in so many of us
(the same conscience, with all its assumptions, that distin-
guishes us as the somewhat "civilized" people we at least some-

times are, or try to be) is no doubt maimed before the heart stops beating.

Let us, who are lucky to have been given by fate the safety to read and ponder *The Sunflower*, to pose its haunting, provocative, thoroughly challenging moral questions to ourselves, not only struggle for (and with) our various responses, answers, but take to heart what may be, finally, the author's real intent for us: that we never, ever forget what happened to him and millions of others; that their experiences become (through the movement of mind and heart that goes with reading, with writing) for now and for the future our very own—an introspective moral legacy we dare not relinquish for our own sakes, never mind out of respect for those whose suffering has enabled that legacy.

# THE DALAI LAMA

I believe one should forgive the person or persons who have committed atrocities against oneself and mankind. But this does not necessarily mean one should forget about the atrocities committed. In fact, one should be aware and remember these experiences so that efforts can be made to check the reoccurrence of such atrocities in the future.

I find such an attitude especially helpful in dealing with the Chinese government's stand on the Tibetan people's struggle to regain freedom. Since China's invasion of Tibet in 1949–50, more than 1.2 million Tibetans, one-fifth of the country's population, have lost their lives due to massacre, execution, starvation, and suicide. Yet for more than four decades we have struggled to keep our cause alive and preserve our Buddhist culture of nonviolence and compassion.

It would be easy to become angry at these tragic events and atrocities. Labeling the Chinese as our enemies, we could self-righteously condemn them for their brutality and dismiss them as unworthy of further thought or consideration. But that is not the Buddhist way.

Here I would like to relate a very interesting incident. A few years back, a Tibetan monk who had served about eighteen years in a Chinese prison in Tibet came to see me after his escape to India. I knew him from my days in Tibet and remember last seeing him in 1959. During the course of that meeting I had asked him what he felt was the biggest threat or danger while he was in prison. I was amazed by his answer. It was extraordinary and inspiring. I was expecting him to say something else; instead he said that what he most feared was losing his compassion for the Chinese.

# EUGENE J. FISHER

Simon Wiesenthal's *The Sunflower* embodies one of the most compelling moral questions to have emerged from the Second World War. Its reissuance challenges a new generation of Jews and Christians to grapple with it. That is an event to be welcomed, painful as the grappling is likely to be for many of us.

When *The Sunflower* first appeared in English, I had not yet begun in my present position in Catholic-Jewish relations for the National Conference of Catholic Bishops. I can remember being relieved that no one, then, asked me to respond to it. I would have had no way to start. In one sense, I still don't. As several of the original responders stated, no one can really know what she or he would have done in such a situation. One can only come up with what one would *hope* to have done. Nor can any Christian really speculate, as other commentators acknowledged, as to what a Jew should have done in the situation described. Christians simply do not have the experiential base to make a moral judgment on Jewish behavior with regard to the Shoah.

Those writing today do have some advantages over the original responders. One, of course, is to be able to draw on their reflections, which plumbed the depths of the issue from numerous angles. The statements supporting the narrator's silence and refusal to pretend to forgive are argued, to my mind, convincingly. Most of these are by Jewish respondents. In both Jews and Christians, however, I can discern an uneasiness with any "either/or" resolution, since repentance and reconciliation are liturgically central to both traditions as seen in the holy days of Yom Kippur and Good Friday. The difference in reaction, then, may not stem from theology as much as from existential stance.

The original collection was so trenchant and complete, it would seem that there would be little substantive to add. There is, however, much that has come out between Jews and Christians through the events of the past two decades of intense Jewish-Christian dialogue and equally intense controversy. We may well find in this second collection, then, a difference in tone and perhaps substance from the earlier responses. If so, this might be a valuable barometer of how the relationship has changed over the years.

Since the first edition of this book we have seen President Reagan's visit to Bitburg and the election of Kurt Waldheim, as well as controversies over Edith Stein, Cardinal Glemp, and the Auschwitz Convent. One of several leitmotifs running through them, often in the form of a charge by the Christian side, has been the question: Why can't they (the Jews) forgive? We Christians do. Why can't they let it alone and get on with living? In other words, the question so presciently raised and profoundly framed by Simon Wiesenthal has emerged as critical to Jewish-Christian relations.

With regard to Bitburg and Waldheim, I participated in what came to be called "the Forgiveness Debate" with two British Christian colleagues, who felt that it would be healthy for the Jewish community, if not to forget, at least to begin to forgive. I argued that it is, on the one hand, too soon for this, since the essential sign of repentance is a "turning away" (*teshuvah*) from evil and toward the good. While well begun by Christians, I believe that if I were Jewish, I would wait a generation or so to see if the official documents and statements of the Churches do, in fact, bring about the transformation toward which they confessedly aim.

Secondly, I believe it is the height of arrogance for Christians to ask Jews to forgive them. On what grounds? We can, as established by evidence of changed teachings and changed behavior, repent and work toward mutual *reconciliation* with Jews. But we have no right to put Jewish survivors in the impossible moral position of offering forgiveness, implicitly, in the name of the six million (as, again, several of the original respondents articulated quite well). Placing a Jew in this anguished position further victimizes him or her. This, in my reading, was the final sin of the dying Nazi.

Bitburg was a classic case in point. There, the Christian leader of the victorious Allies met with the Christian leader of the defeated Germans at a Nazi cemetery to "forgive" each other for what Christians had done and allowed to be done to Jews by Nazis. Jews who raised questions were dismissed by some other Christians as "unforgiving" and even "vengeful." It was a sad replay of the ancient stereotypes that had contributed to the problem in the first place.

Over the years, I have kept getting from my fellow Christians variations of the same refrain. And I keep rejecting them. I also receive the question from well-meaning Catholics and Jews: Has the Church officially apologized to the Jews yet and asked for their forgiveness? "The Church has done more," I reply, hoping that a theological response will satisfy a sociological and psychological question. It has expressed its repentance before God and before all humankind. It has refrained from asking "the Jews" (which Jews speak for all?) for "forgiveness." That could easily be seen as "cheap grace."

In 1990, at a meeting of the International Catholic-Jewish Liaison Committee (ILC) in Prague, which I had the honor to attend, Cardinal Edward I. Cassidy of the Holy See's Commission for Religious Relations with the Jews spoke officially for the universal Church of its proper attitude after the Holocaust being one of "repentance (*teshuvah*)." The Hebrew biblical term was used so that no one could mistake the intent. In December of 1990, at an ILC event in Rome commemorating the twenty-fifth anniversary of Nostra Aetate, the Second Vatican Council's formal declaration on the Church's relations to the Jews, Pope

John Paul II pointedly made the statement of Cardinal Cassidy his own. In the spring of 1992, the statement of repentance was made by a representative of the Spanish hierarchy before a large group of visiting American rabbis at an event in Madrid commemorating the expulsion of the Jews from Spain five hundred years earlier. In late May of 1992, it was repeated as the official position of the Catholic Church by Cardinal Cassidy at the ILC meeting in Baltimore.

These Church statements reflect sentiments expressed since the Second Vatican Council by Catholic bishops' conferences and their Protestant counterparts in the United States, Europe, Latin America, and Australia. So there is little doubt as to what official Catholic teaching is on this matter today. They represent a different sort of answer from the dilemma which *The Sunflower* so trenchantly sets up. In the person of its official representatives, the Christian community asks, through sincere repentance (the test of which is change of behavior) for forgiveness not directly of the Jews (for that would put surviving Jews in a morally intolerable situation) but of God. But one does this publicly, as the Pope has done it, since the offense is not only against the Jews but God and humanity as well.

And then the Churches must follow through with revised textbooks, improved New Testament translations, better sermons from the pulpit, and better lessons in the classroom. For the pulpit and classroom are the Church's key "delivery systems" when it comes to making a difference for the future in the long haul. Perhaps the Jewish community could offer a prayer or two that the efforts in this direction that have been begun by responsible Church leaders since World War II, and especially since the Second Vatican Council, will succeed in changing the face that Christianity presents to Judaism both radically and permanently.

# EDWARD H. FLANNERY

The story in *The Sunflower* presents us with an important moral question: Is it permitted to refuse forgiveness to a sincerely repentant malefactor? The question is embedded in a real-life situation in which Simon, our author, an erstwhile internee in a World War II concentration camp, refuses a forgiveness requested by Karl, an SS man who had been actively involved in a heinous military action, but who now is close to death and repentant.

Simon refused simply by walking away from Karl. But apparently not so simply from himself. Somewhat later, Arthur, a fellow internee, makes this plain in this scolding of Simon:

> And you . . . do stop talking about it. All this moaning and groaning leads to nothing. If we survive this camp— and I don't think we will—and if the world comes to its senses again, inhabited by people who look on each other as human beings, then there will be plenty of time to discuss the question of forgiveness. There will be votes for and against, there will be people who will never forgive you for not forgiving him . . . But anyhow nobody who has not had our experience will be able to understand fully. . . .

> Arthur was right, I could see that. That night I slept soundly (p. 75).

Simon's sleep was not to remain so tranquil. Before the story draws to a close we find him still wrestling with the problem.

His subsequent behavior gives eloquent testimony to the ambivalence that possesses him. His decision to visit Karl's mother gives evidence of his uncertainty and guilt feelings. And the actual meeting gives a further clue of this. He refused to reveal to her the atrocities Karl had indulged in, tempted as he was to do so. It is difficult not to see these waverings as a leaning toward atonement.

What, in final analysis, are we to conclude regarding Simon's refusal to grant Karl the forgiveness he sought?

I can well understand Simon's refusal, but I find it impossible to defend it. I do not arrive at such a position easily. For anyone who holds an allegiance to our Judeo-Christian heritage and who has any sense of the horrors of the Shoah and of the savagery of its Nazi perpetrators cannot come easily to a decision on Simon's painful dilemma.

To comprehend it adequately one must take into consideration two basic components: the psychological or emotive aspects of the situation and its ethical or religious involvement. The psychological or emotive factors are of importance and should have an influence on the decision to be made, but when they are in serious conflict with ethical or religious principles they must give way, as, in my view, they must in the case before us. The eternal and millennial transcend the transient and terrestrial.

It is a cardinal principle of Judeo-Christian ethics that forgiveness must always be granted to the sincerely repentant. The only seeming exception to this in the Hebrew and Christian scriptures is in the New Testament allusion to the "unforgivable sin against the Holy Spirit" (Mark 3:29). But this refers to a person's rejection of God and therefore precludes any relation to forgiveness of humans. Contrariwise, in the same Gospel we read Jesus' answer to the question of how many times one must forgive. Should it be "seven times"? Speaking out of his Jewish tradition, his answer was, "Seventy times seven times"—a metaphorical way of saying "always."

Simon connives with the foregoing principle, though obliquely. When speaking of those bystanders who passively watched Nazi atrocities, he writes, "Was it not just as wicked for people to look on quietly and without protest at human beings enduring such shocking humiliation?" Does not watching the dying Nazi pleading for mercy in his final agony fit within his description of inhumanity?

*The Sunflower* story brings up the question of whether Simon had a right to forgive Karl in the name of all Jews. The question appears to me as irrelevant. The dying SS man did not ask him to speak in the name of all Jews or, for that matter, for the harm done to all Jews but only for what he had done. The situation was interpersonal; the right to speak for all Jews is public and juridical, which does not apply here. One could ask further: If Karl were to extend the scope of forgiveness to collective proportions and should die in this happy illusion, where would be the harm?

The ultimate question posed in *The Sunflower* asks whether the fundamental norms of ethics and morality are exceptionable in certain difficult circumstances. Two answers are generally given. The first, the traditional and religious one, holds to the universality and permanence of basic moral laws and thus finds them unexceptionable. The second denies this and in this way relativizes moral norms in order to render them subject to change and dependent on individual and social needs and desires. Both positions derive from differing religious, ethical, and ideological premises, which explains why in our secularized societies unanimity on such issues is rarely, if ever, attained.

What would I have done in Simon's predicament? I would have—I do hope—forgiven him and, as an obstinate believer, suggested to him that he make his peace with God by asking for his forgiveness, and, taking full advantage of the situation, uttered a prayer for the repose of his soul and those of the victims of his inhuman behavior.

# EVA FLEISCHNER

Simon Wiesenthal's story ends by inviting the reader to change places with him: "Ask yourself the crucial question, 'what would I have done?'" I find it impossible to answer this question. As an outsider to the Shoah twice over—first, as one who was not there, secondly, as a non-Jew—neither the most vivid imagination nor the deepest empathy can enable me to experience even remotely the horror in the midst of which the victims lived and died. Nor can the skill with which Wiesenthal tells this highly dramatic story bridge the gap. I shall therefore, instead, give my reaction to Simon's response to the dying SS man's wish.

Some might call it *lack* of response, since Simon leaves the room in silence. But I find him responding throughout, again and again: allowing the SS man to hold on to his hand, remaining seated on the bed when revulsion—at times fear—make him want to leave, chasing away the fly from the dying man. Simon was forced to come, he had no choice. But he chose to remain and hear Karl out. And years later, when he visited Karl's mother in Stuttgart, he made the decision not to rob the lonely old woman of the fond memories of her "good" son. All this, in my view, constitutes a significant and humane response on his part.

And yet, after leaving the room, and many times over the years since then, Simon is haunted by the question whether he should have granted Karl's request and forgiven him. The question, for me, is not whether he *should* have forgiven, but whether he *could* have done so. Was it in his power to forgive?

Over the past twenty years I have frequently used *The Sunflower* as a text in my Holocaust course; it has invariably led to animated discussions. One striking feature of these has been that, almost without exception, the Christian students come out in favor of forgiveness, while the Jewish students feel that Simon did the right thing by not granting the dying man's wish.

What is going on here? Is there a fundamental difference between Jews and Christians in their approach to the question of forgiveness? And yet, forgiveness is no Christian invention. Along with so much else in our tradition we inherited from Judaism: the image of a loving, merciful God who waits eagerly and, as it were, with open arms, to welcome back the sinner (cf. Isa. 55:6–7; Joel 2:12–13; Ps. 130:7–8, etc.). These texts from biblical tradition—and they could be multiplied many times over—are reflected also in the teachings of the rabbis. To cite just one example:

A king had a son who had gone astray from him on a journey of a hundred days. His friends said to him, "Return to your father." He said, "I cannot." Then his father sent a message to him saying, "Return as far as you can and I will come the rest of the way to you." In a similar way God says, "Return to me and I will return to you."

(Pesikta Rabbati, 184b–85a,
quoted in Harriet Kaufman,
*Judaism and Social Justice,* p. 29)

Jesus' well-known parable of the Prodigal Son stands squarely in this Jewish tradition. The only requirement for being forgiven by God is genuine repentance—*teshuvah,* metanoia. Such a "turning" is required by Christian as much as by Jewish tradition. Without repentance, no forgiveness.

If this is so, if both traditions believe in a merciful God, if both stress the need for repentance, why the difference in response among my students? I attribute it to two factors.

The first is what I believe to be a widespread misunderstanding among Christians of Jesus' teaching of his oft-quoted admonition to his followers in the Sermon on the Mount to "turn the other cheek" (Matt. 5:39). Jesus is here referring to wrong done *to me,* and is asking *me* not to retaliate. He is not saying that, if someone wrongs me, someone else should "turn the other cheek"; or, if another is wronged, that I should forgive the perpetrator. In other words, the call is addressed *to me,* to forgive evil done *to me.* The message is the same in the Lord's Prayer: "Forgive us our trespasses, as we forgive those who trespass against us" (not, "those who trespass against others").

I believe that Christians—and non-Christians in their

wake—have misread, and continue to misread, these texts, interpreting Jesus' teaching to mean that we are to forgive anyone and everyone, whatever the wrong done to anyone. The element that is lost sight of is that Jesus challenges *me* to forgive evil done to *me* (in itself quite enough of a challenge!). Nowhere does he tell us to forgive the wrong done to another. Yet, the widespread impression persists among Christians that, to be truly Christian, we must forgive, plain and simple, no matter who has been sinned against.

Applying this to Wiesenthal's story: Karl asks Simon to forgive him for the horrendous murder of innocent and helpless Jewish women, children, and men in which he, Karl, participated two years earlier, and the memory of which now tortures him so much that he cannot die in peace. But, I ask again, was it possible for Simon to grant Karl's request? And I answer quite emphatically, no. Only the victims were in a position to forgive; and they are dead, put to death in the most inhuman ways conceivable.

The second factor which may account for the difference in attitude among my students relates to the concept of atonement, or restitution. As I write these lines we are approaching Yom Kippur, the holiest day of the Jewish year. Long ago I learned from Jewish friends that one of the most important ways of preparing for Yom Kippur is to look back over the past year, ask forgiveness of anyone you have wronged, and make up for it in some way. Only then, Jews believe, may they come before God and hope for forgiveness. For, as the Mishnah says,

> For sins against God, the Day of Atonement brings forgiveness. For sins against one's neighbor, the Day of

Atonement brings no forgiveness until one has become reconciled with one's neighbor.

(Yoma 8:9, Mishnah,

quoted in Harriet Kaufman's

*Judaism and Social Justice*, p. 30)

I remember one friend writing forty letters between Rosh Hashanah and Yom Kippur to people she felt she had hurt in some way. This is a long way from the "penance" usually given to Catholics in the confessional, "Say an Our Father or Hail Mary"—though the origin of this custom may well have been the idea of atonement, of which hardly a vestige is left nowadays.

Again, coming back to our story: Karl cannot atone for his crime, since the victims are dead. And Simon cannot forgive Karl in their name. It is helpful here to read Abraham Heschel's response (see pp. 164–66).

One concluding thought. Simon could perhaps have told Karl: "There is no way I can forgive you, since I cannot, dare not, speak in the name of the murdered Jews. But the God you believe in, and I too, is infinitely merciful, and asks of us only to repent of our sins. If your repentance is genuine, and I believe it is, and since you cannot make restitution, throw yourself on God's mercy."

But is not this asking a great deal—too much even—of Simon, given his situation? A situation of utter powerlessness and constant terror, totally devoid of hope, with death hanging over him every moment? Indeed, as I reread the story once more I am struck not only by the agony of the dying man, but by his obliviousness to the suffering, the inhuman condition, of Simon and his fellow Jews. The mere fact of having summoned

Simon to his room exposes the Jew to punishment, if not death. Yet Karl insists on seeing "a Jew"—any Jew—in the hope of being able to die in peace. His own suffering completely blinds him to the suffering of the Jews—not of the Jews in whose murder he participated and who continue to haunt him—but of those still alive in the camps and ghettos, also of Simon.

While this is understandable, humanly, given his deathbed agony, I am left with the question: Could Karl have done something to ameliorate their fate, or the fate of at least a few Jews, by speaking to his fellow SS instead of summoning a poor, helpless, doomed Jew to his bedside? Would such an act perhaps have constituted atonement?

# MATTHEW FOX

Simon Wiesenthal is a truth-teller who shakes up our conscience. Like many rabbis of old, including Jesus, he does not tell us so much *about* right from wrong; rather, he puts us in a place where our conscience must make decisions. We thank him for this. But we also curse him—for his challenge is very difficult. What would we have done—what should we have done—were we in his unenviable position in the hospital with a dying SS man?

Let us remember his circumstances. Simon did not know if he himself was going to live through the day; or the week; or the month. (In fact, most of his friends did not survive the camps and eighty-nine close relatives perished.) And still this one young SS man, in a kind of command performance, summoned a Jew to confess to. He wanted Simon to somehow relieve him of his guilt. We have to remember that the sin that so shook up Karl the SS man, his observing and participating in the slaughter of innocents in a torched house, was not his only sin. It was the nightmare that kept him awake at night, but it was by no means his only sin. Long before that fateful night, this SS man had participated time and time again in the mass hysteria and racial hatred that spawned the death camps and the war and many other deaths of innocents even before the deaths in Dnepropetrovsk. He did not express repentance for one-can-only-guess-how-many acts of hatred and sadism and antisemitism he committed on other occasions as an SS man— only for the one gruesome occasion which interfered with his sleep.

This young man as an enthusiastic Nazi had participated in, among other things, the death of eighty-nine of Simon's relatives. Indeed, he was partially responsible for the very camp where Wiesenthal was facing death daily. And so the confession that he made on his deathbed to Simon Wiesenthal was only partial. It was far from the full story.

When a Catholic confesses his sins, and this SS man was a lapsed Catholic, he not only is to tell the whole story but also to undergo penance to demonstrate his sorrow and contrition. It seems to me that in this regard Simon acted as the ideal confessor. He gave Karl the only penance available to him to bestow: Silence. The penance of Karl's having to be alone with his conscience before he died. Simon did not offer him forgiveness as a Jew—how could he forgive in the name of even one in that home of hundreds who were torched or the millions in camps of death? But Simon, summoned as a priest-confessor, let the man speak his heart. Some sins are too big for forgiveness, even for priests. Public penance is required. This man received no public penance but his private penance was considerable, having to die in the silence of the truth staring him in the face. I sense in the wisdom of Simon's decision to walk out in silence a win-win situation. Simon kept his soul and the young soldier may have saved his soul. He did unburden his soul to the best person possible—not a priest offering cheap grace for unmentionable sins, but a relative of his dead victims.

Call it tough love or call it nonsentimental compassion. But Simon offered Karl a morally responsible and adult response. Silence. Be with your sin. Be in the dark in the Via Negativa where so many of your victims and relatives of your victims lie. Be with your conscience. Be with your victims. Be with your God. I get the impression that Karl appreciated the strength of Simon's response and that is why he gave his last human holdings, meagre as they were, to Simon as a thank-you gift. But Simon, again wisely, refused to touch them.

But Simon did take the man's hand and hold it. And he did swat away flies that bothered the dying but guilt-ridden soldier. By holding his hand Simon was being present and being human. Though holding his hand repulsed him after more of the horror story was revealed, still he stayed in the room and listened. Listening was his gift; listening was his act of compassion. This unusual bond between young men—one a killer and another a hunted one for no reason but his race—this touching of hands and stories and hearts: such a rite of passage for a culture lacking authentic rites of passage for its young. Both were victims of older men's decision making. But one was a perpetrator of that older man's sick vision and the other was at the receiving end of it. This was Simon's compassion, to stay and listen and even to remain silent and refuse to offer cheap forgiveness to so heinous a crime. There are sins that God and not humans must forgive. And no one had anointed Simon to forgive in God's name.

Some kind of mysterious grace seems to have passed between these two young men. Indeed, I wonder if Simon did not receive his vocation from this dying SS man. Why do I say that? Because in many ways Wiesenthal's life commitment since surviving the death camp can be understood as a playing out of the scene so powerfully described at the hospital bed. Simon has continued to hunt down Nazis in order, one might believe, to allow them a deathbed conversion, a deathbed confession. Without his hunting these sinners down neither they nor their victims will rest in the next life. Without this remembering, justice dies. Simon was just to the SS man and more than just—he was compassionate. And his whole life commitment since has been a pursuit of justice and therefore of compassion. For there is no compassion without justice. Simon does not condemn the criminals he uncovers; he leaves that up to the judges of the courts. He only provides the witnesses, the testimony, the evidence. They convict themselves. As did Karl.

And in this vocation to tell the truth Simon carries on a lesson that Karl left him. It is a strange exchange, a strange bond between these two men. It is moving to behold. Simon gave Karl a listening ear on his deathbed; and Karl gave Simon a vocation for a lifetime.

Another act of compassion on Simon's part was his visiting Karl's mother and doing so without a preconceived agenda. There he made more bonding with Karl—seeing his face for the first time in a photograph and feeling the pain in his broken family's story. His letting Karl's mother continue in her denial and in her belief that her son was innocent was an act that carries one beyond justice to compassion as well. He intuited that it would do this broken widow no good to tell her the truth. It was too late for that.

Yet it was this clinging to denial that surely constituted the *sin behind the sin* of the Nazi horrors. How many ordinary German citizens—and clergy and bishops—knew something evil was going on and still lived in denial? Willful ignorance is a sin. In this case, a catastrophic sin that made the Holocaust possible. Simon treated mother and son the same—he listened to both and left both in silence. Each to die with their truth, partial that it was. But Simon's work since has been to break the silence, to keep alive the fuller truth of what transpired. And in doing this he has continued his acts of compassion on an international scale.

I believe this story disturbs us so deeply because, like any true morality story, it applies to today as much as to yesterday. Human capacity for evil is not just about isolated, individual decisions and acts. This story—the entire Nazi story—lays bare the *sins of complicity and the sins of omission and denial* that render our participation in evil so profound. These sins occur so readily in mass society when lies and power can be so easily disseminated by propaganda of the press and politicians and commercial interests. Denial allows these sins to take root and prosper—consider Karl's mother. This is happening still today. Sins of complicity are killing the planet and laying waste the souls of many young people as we live in denial of the prisons we are building to house young persons whose violence stems from despair and joblessness and as we lay waste forests and waters and soil and the air itself by our lifestyles of consumption. How different is our denial from that of Karl's mother? What evil is happening all around us and in our name? Is denial more important to us than the truth? These are questions—perennial moral questions—that Simon's story unveils for us.

Forgiving and forgetting are two separate acts. One should forgive—not out of altruism but out of the need to be free to get on with one's life—but we ought not forget. Simon did not forget—therefore he has gifted us with the greatest of gifts— a lifetime dedicated to justice and compassion. A god-like life. His story prevents our forgetting. If we can remember, then maybe we will choose life over death.

# MARK GOULDEN

*The Sunflower* is remarkable for many reasons. In its own right it is a moving, sorrowful, terrifying narrative which holds the reader enthralled as it unfolds.

It tells of a tragic experience in the life of the author, Simon Wiesenthal, whose memorable book (*The Murderers Among Us*) dealt with the German war criminals who tried to escape retribution. But apart from its own narrative value *The Sunflower* is remarkable because it poses a searing question that will challenge the moral conscience of the reader.

The question is concerned with forgiveness—specifically, forgiveness toward the Germans for crimes which they committed less than thirty years ago. Some may say that the whole subject is slightly jejune nowadays, for there is evidence that the world has conspired to forget the monstrous atrocities that shamed mankind and made a mockery of religion and humanity, even though they occurred well within living memory.

I always find it difficult to exercise restraint when I write or think about these fearful crimes. The mind begins to boggle at the sheer enormity of it all. Is it true, one asks oneself, that civilized human beings actually built huge, complex death chambers for the express purpose of destroying millions of other human beings like vermin?

Can it really be that ordinary German soldiers obeyed orders to machine-gun long rows of living people standing at the edge of vast open graves into which the riddled bodies fell in grotesque heaps?

Did the Germans actually feed into their gas chambers over 960,000 innocent children—a number that is equivalent (if you want a visual cognate) to ten Wembley Stadiums filled to capacity with kids under thirteen?

Do our eyes deceive us when we watch those films of the shuffling, living skeletons wandering around mountains of shriveled corpses in the camps of Belsen, Auschwitz, Birkenau, Treblinka, etc., etc.? Were these zombies once ordinary normal human beings like you and me?

To reflect on these things is to plunge oneself into a nightmare of unbearable ghastliness. The human mind is incapable of comprehending the magnitude and the mathematics of such slaughter. But, alas, it isn't a nightmare. It's all too dreadfully true and it is all recorded, in minute detail, in the vast literature on the subject that now exists.

Just ponder this item for instance: At the recent Auschwitz trial in Frankfurt a dispute arose as to the exact number of victims who were massacred in that death camp. Finally it came out in evidence that of 4,400,000 men, women, and children (approximately the entire population of Denmark) who were condemned to Auschwitz, only 60,000 were still alive when the camp was liberated. Which means that 98.5 percent of all the deportees were methodically exterminated by the Germans. This arithmetic of butchery, this harvest of death, would stagger the imagination even if the carnage concerned rats, never mind human beings.

Well, that was the burden of guilt which the Germans bore when the war ended, and for this culpability they have made no act of atonement as a nation. One often asked in the early days whether a people who had done these things—either by active participation or silent acquiescence—could ever live down such a legacy of inhumanity. Dare they ever lift up their heads again in civilized society? Would the brand of Cain stay forever on the German brow just as the tattooed Star of David would remain indelible on the arms of many a victim who escaped?

These were questions which only time could answer, and time indeed has answered them. For it is a fact that within a matter of three decades, that nation which perpetuated the greatest massacre of human souls in all history—virtually before the very eyes of the world—that nation has been able to resume its place in the comity of peoples with utter self-assurance and complete composure, actually being welcomed by the president of America as "our devoted, staunch, and honorable ally."

Today, people don't talk any more about the mass murder of six million human beings. They don't even want to read about it any longer. Books on the subject are now categorized disparagingly as "concentration-camp stuff" and as such are virtually unsalable. The world seems to have agreed to "let the matter drop" and nobody has more sedulously promoted this "forget it" campaign than the Germans themselves—not for any piacular reasons, but simply "to restore our good name," as Adenauer once naively put it. They even tried recently to introduce a law to stop any more Nazi trials because these served only to perpetuate the legends of the gas chambers, the crematoria, and the torturings.

By a sort of tacit consent the very nomenclature of Germany's misdeeds has, over the years, been modified so that euphemisms such as "the Holocaust," "The Final Solution," "Genocide," etc., are now used to mask the inherent and stunning horror of what is plainly massacre, slaughter, and bestiality. And we are reminded always that it was the Nazis—a mythical horde of subhumans from outer space—who did it all. They descended, unbidden, on the most highly sophisticated, Kultured nation on earth and issued orders which they dare not, could not, and *did not* disobey. Apparently no living German was ever a Nazi; very few even saw one, and whatever atrocities did happen, took place during what is known as the "Hitler Era"—or in the "time of the Nazis"—which is the greatest collective alibi ever conceived.

Small wonder then that the world should so quickly forget crimes (which nobody ever saw) committed by external criminals (whom nobody ever knew)?

To forget all may be easy, but to forgive all must be something more than a pulpit platitude. First, we must ask ourselves in whose hands lies the privilege of granting forgiveness? We can, of course, say, with the ecclesiastics, that mercy and forgiveness belong entirely to God, in which case the whole dialogue comes abruptly to an end. Or we can subscribe to the dictum of the poet Dryden—"Forgiveness, to the injured doth belong." But, unfortunately, the injured in this case (six million martyred dead) are incapable of exercising such prerogative or indeed of expressing any opinion at all.

And if the dead can't forgive, neither can the living. How can you possibly forgive monsters who burned people alive in public; in ceremonies, staged in the open, with typical Teutonic pomp and precision? Could we even expect the Almighty to exonerate them? But it is precisely a hideous crime like this that is central to the challenging question posed in *The Sunflower*—was Wiesenthal right in refusing to forgive the dying Nazi? You can ignore the question, or evade it, or hedge it about with casuistic hair-splitting, but the simple issue remains—what would you have done in Wiesenthal's shoes? There is no generic answer; it is an individual dilemma that demands a personal answer.

I, for one, would have had no hesitation in solving the problem. I figure it this way: Wiesenthal himself was about to die—ignominiously and forgotten—as a direct result of all those "ideals" and those "standards" which the dying Nazi and millions like him were proud to defend and fight for. I would have asked myself what might the young Nazi have become had he survived or, indeed, if Germany had won the war? I would have tried to visualize the Christ-like compassion and pity which the victorious Germans would have bestowed on the new million Wiesenthals now in their power. And reflecting on these things, I would have silently left the deathbed having made quite certain there was now one Nazi less in the world!

# HANS HABE

O n reading *The Sunflower* I was greatly excited, as everybody who reads your story must be. However, you have not asked me for literary criticism, but for my views on the problems of forgiveness. The two unspoken questions in your story interest me specially: Whom ought we to forgive, when ought we to forgive? I imagine that you did forgive the man whom you call Karl S. But that is, I fear, too simple an answer. We are not an appeal court from God. He revises our judgments, we do not revise His. God's punishment struck the SS man, bypassing all human courts. He whom men punish can still be acquitted by God: he whom men acquit God still may punish. But he whom God has punished we cannot acquit nor can we increase the Divine punishment. Least of all through hatred. He who has been punished is removed from our jurisdiction, even the words "Requiescat in pace" are a mere suggestion. We can hope that a person may rest in peace, we cannot ensure it.

Immediately there arises the question: Ought we, can we, forgive others, murderers who are still alive?

Here too we must be more precise. Whom do you understand by "we"? If you mean the Jews, mothers and fathers, relatives and friends of the martyred and slaughtered people, then there is a considerable shift of meaning. Murder is neither forgivable nor unforgivable. Morals are not restricted to the victims. I have always doubted the role of so-called counsel who appear on behalf of private individuals in murder cases. To judge crimes against humanity is the affair of humanity. Victor

Gollancz, the English publisher, who immediately after the war wrote the word "Forgiveness" on the Jewish flag, was for me just as dubious as are the Jews who take the sword of revenge from the hand of humanity. By "we" I mean humanity, not the Jews alone.

Is murder unforgivable? Yes, without question. Can one forgive the murderer? That is a question that is closely tied up in the complex of punishment. A desire to punish the murderer is the commandment of Justice. To forgive the murderer after he has suffered punishment is the commandment of Love. You write that Karl was "not born a murderer and did not want to die a murderer." What has that to do with the problem of forgiveness? It is not relevant and in no sense an excuse. Practically nobody is born a murderer. Those who are born murderers are the pathological exceptions—their deeds, as a matter of fact, are more pardonable than those who are born "healthy." The death of Christ on the Cross is the symbol of a free human decision. He who decides to commit a murder is laden with a greater guilt than he who is driven to become a criminal by abnormal environment. Anyhow, there is hardly anybody who wanted to die a murderer, even atheists are afraid of the Hereafter.

So we cannot forgive murderers—so long as the murder is not atoned for, either by us as jurymen or by the Supreme Judge. Every society—every society, I repeat, rests upon certain moral principles, at the head of which stands atonement for capital crimes, and this brings me to your next unspoken question: Can there be any extenuating circumstances for murder?

It stands to reason there must be extenuating circumstances—otherwise every murder trial would be pointless—so we must examine them. In several passages, particularly in your conversation with the SS man's mother, you describe Karl's path to murder. That is the natural, but complicated, thing to do. One must not confuse the question of forgiveness with the question of punishment. If Karl were being tried by an earthly court, there would be such extenuating circumstances in his favor as youth, environment, the times, the general atmosphere, and war conditions. Nevertheless, in this case we are operating in two different dimensions. Forgiveness is a spiritual matter, punishment is a legal matter. The verdict of the court is influenced by extenuating circumstances. Such circumstances induce a milder judgment, but in no way mean that we are forgiving the murderer. The free will given to a man does not merely grant him the choice between committing a murderous deed or refraining from it. It is also a part of man's free will whether he allows justice to take its course or whether he dispenses with it. An amnesty granted to an unpunished murderer is a form of complicity in the crime. It does not foster forgiveness, it precludes it.

Again, who should be the object of our forgiveness or our revenge?

You are a man of high principle, and although you relate the story of the SS man and his victims, the proceedings which initially were directed against the murderer end with the Nazi system as the prisoner at the bar. Here our paths diverge.

For the regime we are discussing there is no "problem" of forgiveness. The crimes of the regime were unforgivable, the regime has been tried and destroyed. Meanwhile we are faced not with Mephistopheles, but with Faust. Corruption, though a force of permanent duration, cannot exist without collaboration from the corrupted. The corrupted, in a word, are not victims of the corrupters, but collaborators. With the words "Terrible vision!" Faust turns away, but the ghost rightly defends himself: "You invited me cordially, you have long dabbled in my domain . . . You have passionately striven to see me, to hear my voice, to gaze on my countenance . . ."

The firm is Faust & Co. or, if you prefer it, Mephistopheles & Co., partners just like Hitler and Karl S. The proof lies in the counterproof. The devilish Nazist regime did not corrupt everybody, and of those whom it corrupted most stopped at murder. I cannot accept the excuse that the system relieves the individual of responsibility. Walt Whitman says: "To the States, or to any individual State, or to any city among the States, offer strong resistance and little obedience!" Resistance to evil is not heroism but a duty. Anyone who thinks that he can get rid of evil "in itself" in the world is a victim of megalomania, and who knows whether megalomania in itself does not contain the germs of evil? The important thing is to strengthen the resistance to evil.

Here, in my view, lies the true problem of forgiveness, and here perhaps we approach the answer as to whom we ought to forgive and when.

Mankind will stay as it is—in itself a terrible prospect—if the principles of love and justice remain obstinately separated instead of complementing each other. Looking on the question from this angle, you will find that in the history of man since the beginning of Creation, love and justice have opposed each other. At one period justice was the human ideal, at another, love. The divine idea of justice in love, love in justice, mankind has magnanimously left to the Creator.

Forgiveness is the imitation of God. Punishment too is an imitation of God. God punishes and forgives, in that order. But God never hates. That is the moral value worth striving for, but perhaps unattainable.

You write at the end of *The Sunflower:* I know that many will understand me and approve of my attitude to the dying SS man. But I know also that just as many will condemn me because I refused to ease the last hours of a repentant murderer.

I belong to neither class of reader. It seems to me immaterial whether you forgave the SS murderer or not, for Providence relieved him of life and punishment, and your conscience from the burden of decision. But at least you did not hate the dying murderer, and that is a beginning. To forgive without justice is a self-satisfying weakness. Justice without love is a simulation of strength.

One of the worst crimes of the Nazist regime was that it made it so hard for us to forgive. It led us into the labyrinth of our souls. We must find a way out of the labyrinth—not for the murderers' sake, but for our own. Neither love alone expressed in forgiveness, nor justice alone, exacting punishment, will lead us out of the maze. A demand for both atonement and forgiveness is not self-contradictory; when a man has willfully extinguished the life of another, atonement is the prerequisite for forgiveness. Exercised with love and justice, atonement and forgiveness serve the same end: life without hatred. That is our goal: I see no other.

## YOSSI KLEIN HALEVI

Wiesenthal's encounter with the dying Karl occurs in a dimension beyond our understanding and judgment. Presuming the right to judge Wiesenthal, the camp inmate, reveals a lack of humility. It risks repeating the mistake of those who didn't experience the Holocaust but who readily condemned its survivors—for not violently resisting, for supposedly collaborating, for remaining alive. The very fact that Wiesenthal and his fellow prisoners debated the question of forgiving Karl is more than we have the right to expect of them.

But we are permitted to judge Wiesenthal the postwar survivor. By deciding to rejoin our world rather than enter a bitter seclusion, he and other survivors assumed the burden of moral normalcy: from 1945 onward, they would be measured by the same standards as the rest of us; their wartime suffering couldn't serve as refuge from scrutiny of their postwar lives.

In responding to Wiesenthal's story, then, I begin where I have the right to begin: with his encounter with Karl's mother, in 1946. Here, there is no moral ambiguity. Rather than tell her the truth about Karl, Wiesenthal allows this woman who has lost everything to at least retain a mother's pride in her son. He rejects his opportunity for vicarious vengeance against the innocent; whatever happened "there" cannot justify cruelty "here." Refusal to forgive belongs to that time and place, not ours.

That simple message took me a long time to learn. Though born after the war, I was one of those Jews who tried to isolate Germany in a cordon of untouchability. I refused to visit Germany or buy German products. When I'd meet Germans my age, I related to them with blatant distaste, delighting in their discomfort. I wanted the Germans—all Germans who identified with that poisoned culture—to be exiled from humanity.

Finally, I traveled to Germany in November 1989 as a journalist. The Berlin Wall had just been breached. In the frozen evenings I joined the dense crowds moving in slow motion along the Ku'damm, West Berlin's main avenue, and was reminded, to my dismay, of Jerusalem in the weeks after the Six-Day War: the same dazed joy, the same incredulous sense of crossing inviolate borders. To exclude myself from the Germans' celebration, I felt, was to deny myself an essential human experience, exiling myself from humanity.

During that same trip I visited a Protestant youth club in West Berlin, "Meerbaum House," named for a German Jew killed in the Holocaust. A poster on a wall announced a trip to Poland, to help clean the sites of former death camps; other posters supported various liberal and fringe radical causes, from antiapartheid rallies to Amnesty International to the Sandinistas. One felt that the dead Jew Meerbaum was the dominant presence of this place, that the young people here were offering their notion of altruistic politics to his memory.

I asked those teenagers whether they felt any pride in being German. They laughed. Did they feel excitement when the Wall fell? Blank stares. I thought of the enthusiasm with which Israelis their age react to a national triumph—the rescue of an endangered Diaspora community, a successful attack against a terrorist leader, and it seemed to me that, as a people, we had emerged from the Holocaust with our life force more intact than had the Germans. The young people of Meerbaum House appeared so intimidated by the Holocaust that they couldn't allow themselves to share their people's celebration. But instead of taking a grim pleasure in their shame, I felt the emptiness of revenge against the guiltless. And I found myself actually urging them not to allow the past to distort the present, not to allow Auschwitz to deny them a moment of well-earned self-respect.

Certainly I don't believe that Germans or Jews should obscure the memory of the past. But since that encounter in

Berlin I have become increasingly committed to German-Jewish reconciliation. Wiesenthal's humane gesture toward Karl's mother reinforces for me the sense that, just as we are commanded to remember all our Egypts, there are times when we must also transcend them. For Wiesenthal the survivor, behaving graciously toward the mother of an SS officer required moral courage; for the rest of us, treating a new generation with decency requires only moral common sense.

# ARTHUR HERTZBERG

This personal history of the dying soldier made him more, and not less, guilty. This young man had not drifted into being a Nazi, for he was raised by a mother who was a pious Catholic and a father who never wavered in his opposition to Hitler and his followers. When he decided to join the Hitler Youth, his mother did not put up much of a struggle, but his father was vehemently opposed. The teenager would not listen, at fourteen, and he was even more defiant when he enlisted in the SS, but on his deathbed he remembered that he had been taught better. He could not, as some convinced Nazis did, "jump gladly into the grave" knowing that they had, at least, succeeded in destroying almost all of the Jews of Europe. He chose to do evil when he was sure that the murderers whom he chose to join would succeed. The Nazi regime did allow "faint-hearted" soldiers to ask for other assignments. Had he heeded that impulse, he could have avoided committing horri-

ble crimes with his own hands, but he chose to slaughter innocent people. Even if he was not entirely sure that the "racially
inferior" should be exterminated, he did know that murdering
such "non-people" would elicit special benefits for him from a
victorious Nazi regime.

Simon Wiesenthal perhaps did not remember, at that tense
moment beside the soldier's bed, the teaching in the Talmud
that no one has the right to commit murder even if he is sure
that he himself will be killed for not complying with such an
order. In the text of the Talmud there is the explanation: "How
do you know your blood is more precious?" The dying member
of the SS should have risked losing his own life rather than become a racist murderer or a careerist killer. He had asked for a
Jew, any Jew, to come to his bedside so that he could make his
peace with his victims, and with God.

Wiesenthal said nothing, and he was right. The crimes in
which this SS man had taken part are beyond forgiveness by
man, and even by God, for God Himself is among the accused.

When He proposed (according to the account in the Book
of Genesis) to destroy Sodom and Gomorrah because they
were sinful, Abraham protested: "Would God destroy the
righteous together with the wicked?" In the story in Genesis,
God agreed that if there were as many as ten righteous people
in these sinful cities, he would spare them, but Abraham could
not find even this small number. But, in this dialogue with
Abraham, the Judge of all the earth did agree that He, too,
must act justly; he accepted the premise that he has no right to
destroy the just. In our time, we must ask Abraham's question:
among the victims, there were many righteous and holy people,
and more than a million children who had not known sin. On
the evidence of the "debate" in Genesis, Abraham could not

have forgiven God for willing, or allowing, such cruelty. God can perhaps be defended by the answer that He gave to Job: the Divine plan is beyond human understanding. I cannot swallow the further extension of this argument, that the Nazis were instruments devised by God to help Him realize his unknowable design. Surely, it is not beyond His power to achieve whatever He wants in the world without the near total murder of a people. Can anyone dare forgive the Nazis, and their helpers, in the name of the hidden and silent God who stood by the Holocaust? No doubt, as the Catholic he had once been, the SS soldier thought that words of contrition would get him Divine absolution. Perhaps, after Wiesenthal left, he confessed to a priest and was given the last rites and assured of Divine forgiveness. But the God who had allowed the Holocaust did not, and does not, have the standing to forgive the monsters who had carried out the murders.

On the other hand, when Simon Wiesenthal visited the dead soldier's mother in Stuttgart some months later, he was right not to deprive her of her illusions about her son. He did not visit his sins on her. Wiesenthal obeyed the biblical injunction that each of us dies for his own sins, and not even for those of our children or of our parents. He could not tell this mother the truth, for the truth would have destroyed her, even if she had continued to live on as a physical being.

These reflections were not elicited from me only by contemplating the moving story that Wiesenthal has told. I was born in Lubaczów, Galicia, in 1921 and escaped the Holocaust because my family was in the United States by 1926. I cannot make peace with my own generation of Germans and their collaborators in the satellite countries, because my contemporaries could have refused to join the Nazis, but the majority hailed

Hitler to the day of his defeat and death. I remember my own relatives—a grandfather, many uncles and aunts and their children—and I cannot fathom the mentality of those who murdered them for being Jews. Those who say that they are sorry and ashamed, I can only leave to their own guilt. I am just as pained by the attempts to "explain" the Holocaust. These writings may, sometimes, be full of historical insights, or even ingenious theology, but together they obscure and cover over a question that can never be answered: Why did man, and God, fail so horribly? Together with Simon Wiesenthal, who said nothing at the deathbed of the SS soldier, we can only be silent.

# THEODORE M. HESBURGH

Who am I to advise a person of another religion who has suffered incredibly more than I have? I would not ordinarily presume to do so, but I was requested to do so, so I do.

My whole instinct is to forgive. Perhaps that is because I am a Catholic priest. In a sense, I am in the forgiving business. I sit in a confessional for hours and forgive everyone who comes in, confesses, and is sorry .

I think of God as the great forgiver of sinful humanity. The greatest story of Jesus is the Prodigal Son. Can we aspire to be as forgiving of each other as God is of us?

Of course, the sin here is monumental. It is still finite and God's mercy is infinite.

If asked to forgive, by anyone for anything, I would forgive because God would forgive. If I had suffered as so many had, it might be much more difficult, but I hope I would still be forgiving, not from my own small position but as a surrogate for our almighty and all-forgiving God.

# ABRAHAM JOSHUA HESCHEL

Over fifty years ago, the rabbi of Brisk, a scholar of extraordinary renown, revered also for his gentleness of character, entered a train in Warsaw to return to his hometown. The rabbi, a man of slight stature, and of no distinction of appearance, found a seat in a compartment. There he was surrounded by traveling salesmen, who, as soon as the train began to move, started to play cards. As the game progressed, the excitement increased. The rabbi remained aloof and absorbed in meditation. Such aloofness was annoying to the rest of the people and one of them suggested to the rabbi to join in the game. The rabbi answered that he never played cards. As time passed, the rabbi's aloofness became even more annoying and one of those present said to him: "Either you join us, or leave the compartment." Shortly thereafter, he took the rabbi by his collar and pushed him out of the compartment. For several hours the rabbi had to stand on his feet until he reached his destination, the city of Brisk.

Brisk was also the destination of the salesmen. The rabbi left the train where he was immediately surrounded by admirers welcoming him and shaking his hands. "Who is this man?" asked the salesman. "You don't know him? The famous rabbi of Brisk." The salesman's heart sank. He had not realized who he had offended. He quickly went over to the rabbi to ask forgiveness. The rabbi declined to forgive him. In his hotel room, the salesman could find no peace. He went to the rabbi's house and was admitted to the rabbi's study. "Rabbi," he said, "I am not a rich man. I have, however, savings of three hundred rubles. I will give them to you for charity if you will forgive me." The rabbi's answer was brief: "NO."

The salesman's anxiety was unbearable. He went to the synagogue to seek solace. When he shared his anxiety with some people in the synagogue, they were deeply surprised. How could their rabbi, so gentle a person, be so unforgiving. Their advice was for him to speak to the rabbi's eldest son and to tell him of the surprising attitude taken by his father.

When the rabbi's son heard the story, he could not understand his father's obstinacy. Seeing the anxiety of the man, he promised to discuss the matter with his father.

It is not proper, according to Jewish law, for a son to criticize his father directly. So the son entered his father's study and began a general discussion of Jewish law and turned to the laws of forgiveness. When the principle was mentioned that a person who asks for forgiveness three times should be granted forgiveness, the son mentioned the name of the man who was in great anxiety. Thereupon the rabbi of Brisk answered:

"I cannot forgive him. He did not know who I was. He offended a common man. Let the salesman go to him and ask for forgiveness."

No one can forgive crimes committed by other people. It is therefore preposterous to assume that anybody alive can extend forgiveness for the suffering of any one of the six million people who perished.

According to Jewish tradition, even God Himself can only forgive sins committed against Himself, not against man.

# CHRISTOPHER HOLLIS

*The Sunflower,* whether wholly autobiographical or in parts fictional, is an intensely moving and vivid book. Were it my task to write a literary criticism of it, I should be loud in its praise. But the request that has been made of me is to give an opinion on one definite point. Did the author do right in refusing a word of compassion to the dying SS man who had made to him the confession of the atrocious murder of a Jewish child?

The author does not admit of any repentance for his refusal. But his two Jewish friends, now dead, thought that he would have done very wrong to have admitted such compassion. Only the Polish seminarist thought otherwise and he has vanished from the author's life so that he is no longer able to keep in touch with the developments of his thought. But it is clear from the author's visit to the SS man's mother that his mind is not at ease. It is indeed not clear what purpose that visit had or what purpose he could have supposed that it would have had, since he was not willing to tell the mother the truth about her son, but the fact that he made it is proof of a disturbed, uncertain, and restless mind.

I am asked what, absolutely, he ought to have done under

these circumstances. Let me first make it clear that that is quite a different question from the question "what would I have done?" To that second question I can make no answer. I claim no capacity to resist temptation above the average and what fortitude I would have been able to show in face of horrors so incomparably greater than any that I have ever been called on to face I cannot say. We can all say that men ought to be martyrs if challenged on their faith. We can none of us say whether in the day of trial we ourselves would have the hardihood to be martyrs.

But on the absolute challenge what the author should have done I have no doubt that he should have said a word of compassion. The theology of the matter is surely clear and, as the Polish seminarist truly says in this book, there is no difference on it between Christians and Jews. Differences are here irrelevant. The law of God is the law of love. We are created in order to love one another, and, when the law of love is broken, God's nature is frustrated. Such bonds when broken should be reforged as soon as possible. We are under obligation to forgive our neighbor even though he has offended against us seventy times seven.

On the other hand we are all born in original sin. (Jewish orthodoxy, I understand, does not admit that exact phrase but the language in which they repudiate it shows very effectively that they do in fact believe in it as much as any Christians.) Indeed one could not well do otherwise, for original sin, unlike the other Christian doctrines, is a definite necessity of thought. Men are born in sin and when God has been defied by actual sin there cannot be forgiveness unless there is repentance. We are indeed told to be reluctant to condemn others. "Judge not that ye be not judged." It is our duty to reflect how small is our own understanding and that, if we knew all of a story, we should often see how much more there was to be said for another's action, how much more—it may be—of the blame really is ours than appeared at first sight.

But these considerations, so often just, are here irrelevant. Here the SS man had committed an appalling crime. It was perhaps relevant for him to recount the impulses that had caused him to join the SS, the appalling corruption of Nazi propaganda to which he had been subjected, the military discipline of which he was the slave at the time of the act, but these are explanations. They are not excuses. The SS man does not pretend that they are excuses. He does not attempt to excuse himself. He was guilty of an appalling crime and he was frankly confessing his crime. Nor has the author any doubt of the sincerity of his repentance. Therefore, however difficult it was, there is surely no doubt that a word of compassion, indicative of his recognition of that sincerity, should have been said.

It is of course true that penitence involves a willingness to make restitution to the person wronged and, had the circumstances been other, it would have been reasonable to have demanded of the SS man that, even if he could not bring back to life the little child whom he had killed or discover any of his immediate relatives, yet he should in some notable way have attempted some service to the Jews which would have given evidence of the sincerity of his repentance. Whether he could or would have satisfied such a challenge had he lived and been restored to health, who shall say? Since he was to die in a few hours, the question is meaningless. Even if the author had doubted, one should give the benefit of the doubt.

'Tis God shall repay. I am safer so.

Nor indeed is it easy to see, as indeed the author himself

confesses, for what reason the SS man should have sent for and made this confession to a Jew unless he was sincerely ashamed of what he had done.

Of course I am stating what seems to me to be the absolute moral law. I am not suggesting that obedience to that law could under the circumstances possibly have been easy or passing any personal condemnation. But surely the absolute moral law was stated by Christ at the Crucifixion when He prayed for the forgiveness of His own murderers. It is of course true that the persecution and murder of Jews was still going on and that the author fully expected that he himself would be murdered before long. But that, I should have thought, in the moral order made forgiveness easier rather than more difficult.

The author's two Jewish friends, Arthur and Josek, argued with him that maybe he had a right to forgive injuries against himself but that he had no right to forgive injuries against other people. But insofar as this act was not merely a personal act of one SS man against one Jewish child but an incident in a general campaign of genocide, the author was as much a victim—or likely to be soon a victim—of that campaign as was the child, and, being a sufferer, had therefore the right to forgive. His forgiveness could not in the nature of things be the casual, idle word of someone who pardoned without caring the perpetrator of a distant crime to which he was really indifferent.

Nor of course has forgiveness anything to do with the refusal to punish. In this case since the SS man was just about to die the question of punishment did not arise, but, had he survived, the fact that he had been spiritually forgiven would of course have been no reason why he should not have been subjected to the appropriate punishment.

It is interesting to understand why the SS man wanted thus to confess to an unknown Jew. The SS man had been brought up as a Catholic but he had abandoned his religion when he joined the Hitler Youth. There seems some suspicion that on his deathbed he had a certain return of faith—or at least a desire to return to his faith. If that was at all so, if he had come to think that there was at least a possibility of future life and a judgment awaiting him, then it would of course have been reasonable that he should have confessed to a priest had one been available. If there were no priest he could be confident that the verdicts of God would be just and, if his repentance was sincere, need be under no fear that God would not show mercy.

Whichever way round, why was his state made any better, his mind at all relieved, by confessing to an unknown Jew? The Jew had no power to give him absolution. It is not easy to see but it is a psychological fact that sinners on their deathbed do often wish to relieve themselves by telling their story to someone and under any normal circumstances who would be so hard-hearted as to refuse to listen to such a story?

The real issue is whether the Jew and Nazi were two of God's children sharing a common humanity or whether they are two different sorts of being, irrevocably at war with one another. If the second interpretation was that accepted by the Jews it was assuredly the Nazis who were responsible for it and they could not complain if the Jews accepted it. Yet for all that, whatever the temptation to think otherwise, it is surely the inevitable consequence of any monotheistic faith that all men—even the least naturally lovable—are the children of God, in Christian belief that they are those for whom their Omnipotent Creator did not disdain to die, in Jewish belief that they are God's creatures.

One can well understand how the Jews in their camps had come to tell one another in the bitter sick joke which the author recounts to us that God was on leave. Yet it was precisely the rejection of this blasphemy that surely religious faith demanded—demanded the belief that somehow, however difficult it might be to see how, "God is not mocked" and that, as with Job, "though He slay me yet will I trust in him."

Man, what is this and why art thou despairing?

God shall forgive thee all but thy despair.

According to an old medieval legend the Apostles assembled together in heaven to recelebrate the Last Supper. There was one place vacant, until through the door Judas came in and Christ rose and kissed him and said, "We have waited for thee."

# RODGER KAMENETZ

Dear Simon Wiesenthal,

I feel silence, under the circumstances, was the best response. As a captive marked for death, you did not have the full freedom to speak. Either to forgive or to condemn, or both as the situation required. For this person, even by the manner he was treating you in that hospital, needed to hear your criticism before the conversation could ever move to forgiveness. Yet how could you know how your words would be taken, or what their consequences would be to your survival? You were under duress—the best choice was to remain silent.

That leads to my main objection to the situation: you were

not addressed as a person. You were addressed, from his perspective, as Jew. Not as *a* Jew, a Jewish person, as an individual, with a life, a history, a heartbreak of your own, but merely as *Jew.* For his purposes, any Jew would do.

That did not give you proper respect. And in your condition at that time, respect was also precious. I cannot encounter another person's humanity as a category, but only when I meet him or her as a particular individual. That was the insult hidden within his approach. Yes, he saw the suffering he had inflicted, and he felt the guilt. But he had not moved past the deeper sickness of his soul and of his time—and our time as well. He could not see you as a person because he could only see you as Jew.

You yourself saw him as a particular person, a human being. That is to your credit. If he had also reached the same point, then the conversation about forgiveness could begin.


# CARDINAL FRANZ KÖNIG

*Archbishop of Vienna*

Reading about your experiences moved me very deeply. Your story is shocking, and not only because of the horrors you had to witness as a concentration camp prisoner. I found just as shocking your account of your student days and previous life at the university. The recurring symbol of the sunflower in your narrative, on the one hand, shows literary brilliance; on the other hand, it begs for a psychological interpretation which I would not attempt.

As for the difficult question you finally address to the reader—whether you behaved correctly toward the dying young SS man who "confessed" to you his participation in a horrible murder of Jews and asked you for forgiveness by proxy, as it were—I do not want to get into the general questions it raises concerning justice, mercy, sin, etc. However, I would like to answer your personal question as follows:

Even though an individual cannot forgive what was done to *others*, because he is not competent to do that, there is still a question of whether one *may* forgive. For Christians, the binding answer is in the Gospels. The question of whether there is a limit to forgiveness has been emphatically answered by Christ in the negative.

The distinction between whether we *can* forgive and whether we *may* forgive still leaves unresolved the question of whether we *should* forgive. You did the dying man a great service by listening to him despite your internal reluctance, by showing him sympathy, by giving him an opportunity to confess his crimes and express his regret, which means you acknowledged his inner conversion. We have reasons to assume that the dying man still believed in God, and that, through his personal confession to you, he did what he could under those circumstances, in the hope of finding God's mercy. Even though you went away without formally uttering a word of forgiveness, the dying man somehow felt accepted by you; otherwise he would not have bequeathed you his personal belongings.

Considering your situation at the time and recalling what you went through, an explicit pardon would have surpassed our concept of the human. Nevertheless, you had an opportunity to put forward an act of almost superhuman goodness in the midst of a subhuman and bestial world of atrocities. The fact that you did not take advantage of this opportunity may be what still haunts you as a striving human being.

Summing up, let me conclude my reply with the words of the Psalm: "If thou, O LORD, shouldest mark iniquities, O LORD, who shall stand?" (130:3). Thank you so much for your confidence in entrusting this manuscript to me.

# HAROLD S. KUSHNER

I am not sure there is such a thing as forgiving another person, though I know there is such a thing as being forgiven. To be forgiven is to feel the weight of the past lifted from our shoulders, to feel the stain of past wrongdoing washed away. To be forgiven is to feel free to step into the future unburdened by the precedent of who we have been and what we have done in previous times.

My imagination, contaminated by computer imagery, sees the human soul as possessing a "feedback mechanism." Every time we are called on to make a decision, we not only weigh the alternatives, we deal with the memories of how we have responded to similar situations in the past. A voice inside our head tells us "these are the choices, and this is the way you have chosen on other occasions." Thus Maimonides and Erich Fromm see that every time the Pharaoh of the Exodus story says no to Moses, he makes it more likely that he will say no the next time and harder for him to change course and say yes, because his feedback mechanism keeps telling him "you are a person who says no to such demands."

If we feel that our past behavior was wrong, being forgiven means erasing that message, liberating ourselves from the idea that we are still who we used to be, and freeing ourselves to become a new person.

To be forgiven is a miracle. It comes from God, and it comes when God chooses to grant it, not when we order it up. That is why, in the Amidah, a Jew prays three times a day for the miracle of God's forgiveness. To say that God forgives is not a statement about God, about God's emotional state. God's forgiveness is something that happens inside us, not inside God, freeing us from the shame of the past so that we can be different people, choosing and acting differently in the future.

That was the mistake of the Nazi soldier in *The Sunflower.* His plea for forgiveness was addressed to someone who lacked the power (let alone the right) to grant it. If he wanted to die feeling forgiven, he should have said to himself: "What I did was terribly wrong and I am ashamed of myself for having done it. I reject that part of myself that could have done such a thing. I don't want to be a person who would do such a thing. I am still alive, though I don't know for how much longer, but the Nazi who killed that child is dead. He no longer lives inside me. I renounce him." And if God chose to grant him the miracle of forgiveness, he would feel that he had expelled the Nazi within him as our body expels a foreign object, something that is not us, and he would die a different person than he had lived.

Of course, had he repented of his crime earlier and not at the point of death, he would have had the opportunity of experiencing the cleansing power of repentance by facing the same situation and acting differently. Unfortunately, by summoning one Jew to absolve him of what he had done to other Jews, he leaves us doubting whether he has in fact transcended the Nazi view of seeing Jews as less than human, interchangeable entities rather than unique human beings, even as a person sins by hating all blacks, whites, Christians, Jews, Germans because of what some other blacks, whites, etc., may have done to him.

That is what it means to be forgiven. What does it mean to forgive? A woman in my congregation comes to see me. She is a single mother, divorced, working to support herself and three young children. She says to me, "Since my husband walked out on us, every month is a struggle to pay our bills. I have to tell my kids we have no money to go to the movies, while he's living it up with his new wife in another state. How can you tell me to forgive him?" I answer her, "I'm not asking you to forgive him because what he did was acceptable. It wasn't; it was mean and selfish. I'm asking you to forgive because he doesn't deserve the power to live in your head and turn you into a bitter, angry woman. I'd like to see him out of your life emotionally as completely as he is out of it physically, but you keep holding on to him. You're not hurting him by holding on to that resentment, but you're hurting yourself."

Forgiving is not something we do for another person, as the Nazi asked Wiesenthal to do for him. Forgiving happens inside us. It represents a letting go of the sense of grievance, and perhaps most importantly a letting go of the role of victim. For a Jew to forgive the Nazis would not mean, God forbid, saying to them "What you did was understandable, I can understand what led you to do it and I don't hate you for it." It would mean saying "What you did was thoroughly despicable and puts you outside the category of decent human beings. But I refuse to give you the power to define me as a victim. I refuse to let your blind hatred define the shape and content of my Jewishness. I don't hate you; I reject you." And then the Nazi would remain chained to his past and to his conscience, but the Jew would be free.

# LAWRENCE L. LANGER

I have no idea what I might have done in Simon Wiesenthal's place, nor do I believe that the question is a legitimate one. Role-playing about Holocaust reality trivializes the serious issues of judgment and forgiveness that *The Sunflower* raises. In my opinion, discussion should focus on the SS man's request, and Wiesenthal's response to it.

The mass murder of European Jewry is an unforgivable crime. By his own description, the SS man provides the details: Jewish men, women, and children are herded into a building, hand grenades are thrown in, setting it on fire; the SS men then shoot Jews—including little children—trying to escape the flames through exits or by jumping from windows. *Can* one repent such a monstrous deed? I do not see how. The real test of the SS man's spiritual integrity came at the moment he received the order to shoot. At that instant he was still a morally free man (assuming he had not taken part in earlier crimes). By agreeing to shoot instead of deferring to a higher authority and disobeying the order, he failed the test and permanently cut himself off from the possibility of forgiveness. This may not be true for other crimes—but the mass murder of European Jewry is not an ordinary crime.

No matter what the criminals—the men and women who planned, authorized, collaborated in, and carried out such actions—say afterward, the crime of the Holocaust remains unforgivable. How can a criminal be forgiven for an unforgivable crime?

It seems to me that in refusing to extend forgiveness to the culprit, Wiesenthal unconsciously acknowledged the indissoluble bond fusing the criminal to his crime. Although many have hailed the sincerity of the SS man's repentance, we have no way of verifying this. All we have is Wiesenthal's remembered account, a reproduced voice, not an authentic one. The long monologues of the dying SS man cannot be verbatim, only approximate. Hence the mystery of his inner feelings remains swathed in the bandages that encase his body. Wiesenthal does not enter into a dialogue with him, which might have revealed much; he only listens.

He does carry on dialogues with his fellow Jews, and with an apprentice priest named Bolek. These dialogues give us an important clue to the dilemma we are facing: the *language* of the exchanges does more to shape our attitude toward the SS man's request for forgiveness than the actual crime he has committed. For example, Bolek understandably chastises Wiesenthal for his failure to forgive: "Whom had the SS man to turn to? None of those he had wronged were still alive." When we call the murder of a helpless Jewish father and child a "wrong," we ease the crime into the realm of familiar and forgivable transgressions and relieve ourselves of the burden of facing its utter horror.

Perhaps unwittingly, Wiesenthal fills Bolek's mouth with questionable platitudes: "When one is face to face with death one doesn't lie"; "he had no opportunity to expiate the sins which he had committed"; he showed "genuine, sincere repentance for his misdeeds." I believe that anyone capable of labeling the murder of defenseless Jews a "misdeed" sacrifices his right to comment on the subject. Trapped by his theological word-horde, the novice weaves around the by now unmentioned details of the crime a verbal tapestry of exculpation that shifts the onus of responsibility from the criminal to the victim. Of course, Wiesenthal and not Bolek records these words for the reader, and this raises a question of narrative authority in the text of *The Sunflower* that would require separate investigation.

The "disappearing criminal" is one of the most dangerous and lamentable legacies of the Holocaust experience. Ironically, in asking forgiveness of a Jew, the SS man transfers the weight of moral decision from himself to one of his potential victims. This dynamic, unfortunately, recurs in numerous testimonies of Holocaust survivors who, in the absence of real malefactors like the dying SS man, sometimes blame *themselves* for acts or consequences of which they are perfectly innocent. For me, the SS man's request betrays his utter failure to understand the nature of his crime: it seems a desperate last gesture to escape his guilt, though we will never know what his buried motives were. He may not know them himself.

Words like "wrong" and "misdeed" grew up in a universe of discourse oblivious to places like Auschwitz and Majdanek, where gas chambers and crematoria flourished. The long list of exonerating terms that appear in *The Sunflower*—atonement and expiation, repentance and absolution, guilt and forgiveness—

to me reflects a valiant but misguided and ultimately doomed effort to reclaim for a familiar vocabulary an event that has burst the frame of conventional judgmental language. Jean Améry's classic study of his ordeal at the hands of the Gestapo and in Auschwitz, *At the Mind's Limits*, had for its original German title *Jenseits von Schuld und Sühne* (Beyond guilt and atonement). Améry not only promotes Nietzsche's *Beyond Good and Evil* (Jenseits von Gut und Böse) to modern times, but also invites us to reconsider the terminology with which we will evaluate the most hideous crime of the twentieth century.

Deep in the bowels of Dante's Inferno is a sinner whose presence must have confounded Dante's readers, because they believed that this sinner was still alive. In fact, he was; but Dante the poet invents the heretical idea of acts so outrageous that they condemn the soul of the sinner to eternal damnation before his death. Hence the possibility of an unrepentable and thus unforgivable crime is not a new one, though Dante could not have known how this quirk in his orderly design for Hell might herald our current threatening impasse about atrocities that are beyond guilt and atonement.

Imagine an SS man today standing by a mass grave at Chelmno or Treblinka or Babi Yar, and saying "I'm sorry; I repent what I have done." His words would drift down among the hundreds of thousands of wasted corpses or their ashes, and then sink further, to that lower place where they would echo amidst the unforgiven and unforgivable spirits of those eternally damned for having consented to these monstrous acts to begin with. That is where our search for guilt should begin—and end.

*The Sunflower* should prompt us—has always prodded me—to shift the locus of our discussion. The vital question to ask about this text is not whether Wiesenthal should have forgiven the SS man. It is rather why the SS man, as a young boy, against his father's wishes, joined enthusiastically in the activities of the Hitler Youth; why, again presumably against his father's wishes, he *volunteered* for the SS (as free a choice as a man could make at the time); why he then pursued a career in that murderous league of killers without protest, including the episode he tells of on his deathbed; and most important of all, why he had to wait until he was dying to feel the time had come for repentance and forgiveness. On these issues, the SS man is deftly silent.

Such are the questions, only implicit in Wiesenthal's narrative, that should challenge our imagination. Simon Wiesenthal himself was and remains innocent of any wrong.

# PRIMO LEVI

The events you evoke occurred in a world which was shaking on its foundations and in an atmosphere completely impregnated with crime. Under these conditions, it is not always easy, indeed it is perhaps impossible, to assign an absolute value to right and wrong: it is in the nature of crime to create situations of moral conflict, dead ends of which bargaining or compromise are the only conditions of exit; conditions which inflict yet another wound on justice and on oneself.

When an act of violence or an offense has been committed it is forever irreparable: it is quite probable that public opinion will cry out for a sanction, a punishment, a "price" for pain; it is also possible that the price paid be useful inasmuch as it makes amends or discourages a fresh offense, but the initial offense remains and the "price" is always (even if it is "just") a new offense and a new source of pain.

This having been said, I think I can affirm that you did well, in this situation, to refuse your pardon to the dying man. You did well because it was the lesser evil: you could only have forgiven him by lying or by inflicting upon yourself a terrible moral violence. But, of course, this refusal is not the answer to everything, and it is quite easy to see why you were left with doubts: in a case like this it is impossible to decide categorically between the answers yes and no; there always remains something to be said for the other side.

In your case, as you were a Häftling, that is a predestined victim, and since, at that moment, you felt that you represented the entire Jewish people, you would have been at fault in absolving your man, and you would perhaps today be experiencing a deeper remorse than you feel at not having absolved him.

What would this pardon have meant for the dying man and for you? Probably a great deal for the former; a kind of sacralization, a purification which would have freed his religious conscience, all too tardily aroused, from the terror of eternal punishment. But I think that, for you, it would have been meaningless: certainly it would not have meant "you are guilty of no crime," nor "you committed a crime against your will or without knowing what you were doing." On your part it would have been an empty formula and consequently a lie.

I should like to add this: the figure of the SS man as portrayed in your book does not appear as fully reinstated from the moral point of view. Everything would lead one to believe that, had it not been for his fear of impending death, he would have behaved quite otherwise: he would not have repented until much later, with the downfall of Germany or perhaps never. The act of "having a Jew brought to him" seems to me at once childish and impudent. Childish because it is too reminiscent of the defenseless child who cries out for help: it is quite possible that in his mind, bent as it was by propaganda, the "Jew" was an abnormal being—half-devil, half-miracle worker, capable in any case of supernatural deeds. Did Himmler not believe something similar when he ordered the suspension of the Lager massacres, in the hope that the "Jewish International" would assist Germany in concluding a separate peace with the West?

And impudent, because once again, the Nazi was using the Jew as a tool, unaware of the danger and the shock his request must have constituted for the prisoner: his action, examined in depth, is tinged with egoism, since one detects in it an attempt to load onto another one's own anguish.

# DEBORAH E. LIPSTADT

*T*eshuvah, repentance, derived from the Hebrew word "to return," is Judaism's process of saying I'm sorry to those we have wronged. It is more than repentance but is designed to make our relationship with both God and those around us whole again. Judaism believes that God more than accepts the repentant person, God *desires* people to return. Done properly, *teshuvah* can result in the sinner returning to a repaired relationship with both God and with his/her fellow humans, even as God returns to the sinner. In the Talmud we read: "In a place where people who have done *teshuvah* stand, the purest *zadik* (righteous person) cannot stand." The fact that a repentant sinner is more righteous than a pure *zadik* doesn't seem to make sense. Maimonides offers an interesting insight on *teshuvah* which may explain this dilemma. Citing the verse from Genesis, after Adam and Eve eat from the forbidden fruit, God says: "Now Adam is like one of us [*c'echad memenu*], knowing the difference between right and wrong."

The simple explanation that after humans have sinned they become Godlike seems puzzling. In the Mishnah Torah Maimonides reads the verse differently. He puts a period after *echad*, which he translates as unique, and then translates *memenu*, as from within himself. "Now Adam is *echad*, unique. *Memenu*, from within himself, he knows the difference between right and wrong." The human species is unique in the world, in that humans use their own intelligence and reason to distinguish good and evil.

So too those who have done wrong and then performed *teshuvah* have reached a new level: *from within themselves*, they know the true difference between right and wrong. It is this unique human ability to know the difference between right and wrong which makes *teshuvah* transformational. But repentance is not a simple thing. Before we can evaluate the prisoner's response to the soldier from a Jewish perspective it is necessary to delineate the various steps entailed in repentance.

First one must ask forgiveness of the aggrieved party. This personal encounter is a sine qua non when it comes to sins between two human beings. A number of years ago, on *60 Minutes*, Mike Wallace interviewed Chuck Colson, former head of the Nixon White House Plumbers, the Watergate era dirty tricks unit. Wallace asked Colson, who while in jail had become a devout Christian, if he felt any need to go to the people whose lives he so severely dislocated and apologize to them. "No," Colson answered, "I have made peace with God in my heart." This is in striking contrast to *teshuvah*, which calls for going to the wronged party first. Judaism believes that it is only through human interaction that the victim can best be healed and the wrongdoer most profoundly changed. Making peace with God comes later. By forcing a face-to-face encounter with the aggrieved party Jewish tradition teaches that sin is not a generalized amorphous act but something quite specific done against a particular person or group of people. If I sin, I cannot go to someone else who has some remote connection with the person I have harmed and ask that third party for forgiveness.

After confronting the person against whom the sin has been committed and trying to correct that wrong, one turns to God. Then one verbally confesses one's sins, expresses shame and regret for having committed this act, and resolves never to act that way again. But this does not yet bring one to the highest or most complete level of the process, *teshuvah gemurah*, complete *teshuvah*. This is achieved when the individual is in the same situation in which he or she originally sinned and chooses not to repeat the act. The person still has the potential to commit that sin again; i.e., his/her strength has not diminished nor has the capability been lost. Nonetheless, they choose not to repeat it.

Finally, it is important to differentiate between *teshuvah*, repentance, and *kaparah*, atonement. Atonement only comes after one bears the consequences of one's acts. Some might ask, is not repentance enough? Why is punishment also necessary? Judaism is founded on the notion that actions have consequences:

righteous acts result in blessing, evil acts in punishment. When King David sinned by scheming to have Bathsheba's husband killed so that he could have her for his own, he subsequently performed *teshuvah*. (His genuine remorse is evident in Psalm 51, written after he committed his heinous crime.) Nonetheless he was punished for his actions. Only then was his relationship with God returned to its original place.

The question to be asked is not *should* the prisoner have forgiven the SS man but *could* the prisoner have forgiven him? The prisoner could have told the soldier that he personally forgave him because he was different from his fellow SS soldiers who had shown no remorse. But this Jew could not have offered the soldier atonement. The SS man had done nothing against him specifically. The Jews who had been burned to death by this soldier had not authorized anyone to forgive on their behalf.

The prisoner's dilemma has contemporary reverberations. Jews are often asked by non-Jews, "Isn't it time 'you Jews' forgave the German perpetrators? Isn't it time you forgot?" (It is interesting to note that few other people who have suffered the consequences of persecution, including persecution of a far less heinous nature, are asked this question.) When asked, I respond that I am yet to encounter a perpetrator who is actually seeking forgiveness. Citizens of Germany, Austria, and other countries which took part in the Holocaust who were born after the Holocaust bear no direct guilt for what happened. They may bear a national responsibility and their country may have an indelible blot on its historical record, but they bear no direct guilt. More importantly, even if I did encounter a perpetrator asking forgiveness, who am *I* to offer forgiveness? *I* cannot speak on behalf of those who have been wronged—particularly those who have been killed.

Ultimately we have no way of knowing if the soldier had actually performed complete *teshuvah*. This SS soldier who lay on his deathbed did not have the ability to repeat his heinous crimes. Would he have felt so contrite if he had not been at death's door? It is also important to remember that the soldier's apparently genuine struggle with his past did not obviate his responsibility to bear the punishment for what he had done. Even if the prisoner had offered the soldier verbal forgiveness, that would not have resulted in an automatic cleansing of the slate. Such atonement would only have come when the guilty man had borne the consequences of his act and had demonstrated by his subsequent behavior that he had returned to that "place" he had occupied prior to committing his heinous crime.

# FRANKLIN H. LITTELL

Guilt is the question. The problem of the dying perpetrator was the fact that the only human persons who could have forgiven him were dead.

This story is told repeatedly in discussions of the Holocaust and its perpetrators and complicit spectators. The question of individual guilt slides easily into collective guilt. The matter of moral guilt arises inevitably from the fact of political guilt that is displayed to view.

Christians believe that in the end only a Divine intervention can clarify and release the soul burdened with guilt. They also believe that God loves the broken-hearted penitent. No person or nation, however, will "turn from the ways of evil" and "turn again unto the Lord" without a strong sense of the reality of sin and guilt.

During the more than four decades since Rafael Lemkin coined the term "genocide," progress on both fronts—political and moral—has been slow. But to date the scholars and statesmen have moved further in creating the structures to inhibit and punish the slaughter of targeted ethnic, religious, and cultural groups than the religionists have moved to create the moral and religious energy to outlaw genocide and enforce the laws against it.

The political leaders seem less afraid of exercising the power to restrain the incidence of genocide than the religious leaders are to proclaim the sin and guilt of the perpetrators *and* the bystanders. Perhaps this is because—again—the leaders of the churches of "Christendom" have not yet allowed their imaginations to transport them to the SS man's deathbed moment of crystal clarity.

In the meantime, the civilized world is struggling to find legal ways, insulated by due process of law, to punish criminals guilty of genocide. The principle was staked out at Nuremberg, and it became part of international law with the Genocide Convention. Now the first efforts are being made to punish perpetrators of genocidal acts in the ruins of Yugoslavia.

Many feel despair that the way is so difficult. But there are always time lags between the several stages in translating moral and religious guilt into civil and juridical guilt. First there is the realization that some wickedness is not like an earthquake or a flood: it is wrong, and someone did it. Then there is the time lag until the thought penetrates the communal mind that if someone did it, that person can be punished (and others so inclined be discouraged). There follows the time lag until the crime is defined and punishment decreed for perpetrators. Finally, there is a time lag until the laws that are on the books generally can be enforced.

This has been the sequence in the history of murder, polygamy, dueling, feuding, infanticide, slavery, and a dozen other greater or lesser evils that were sins before they were seen as crimes and treated as matters of criminal law. Rather than being discouraged by our seeming impotence in the face of great genocidal evils in Rwanda, Burundi, "Bosnia," and elsewhere, we might take courage in the thought that everyone is miserable about it. We are in the time of the last "lag," when the law is written down but enforcement is partial and sporadic.

In earlier times there was neither hesitation nor embarrassment on the part of rulers. The makers and shakers of primitive societies have always piled the skulls high to vaunt their power over others. Then came the stage when civilized peoples didn't like what they heard but felt unable to do anything to limit and/or punish the crime. "That's the way things are" was the general and fatalistic expression, and a few generations ago it would have been applied to the horrendous crimes committed by all sides in the ruins of Yugoslavia. Now the spectators are all miserable, and that is a sign of progress.

In the not too distant future the last gap will be closed, and the murder of peoples—widespread before the word "genocide" was even invented—will be inhibited by law and criminals who breach the law in this sector will be punished.

On the moral and religious front, progress is less evident.

What was the guilt of the German, Croatian, Austrian, French, Ukrainian, and Baltic churchmen who were either running with the perpetrators or at least complicit spectators of the genocide of the Jews? What was the guilt of those American churchmen who were eager to remain bystanders during the Holocaust?

So far, the Christian establishments are in a "full press" defensive formation. Only in a rare case, such as the January 1980 Declaration of the Protestant Church of the Rhineland, have the Christian social and/or legal establishments in Europe and America dug deeper than pious expressions of regret for "anti-Judaic teaching" and sometime anti-Jewish "race prejudice." The Christian doctrines of Sin and Guilt are thereby whittled down to the relatively painless pagan idea of error or mistaken judgment.

The Christian churches have yet to confront the truth that during the Holocaust there opened up a yawning chasm between traditional Christian words and actual Christian actions and inactions. The guilt that rests upon Christendom is more than the sum total of individual mistakes, and it has confronted the faith with a credibility crisis. Among outsiders, cynicism and atheism have been fortified. Among communicants or constituents, uncertainty and distrust prevail. The pronouncements of church leaders carry no special authority even among members, let alone in the nations at large.

We are returned, willing or unwilling, to the most fundamental factor in law and order: even the most ruthless despot or dictator cannot rule without the at least passive complicity of his subjects. On the other face of law and order: no crime can be inhibited or punished unless there is a strong conviction that to commit it is sinful. To achieve a higher level of human interaction and concern, progress must be made on two fronts: one, in the enforcement of law by reliable stewards of public power; two, through deepening of individual and group awareness of the earnest nature of the choice between good and evil, between innocence and guilt.

# HUBERT G. LOCKE

Silence hangs like a pall over this wrenching experience that you have shared with us, Mr. Wiesenthal. When the dying Nazi turns to you and tries to beg forgiveness, you remain silent. At that moment, you tell us, "there was an uncanny silence in the room." Later, when you visit his mother, you stand before his portrait in silence and finally you leave the old woman without having answered her entreaties. By remaining silent, you kept the truth about a son from his mother—in your words "without diminishing . . . the poor woman's last surviving consolation—faith in the goodness of her son." You gave, on one hand, silent assent to a dying man's truth about himself and, on the other, you kept the truth, by silence, about a son from his mother. In your silence, both revelation and concealment are manifest; is it possible that you said more in your silence than if you had spoken?

You ask if your silence to the dying Nazi's pleas for forgiveness was right or wrong. You wonder if it was a mistake not to have told his mother the truth. You also ask those of us who read your account, if we had been in your place, what we would have done. Only those who are certain of their answer to your final query can have the arrogance to pose answers to the first two. Silence, in fact, may be the better response—our silence to yours—in the hope that by listening quietly and more closely to your experience, we might learn from it, rather than moralize about it.

Why is it, in fact, that we mortals are so averse to silence, that we feel we must greet each experience with dissection, discussion, and analysis, that to speak is to know? There is, to be sure, the conviction that we gain understanding by rational effort, that by asking questions and weighing evidence and considering alternatives and demanding proofs and debating various positions and interpretations, we somehow arrive at the "right" answers to life's mysteries. Much of our much-touted human progress has been achieved because we are so wedded to such efforts—but then we come up against an experience such as you have placed before us and our response—my response, at least—is to shudder. I find myself unable to ask the probing questions of morals and ethics regarding your situation; instead, I am conscious of a cold chill that comes over me when I sense what it may have been like to be in your or a similar circumstance. No, I cannot answer your question of right and wrong; your silence was your answer and perhaps it should be ours as well.

There is much that silence might teach us, if we could but learn to listen to it. Not the least of its lessons is that there may well be questions for which there are no answers and other questions for which answers would remove the moral force of the question. There are matters that perhaps should always remain unanswered; questions which should lay like a great weight on our consciences so that we continually feel an obligation to confront their insistent urging. There are questions that are unanswerable queries of the soul, matters too awe-full for human response, too demonic for profound rational resolution. By our silence, perhaps we acknowledge as much; we own up to our humanness. We concede that we are not gods and that we lack, as much as we might be loath to admit it, the capacity to provide understanding and assurance for every inexplicable moment in life.

Perhaps we should be reluctant to answer your questions for another reason as well. The Latin verb "to answer," which is reflected in the English word "response," carries with it the meaning of "to assure" or "to promise or vow" or "to engage oneself." It suggests that there is much more here than a mere intellectual exercise which you have given us. It implies that if we think we have answers or an answer, we are also offering assurances that what we propose will somehow satisfy the moral dilemma. It also suggests that we who answer also are prepared to engage ourselves in validating the accuracy (dare one say, the truth) of our response. An answer involves our willingness to attest to or affirm, by our personal involvement and commitment, the genuineness of our assertion. I dare not answer unless I am also ready to act; that is reason enough for pause.

Your experience was part and parcel of a moment in history, as it is often observed, when even God was silent! I am struck most by your recounting your conversation with Arthur who tells you of the old woman in the Ghetto. When asked for news of when you and your comrades might get out of the camp or when you might be slaughtered, she says in effect, there is no news, for God is on leave. Perhaps there was a moment—one which you and millions of others experienced—which was so beyond the pale of comprehension that even God was silent. If God was silent, dare any of us speak?

# ERICH H. LOEWY

Anyone who has never been in such an almost inconceivable situation like Simon Wiesenthal's cannot judge the events related in *The Sunflower*. Any judgment we would offer about such a situation is truly a form of hubris. I was personally lucky to escape from the Nazis in 1938. While what I experienced was, to put it mildly, distinctly unpleasant, it cannot compare to what those underwent who were—due to the Nazis but also to the policies of the western states and of the churches—locked in. My comments, therefore, are not a way of judging a situation which is entirely beyond being judged by normal standards but rather a way of examining some more common ethical problems.

The relationship we are confronted with here is not simply one between strong aggressor and supine victim; nor is it a relationship of former victim to former aggressor with strength and weakness of each having, so to speak, changed places. The existential situation is one in which the context is unchanged: Wiesenthal continues to be a prisoner, the victim of rapacious forces which surround him. But in the particular context in which Wiesenthal experienced this story—in the sickroom of the wounded SS man—the situation is, for the moment, changed: it is the aggressor who, in a significant sense, is now the weaker, psychologically dependent upon his former victim and, in a sense, pleading with him. But he is pleading in a strange context: at any moment the SS man, although in one sense weakened, can call upon overwhelming forces which could and would crush Wiesenthal. Thus, for Wiesenthal, not doing what the weaker SS man wants still carries an inevitably grave risk. The relationship is extremely complex and the strengths and weaknesses of the actors, in the situation with which we are presented, may shift at any time.

Not enough has, I think, been made of Wiesenthal's behavior during the time that the SS man "confessed": evidently a matter of hours and agonizing hours for both. Too much has been made of the final question of forgiving or of not forgiving. What matters here, and what deserves more attention, is the basic humanity of the situation: a blind, fatally wounded aggressor pleads with one of his (potential) victims and that victim, let's face it, feels sorry for him. His compassion—incredible under the circumstances when one thinks where Wiesenthal is coming from and inevitably going back to—is aroused and he can in a sense place himself in the shoes of another suffering being, even of one who has brought unimaginable harm to persons just like Wiesenthal. He touches the man (the very thought makes my blood curdle), he chases away a fly which bothers the SS man, and he stays. By his behavior Wiesenthal tacitly admits the SS man back into a human company from which such a person must, when the truth strikes, feel himself permanently excluded. That is a form of acceptance, of acceptance of common humanity if not forgiveness or even understanding. One wonders if, rather than empty words of forgiveness, such human acceptance was not far more what the SS man truly wanted and hoped for. Showing the SS man that despite all that he had done he remained in Wiesenthal's eyes and heart, at any rate, a human being, is something Wiesenthal could, and did, do. The fact that he could do it, the fact that he sat by the bed, touched the SS man, and chased away a fly shows, I think, the measure of the man. It is,

I think, the most important element in this story and perhaps the one which, when all is said and done, brought more comfort to the SS man than he could have hoped for or, in a strictly rational sense, deserved.

Of course, Wiesenthal could not forgive the SS man: no one can forgive others something that has not been done to them directly. Nor is it, I think, Wiesenthal's role to point out the possibility of forgiveness by God. Wiesenthal is neither a priest nor a rabbi and pointing out that God might have mercy under these circumstances may easily irritate rather than comfort. The SS man chose not to confess to a priest, although he is Catholic, or to receive absolution. He chose to speak to a victim and to seek human forgiveness from someone who represented for him those he had hurt. God or Divine forgiveness is altogether another matter. Ignoring such a request is all that Wiesenthal could do.

The question of Simon Wiesenthal's relationship with the mother likewise bears examination. Obviously Wiesenthal was motivated by a deep concern for the truthfulness or falseness of what he had been told by the SS man about his previous life as well as by compassion for a severely damaged and bereaved mother. Soon after the war Wiesenthal subjects himself to an arduous journey (how arduous only those who are familiar with conditions in postwar Germany can understand) and finds a widow in a cold, bombed-out, and devastated building. He sees that she has her only son's picture on the wall, an only son whose story of his previous life at home she corroborates: he joined the SS, and since he became a Nazi had been totally estranged from his father; despite this, according to the mother, he had always been a good boy who would never harm anyone. When asked, Wiesenthal lies: he never met her son personally and only received his name through the window of a transport of wounded soldiers. Some have said that lying to the mother was wrong: had she known the truth, she could have come to terms with it, could have received solace from the Church and been reassured of Divine forgiveness. I cannot agree with this: she may very well not have been religious or even if she was religious such solace may not have been meaningful to her. Just as cogent would be the argument that knowing about her son could drive her to final despair and, perhaps, to suicide. Wiesenthal chose, humanely and I think wisely, to hide the truth.

What can we learn from all this? I think it is that rationality without compassion and compassion without rationality are both ineffective when it comes to grappling with ethical problems. If only compassion would have counseled Wiesenthal, an empty forgiveness might easily be granted when in fact forgiveness was not only out of place but in truth impossible. Reason alone might suggest that the suffering of the SS man was well deserved and prompted Wiesenthal to treat him inhumanely. Reason prevented the sentiment of compassion from degenerating into sentimentality and compassion prevented unmodified reason from prompting a less humane act. In dealing with the mother, on the other hand, reason (helped along, perhaps, by a desire for revenge) could easily have led Wiesenthal to divulge the truth. Compassion prevented bludgeoning the mother with the naked truth and reason allowed Wiesenthal to hold his compassion in check. Without reason compassion could readily have led to a more active form of lying and transformed an SS villain into a hero. Since some personal contact with her dead son had been established, perhaps Wiesenthal left the mother more capable of bearing her grief. Humanity, once again, became shared.

I cannot judge Wiesenthal or his actions wrong under these circumstances. If, God forbid, I should ever be in a similar situation I could only hope that I would have the strength to act in a similar fashion. I am afraid I might not.

# HERBERT MARCUSE

I think I would have acted the way you did, that is to say, refused the request of the dying SS man. It always seemed to me inhuman and a travesty of justice if the executioner asked the victim to forgive. One cannot, and should not, go around happily killing and torturing and then, when the moment has come, simply ask, and receive, forgiveness. In my view, this perpetuates the crime.

By the way, the question transcends the Jewish problem. As a member of the National Liberation Front, would one forgive a Marine sergeant the killing and torturing of one's friends, wife, children? Is anyone justified, entitled to forgive?

I still remember the traumatic shock I had when I read that, after the assassination of Rathenau, his mother went to the assassin's mother and comforted her!

I believe that the easy forgiving of such crimes perpetuates the very evil it wants to alleviate.

# MARTIN E. MARTY

What would I have done?"

The author's final question is designed to haunt. The word that leaps, nags, and accuses is "I." Here there is no thought of categorical imperatives or universal principles. What would *I* have done? Ortega reminds us: "I am I and my circumstances." My circumstances are unimaginably different from his. It is difficult, then, to imagine an answer to his question.

Almost two thousand years after the early Christians were martyred by the Romans we Christian children were taught to prepare ourselves. We, too, might be called upon to witness even unto death. Strange how powerful a story can remain for two millennia. So it shall be with the recall of the Holocaust for the descendants of Jews. Astute teachers would remind us that martyrdoms continued. Even as we sat in school, Christians were dying for their faith in Russia, Germany, and elsewhere. At the time I was in third grade Dietrich Bonhoeffer, a Christian who was later to die in one of Hitler's camps, was writing a book on discipleship. Its first line told us that when Jesus Christ calls a man he calls him to die.

Without doubt I prepared myself intellectually as a child for such discipleship. I am not sure that if my circumstances called me to such extremes I would be ready. I, who cower in the dentist's chair and shrink from minor pain—would I be able to stand torture? I, who have been trained or who have trained myself to look past or to overlook injustices and suffering every day—would I be ready to witness? "What would I have done?" I do not know. But the author's question pursues beyond that first evasion.

"What would I have done?" becomes "What *should* I have done?" But to answer that question would identify me again with the author and his circumstances, something that is impossible for me to do. Even the author's fellow prisoners do not satisfy him with the counsel they offer. Were I to respond directly, it would be necessary for me to get almost as close as they, to share the experience of the author's people. But is there then a single prescription, a single "ought" or "should"? His committee of counselors sometimes seems to imply that there is. To act one way would be to deny the Jewish people. To act another way would be to affirm them. I prefer his lifelong uncertainty to their counsel. To say that all persons in a people must act a specific way is to routinize them, to program them, to deprive them of elements of their humanity.

Viktor Frankl, the psychiatrist who survived the death camps, has pondered the question of exceptionality there and thenceforth. Why did some prisoners who knew they were to die that day still spread comfort and share bread? He could not answer, but he did note that they demonstrated that one freedom cannot be taken away: the freedom to choose one's own attitude in the face of any circumstance. The author chose the attitude of perplexity and bemusement. He chose to let himself be haunted all his life. Who is to say that his choice is inferior to the counselors', for they were more sure of themselves and the impact of peoplehood.

Speaking of peoplehood and circumstances, one more thing must be said. I am a Christian, and I hear the question framed against Wiesenthal's experience. So it sounds like this:

"What would/should a Jew have done?" I cannot imagine being asked to this symposium except for the fact that I am a Christian. So I hear, "What does a Christian say?" And in that way of stating it I can only respond with silence. Non-Jews and perhaps especially Christians should not give advice about the Holocaust experience to its heirs for the next two thousand years. And then we shall have nothing to say.

This does not mean that the Holocaust has to be set apart qualitatively from the experience of all other genocides and victimizations in history. To do so would be to dishonor innocent sufferers elsewhere. Modern Armenians, tribesmen in Africa, peoples of the Asian subcontinent have all experienced hatreds and madnesses as have the Jews. They may appear on statistically smaller scales, but I do not begin to comprehend the Holocaust if I say that others' suffering was less meaningful or less valid. But it happens that the Holocaust is webbed into "our" history—Western and Western religious history. This circumstance impels silence. Cheap instant advice from a Christian would trivialize the lives and deaths of millions.

Forget, then, the author's circumstance and keep the essence of his question for me. Is there any kind of situation in which the offense is so gross and enormous that I should withhold forgiveness in the face of what appears to be true penitence? My answer would be that in every circumstance that I can picture, more value would grow out of forgiveness than out of its withholding. But I must ask what am I afraid of or concerned about, and what is it that causes me to hem and hedge, to shuffle and clear my throat, to be suspicious of that answer?

First, I am afraid of "cheap grace," as were *The Sunflower* people. W. H. Auden's Herod parodies a version of Christian forgiveness. He sees every corner newsboy remarking that he likes to commit sins and God likes to forgive them so the world is admirably arranged. No. Nothing should happen that would let haters or murderers off the hook by assuring them that grace is readily available. The author's silence in that hospital room was a guard against the cheapening of grace.

A second fear: crimes against a people will be taken less seriously if individual persons start forgiving in their name. The question is here raised, then, whether latter-day Germans who do express repentance should be allowed to feel forgiven. Here I must raise the question whether it is always valuable to prolong a people's sense of guilt. As a white, they tell me that I must always feel guilty and grovel over what whites in the American past did when they killed Indians and enslaved blacks. And, to a measure, I do. But I have sufficient guilt for my own faults in relation to the heirs of the Indians and blacks, and to many other people. Is there not a limit to the good that can be achieved by my groveling, my self-hate, my loss of pride in the positive features of my heritages? Did not Nazism in part grow out of such negative and resentful views? Must I not also be given a means for retrieving from a people's history some moments, models, motifs that can give dignity and nobility to a history?

The third reason for pause: if grace be cheap and splattered at random, will we not soon forget to tell the story? Theodor Adorno and Alexander Solzhenitsyn have both reminded us that to forget to tell the story is to deprive past sufferers of the meaning of their act. But there are many ways to tell the story. Wiesenthal's ambivalence stays in our mind because he has taken pains to tell us of it. So would other attitudes, if there be storytellers to broadcast them.

We do not want cheap grace, a casual people, or a forgotten victim. What do we want? I am on a search for grace in the world. While my colleagues write on the phenomenology of evil or of the will, I want to see what grace feels like. As a Christian I am told that God is a gracious Other, but I also need to be a gracious brother. Gracelessness helps produce totalitarianisms as much as cheap grace might. If there is to be grace, it must be mediated through people. We have to see potentials in the lives of even the worst people, have to see that it is we who can dam the flow of grace. I do not for a moment claim that this insight is mine because I am a Christian; phenomenologically speaking, such a concept of grace is shared by people of many faiths and of no clear faith. Reportorially, it often has not been visible on Christian soil. But that does not mean that a turn cannot now be taken.

If I forgive in the face of true repentance and new resolve, I am free. Wiesenthal successfully works on the basis of his uncertainty; it motivates him. But I can let my being haunted preoccupy me so that I do not notice "the other." Forgiving and being forgiven are experiences that allow me to be free for a new day. I cannot say that I would be more free or more creative than is Wiesenthal. That is because I cannot say what he should have done but only what I would like to think I would want to do.

# CYNTHIA OZICK

*Notes Toward a Meditation on "Forgiveness"*

### 1. THE USES OF JESUS

The SS man had a Catholic education. As a boy he was a "server in the church." Should not a Christian education make it impossible for a child to grow up to be an SS man? Should not a sentence like "The SS man had a Catholic education" be so thoroughly a contradiction of its own terms that the words come out jabberwocky?

The words do not come out jabberwocky; the SS man *did* have a Christian education.

Does the habit, inculcated in infancy, of worshiping a Master—a Master depicted in human form yet seen to be omnipotent—make it easy to accept a Führer?

### 2. THE SOURCES OF PITY

Pity is not "felt," as if by instinct or reflex. Pity is taught. But what is the original source of pity? What teaches it? The Second Commandment—the one against idols.

Every idol is a shadow of Moloch, demanding human flesh to feed on. The deeper the devotion to the idol, the more pitiless in tossing it its meal will be the devotee. The Commandment against idols is above all a Commandment against victimization, and in behalf of pity.

Moloch springs up wherever the Second Commandment is silenced. In the absence of the Second Commandment, the hunt for victims begins.

The Second Commandment is more explicit than the Sixth, which tells us simply that we must not kill; the Second Commandment tells us we must resist especially that killing which serves our belief.

In Germany, did the Church say, "Hitler is Moloch"?

Moloch's appetite for victims cannot be stemmed. Begin by feeding it only Jews, and in the end it will eat even the little boys who are servers in their church.

There are no innocent idols. Every idol suppresses human pity. That is what it is made for.

### 3. VENGEANCE AND FORGIVENESS

Is the morally obsessed human being more drawn to vengeance or to forgiveness?

What is vengeance, what is forgiveness?

Often we are asked to think this way: vengeance brutalizes, forgiveness refines.

But the opposite can be true. The rabbis said, "Whoever is merciful to the cruel will end by being indifferent to the innocent." Forgiveness can brutalize.

You will object, "Only if it seems to condone. But forgiveness does not condone or excuse. It allows for redemption, for a clean slate, a fresh start; it encourages beginning again. Forgiveness permits renewal."

Only if there is a next time. "I forgive you," we say to the child who has muddied the carpet, "but next time don't do it again." Next time she will leave the muddy boots outside the door; forgiveness, with its enlarging capacities, will have taught her. Forgiveness is an effective teacher. Meanwhile, the spots can be washed away.

But murder is irrevocable. Murder is irreversible. With murder there is no "next time." Even if forgiveness restrains one from perpetrating a new batch of corpses (and there is no historical demonstration of this in Nazi Germany), will the last batch come alive again?

There are spots forgiveness cannot wash out. Forgiveness, which permits redemption, can apply only to a condition susceptible of redemption.

You will object: "If forgiveness cannot wash away murder, neither can vengeance. If forgiveness is not redemptive, surely vengeance is less so, because vengeance requites evil with an equal evil, thereby adding to the store of evil in the world."

But that is a misunderstanding. Vengeance does not requite evil with evil; vengeance cannot requite, repay, even out, equate, redress. If it could, vengeance on a mass murderer would mean killing all the members of his family and a great fraction of his nation; and still his victims would not come alive.

What we call "vengeance" is the act of bringing public justice to evil—not by repeating the evil, not by imitating the evil, not by initiating a new evil, but by making certain never to condone the old one; never even appearing to condone it.

"Public" justice? Yes. While the evil was going on, to turn aside from it, to avoid noticing it, became complicity. And in the same way, after three or four decades have passed and the evil has entered history, to turn aside from it—to forget—again becomes complicity. Allowing the evil to slip into the collective amnesia of its own generation, or of the next generation, is tantamount to condoning it.

You will object: "Here you are, naming vengeance as public justice because it does not condone evil. But forgiveness too does not condone evil. It doesn't matter that it may sometimes appear to; the fact is it doesn't. And you have already demonstrated that there are some evils forgiveness cannot wash away. Yet now you say that vengeance, like forgiveness, neither condones nor washes away the evil. How, then, do vengeance and forgiveness differ?"

In this way: forgiveness is pitiless. It forgets the victim. It negates the right of the victim to his own life. It blurs over suffering and death. It drowns the past. It cultivates sensitiveness toward the murderer at the price of insensitiveness toward the victim.

What is always characterized as "vengeance"—which is to say, a justice that enlightens the world as to the nature of evil (and by "nature of evil" I do not mean something philosophical or metaphysical, but the exact conduct of the evildoer: what precisely was done; when and where; by whom; to whom)—this so-called vengeance is fired by the furnaces of pity. This so-called vengeance—justice in apposite dress—generates fire after fire of pity.

I forgot for a moment where I was and then I heard a buzzing sound. A bluebottle . . . flew round the head of the dying [SS] man, who could not see it nor could he see me wave it away.

"Thanks," he nevertheless whispered. And for the first time I realized that I, a defenseless subhuman, had

contrived to lighten the lot of an equally defenseless superman, without thinking, simply as a matter of course.
(p. 37).

The young man who will become Simon Wiesenthal, who will
become the world's "Nazi-hunter," waves a fly from the wound
of the dying Nazi "without thinking, simply as a matter of
course." A hand striking out for pity. At that moment the SS
man is seen as the victim of a fly.

Vengeance, only vengeance, knows pity for the victim.

You will object: "Oratory! And if he had forgiven the SS
man, he would *not* have waved away the fly?"

He would not have noticed it at all. Whoever forgives the
murderer blinds himself to the vastest letting of blood—how
then should he see the smallest mite?

It is forgiveness that is relentless. The face of forgiveness is
mild, but how stony to the slaughtered.

### 4. MORAL TENDERNESS, MORAL RESPONSIBILITY

Consider this dying SS man. Is he not unlike so many others?
He, at least, shows the marks of conscience, of remorse, of
sickness at his life. He is not arrogant; he is not self-justifying;
he feels disgust at everything he has witnessed, he recoils from
everything he has committed. He is a man at a moral turning.
Ought he not to be delivered over to his death—to use the old
Christian word—shriven? *He* is penitent, so many others are
not—should the penitent be treated like the impenitent?
Should a revived goodness, a recovered cleanliness of heart, be
dealt with exactly as one would deal with the recalcitrance of
an unregenerate brute?

Consider now the brute. He exults in his brutishness. Remorse never touches him; even in memory, even thirty years after those butcheries of his, he exults in them. His mind, dim for other matters, is a bright and secret screen on which he renews and replenishes these triumphs of his old lost barbaric power over the weak. He was a great man then; he was like an angel, he served in fact the Angel of Death, lives were in his hands and under his feet, his boots were on the necks of the doomed. As he never experienced regret then, so now he never dreams of wishing away the old sensations and reminders.

But the dying SS man has had twinges all along. He has, in fact, a moral temperament. He is intelligently contrite; he knows there is no way for him to atone, but he understands what atonement is, he understands the force of contrition. He is a man with a vigorous insight into his own moral nature. He is a man with a conscience.

Should not some special recognition—some softening of condemnation—be given to the man of conscience? We condemn the brute; he is a barbarian; we condemn him as we condemn every barbarian. How then can we dare to condemn the man of conscience, as if there were no difference between him and the barbarian?

We condemn the intelligent man of conscience because there *is* a difference;* because, though at heart not a savage, he allowed himself to become one, he did not resist. It was not that he lacked conscience; he smothered it. It was not that he lacked sensibility; he coarsened it. It was not that he lacked humanity; he deadened it.

The brute runs to feed Moloch because to him Moloch is

*For the root of this insight I am indebted to Professor Melvin L. Plotinsky of Indiana University.

not a false god, but a Delightful True Lord, the Master who brings him exaltation. In exaltation he shovels in the babies. He has no conscience to stop him, no moral education, no moral insight. Perhaps he was never a server in his church. Does he even know what wickedness is?

The intelligent man of conscience also shovels in the babies, and it does not matter that he does it without exaltation. Conscience, education, insight—nothing stops him. He goes on shoveling. He knows what wickedness is. By now he has been shoveling for so long that he knows what Moloch is, he is intimate with Moloch. He is a morally sensitive man, and he shovels babies to glut the iron stomach of the idol.

The morally sensitive SS man goes on shoveling, and shoveling, and shoveling.

A virtuous childhood as a server in his church lies behind him; he shovels. A virtuous future as a model of remorse lies ahead of him; he shovels. He shovels and shovels, all the while possessed of a refined and meticulous moral temperament—so refined and so meticulous that it knows the holy power of forgiveness, and knows to ask for it.

I discover a quotation attributed to Hannah Arendt: "The only antidote to the irreversibility of history is the faculty of forgiveness." Jabberwocky at last. She is the greatest moral philosopher of the age, but even she cannot make a Lazarus of history.

Graham Greene explains the Catholic idea of hell—no longer that medieval site of endless conflagration; instead, an eternal separation from God.

Let the SS man die unshriven.

Let him go to hell.

Sooner the fly to God than he.

# JOHN T. PAWLIKOWSKI

To respond adequately to the questions raised by Simon Wiesenthal in *The Sunflower* may exceed human capacity. But we can begin to get some hold on them if we come to understand the significant difference between *forgiveness* and *reconciliation.* Unfortunately, in the popular mind, and perhaps in Wiesenthal's conception as well, the two notions easily become intertwined. While Wiesenthal refuses to speak the words of forgiveness the dying Nazi soldier wishes to hear, one has the sense that in his heart he has come close to such an act. His dialogue with the priest who was his fellow inmate, as well as his conversation with his camp partners Arthur, Adam, and Josek, coupled with his unwillingness to destroy the "good boy" image of her son held by the mother of the dead Nazi soldier leaves me with the impression that his public silence may not fully represent his innermost feeling.

His willingness to forgive in a way at the inner level of his being was no doubt rooted in part in a remark he makes early on in the narrative where he reflects on the question "Were we truly all made of the same stuff?" (p. 7). While Wiesenthal leaves the answer rather ambiguous at that point, subsequently one is left with the impression that he recognizes a certain basic human equality as common both to "victim" and "perpetrator," even if we must continue to condemn publicly the perpetrator's crime. And his willingness to acknowledge the dying soldier's "warm undertone in his voice as he spoke about the Jews" (p. 40) further confirms this perception.

The public form of forgiveness is reconciliation. And this

is of necessity a much longer, more complex process, especially in a case such as this where Wiesenthal is being asked to reconcile publicly with the Nazi soldier through word and gesture in the name of a community of victims. Reconciliation entails several stages: repentance, contrition, acceptance of responsibility, healing, and finally reunion. Clearly in the limited and confined circumstances in which Wiesenthal encountered the dying Nazi soldier reconciliation was an impossibility. The various stages cannot be traversed quickly. They require demonstrated changes that go beyond the merely verbal. The dying soldier, as I perceive him through Wiesenthal's description, was seeking not merely forgiveness in the more limited sense, but also a sense of reconciliation not only with Wiesenthal as an individual but through him with the Jewish people at large.

In my judgment Wiesenthal was correct in withholding such reconciliation, for it would have provided the man with what theologian Paul Tillich referred to as "cheap grace." That Wiesenthal might have said or done something to provide the dying man with a limited sense of personal forgiveness is certainly open to discussion, although the fact that the soldier seemed to regard Wiesenthal primarily as a "communal symbol" rather than a single human person complicates the matter considerably. If Wiesenthal had possessed a better grasp of the distinction between forgiveness and reconciliation, however, he might have found a way to offer the man some sense of forgiveness while making it clear that under the circumstances it was impossible to effect reconciliation with the Jewish victims as a whole. In so doing Wiesenthal may have alleviated that burden of uncertainty about the encounter with the dying soldier he appears to carry to the very end of the story. He would have responded positively to the sense of human bonding, despite the soldier's terrible crime, of which he seems keenly aware, while safeguarding against any premature feeling of reconciliation on the part of the soldier.

Apart from the moral dilemma about forgiveness/reconciliation that permeates the entirety of *The Sunflower*, two other issues strike me as worthy of further reflection. The first relates to Arthur's reaction to the comment made on the radio by the anonymous woman who remarks that "God is on leave" (p. 8) when asked whether Divine intervention on behalf of the victims was conceivable. For Arthur this seems a somewhat liberating idea. Wiesenthal remarks that for the first time since he and his friends had come to the stable they were laughing. But he was not. His personal reaction to the woman's "theological" observation was a rather dismissive "Tell me when He gets back" (p. 8).

In hindsight one can say that both Arthur and Simon were partially correct. Yes, the Holocaust was not to mark the end of all God-talk and God-belief. It was too easy to lay all the blame on God's failure to take the Divine covenantal responsibility with sufficient seriousness and stop the Nazis in their tracks. But, on the other hand, Wiesenthal's curt reply serves as a reminder that easy theodicy answers in terms of the Holocaust will not work any more than "cheap grace" will work in terms of reconciliation. The struggle to find a meaningful understanding of Divine presence is a far more wrenching process than either Arthur or Simon would seem to realize. As Elie Wiesel has poignantly shown in some of his writings many Holocaust victims, despite everything, could not in the end simply let God disappear from their lives. Yet, as Irving Greenberg and others have rightly observed, a deeper appreciation of God's role during the Holocaust, and afterward, will involve an understanding of a continual absence/presence relationship ("moment faith") rather than a total leave of absence as the woman on the radio suggested. And it will include as well a major redefinition of human and Divine agency in the world. God's control and God's interventionist possibilities can no longer be envisioned in the same way as they were in biblical and classical versions of Judaism and Christianity.

One has the sense after a reading of *The Sunflower* that Wiesenthal's rather cryptic response to his friends' discussion of the God-question in light of the woman's remark about God being on temporary leave in fact played a more significant role in his eventual encounter with the dying Nazi soldier than may appear to be the case at first glance. It may just be that Wiesenthal's inability to come to grips with the issue of Divine presence which he externally shrugs off but which may well have haunted him internally more than he reveals was in part the cause of his uncertain approach to the Nazi soldier. If he had personally not come near to resolving his own difficulty with God over the Holocaust, there was little possibility that he would have the inner strength to reach out to the dying Nazi in a genuinely merciful way without pretending to forgive him in the name of the Jewish people.

My final words have to do with a painful subject—Polish/Jewish relations—raised in *The Sunflower*. But they must be spoken. Wiesenthal is quite aware in *The Sunflower* of the suffering, actual and potential, of the Polish nation that was part and parcel of the Nazi plan. He acknowledges, for example, that "the Poles and Ukrainians formed a special stratum between the self-appointed German supermen and the subhuman Jews, and already they were trembling at the thought of the day when there would be no Jews left" (p. 10). Nonetheless, his overall portrayal of Polish-Jewish relations may easily feed the stereotypical image of Poles and Poland as a hotbed of anti-semitism. He plays off the remark that "A wise man once said that the Jews were the salt of the earth," adding that ". . . the Poles thought that their land had been ruined by over-salting. Compared with Jews in other countries, therefore, we were perhaps better prepared for what the Nazis had in store for us" (p. 70).

Without question Polish society in the period between the two world wars was characterized by a pervasive antisemitism rooted in classical images of Jews and in more modern nationalistic theories. Certainly such antisemitism deserves repudiation as the Polish bishops have done in recent years. But there is another aspect to the Polish reality that one will not understand from reading *The Sunflower*. It is that of the Zegota movement, the only organization aimed at saving Jews during the Holocaust. There are the individual righteous, Christians and Socialists, whose number exceeds that of any other nation in Europe. There is also the story of the long, reasonably constructive presence of the Jews in Polish society. And finally there is the fact that Poland was home to Europe's largest Jewish community between the world wars, an extremely complex community ranging from the extreme Orthodox to Socialists and Marxists and Zionists. None of these "facts" in any way ameliorate the horror of Polish antisemitism, including Wiesenthal's obviously painful personal experiences chronicled in *The Sunflower*. But they are important in terms of an accurate overall picture of Polish-Jewish relations which has yet to be written.

# DENNIS PRAGER

I am a religious Jew who has come to admire many Christians and to appreciate Christianity. I have come to see it as a holy path to God for non-Jews (this is not a small theological metamorphosis for a Jew raised in the Orthodox yeshiva world), and I deeply fear the consequences of a de-Christianized America. Yet, more than a decade of weekly dialogue with Christians and intimate conversations with Christian friends have convinced me that, aside from the divinity of Jesus, the greatest—and even more important—difference between Judaism and Christianity, or perhaps only between most Christians and Jews, is their different understanding of forgiveness and, ultimately, how to react to evil.

When the first edition of *The Sunflower* was published, I was intrigued by the fact that all the Jewish respondents thought Simon Wiesenthal was right in not forgiving the repentant Nazi mass murderer and that the Christians thought he was wrong. I have come to understand that this is not because the Holocaust was particularly the Jews' catastrophe, but rather because of the nature of the Jewish and Christian responses to evil, which are related to their differing understandings of forgiveness. I do not know which came first, the different Christian approach to forgiveness or the different Christian approach to evil.

First, forgiveness. As Wiesenthal's fellow sufferers and as a number of Jewish respondents noted in the first edition, the relevant Jewish view of forgiveness is that a person who hurts another person must ask forgiveness from his victim and that only the victim can forgive him. God Himself does not forgive a person who has sinned against a human being unless that human being has been forgiven by his victim.

Therefore, *people can never forgive murder*, since the one person who can forgive is gone, forever. Under circumstances of awesome contrition (which, I believe, must include the murderer giving up his life), God presumably can forgive a murderer, but as far as people are concerned, *murder is unforgivable.* Even parents cannot forgive the murderer of their child (to assume that parents can forgive their child's murderer is to render children property rather than autonomous human beings).

This belief of Judaism that only victims can forgive and that murder is therefore unforgivable reinforces its belief that murder is the most terrible thing a human can do (though there are gradations of sin even in murder—for example, murder accompanied by torture is worse than other forms of murder). Murder undermines the very foundations of the world God created. That is why the third Commandment given by God to humanity after the Flood (the first two are to be fruitful and multiply and not to eat the limb of a living animal) is that "he who sheds blood shall have his blood be shed by man." Not tolerating murder (and to the Torah, allowing all murderers to live is a form of murder-tolerance) is the moral foundation of civilization.

Conversely, tolerance of murder is the characteristic of a world in decay. Yet, as I write this essay in the last decade of the twentieth century, my country, especially its elite, has come to tolerate murder. There is no other way to explain the fact that in the United States of America the average murderer serves but eleven years in prison. We not only forgive most murderers—when they leave prison, murderers are said to have "paid their debt to society"—we do so even if they are unrepentant.

The best educated of Western society view murder as an unfortunate act of "antisocial" behavior and seek the rehabilitation of the murderer, not his punishment (let alone his death).

Is this a function of a society deeply influenced by Christian notions of forgiving everyone? Or is it a society whose secular elite has rejected Judaism's and Christianity's notions of moral absolutes? Probably a combination of both.

In *The Killing of Bonnie Garland*, a book as depressing in its way as *The Sunflower* is in its, psychiatrist Willard Gaylin describes the Catholic priests who took a murderer—a Hispanic Catholic college student who had bludgeoned his girlfriend to death—under their wing and did everything they could to ensure that he was not prosecuted. While I could well imagine a group of secular Jewish therapists or social workers engaging in such behavior, I cannot imagine any group of rabbis, even the most liberal, acting that way.

Indeed, I tested my thesis in real life.

As noted, for ten years I moderated a weekly radio show on which my guests were a Protestant minister, a Catholic priest, and a rabbi, different individuals each week. During that time, the notorious rape and beating of a woman jogger by a gang of young men in New York's Central Park took place. After their arrest, a *cardinal* of the Roman Catholic Church visited the boys at prison to tell them only one thing: "God loves you."

I was so furious that I publicly noted then that someone ought to write an article "How to Get a Personal Visit from a Cardinal." I thought of all the beautiful Catholics in New York, devoting their lives to the poor and the sick, who would give almost anything for a personal visit from a cardinal of their church. But the lucky recipients of such a visit were sadistic batterers and rapists who would have been murderers were it not for the wonders of modern medicine (they left the woman to bleed to death).

On my show, I wondered aloud whether my fury at the cardinal (a good man, hence I omit his name) was a personal or a Jewish response. I assumed the latter since virtually all my Christian callers agreed with the cardinal, and all my Jewish callers agreed with me. But I decided to test my thesis on the clergy. For four weeks, I asked the clergy what they would say to these torturers if they had met with them. Every Protestant and Catholic clergyman, liberal and conservative, essentially echoed the cardinal's words. All the rabbis, Reform, Conservative, and Orthodox, said that they would not meet with the youths, but if forced to, they would tell them of their disgust with them, that they should be severely punished and spend the rest of their lives seeking to redress their evil; and they certainly would not tell them that God loved them.

The Christian view of forgiveness and, as exemplified in the case of the rapists, the Christian view of God's love—in a lifetime of Jewish study and teaching, I have never heard a Jew say that God loves an evil person—have led me to conclude that Christianity and Judaism, or perhaps only Christians and Jews, have differing views of evil and what to do about it. Another example is necessary.

Under the totalitarian Soviet regime, both Soviet Jews and Soviet Christians were oppressed. Indeed, by the end of the Cold War, Soviet Christians were more oppressed than Soviet Jews. Thanks to worldwide Jewish efforts on behalf of Soviet Jews, by the 1980s no Soviet Jew was incarcerated for practicing Judaism, while quite a number of Soviet Christians were incarcerated for practicing Christianity. Why was there no outcry from the world's billion Christians while the thirteen million Jews of the world made Soviet Jewry a household word?

I believe that there are four reasons: the Christian doctrine of forgiveness has blunted Christian anger at those who oppress them; the notion that one should pray for one's enemies has been taken to mean "pray for them, do not fight them"; the belief that God loves everyone, no matter how evil, makes it impossible for a believing Christian to hate evil people and therefore difficult to fight them (I assume those who love mass murderers are less likely to want them dead than those who hate them); and the Christian emphasis on saving souls for the afterlife has led to some de-emphasis on saving bodies in this life.

Thus, in 1982, when the world's best-known Protestant, the Reverend Billy Graham, went to the Soviet Union, instead of taking the side of his tortured coreligionists, he repeatedly took the side of the Soviet authorities, telling churches that "God gives you the power to be a better worker, a more loyal citizen because in Romans 13 we are told to obey the authorities." Had a rabbi made a similar pronouncement in a speech in a Soviet synagogue—something altogether unimaginable—he would have been read out of Jewish life.

None of this is meant to denigrate Christians; indeed I hold Christians responsible for the greatest social experiment in history, the founding of the United States. Nor is it an ode to Jews; their preoccupation with fighting evil has too often led to embracing terrible ideologies such as Marxism and its myriad nihilistic offshoots. It is only meant to explain why to Jews it is so patently obvious that it is morally wrong to forgive a man who has burned families alive, and to Christians it is equally obvious that one ought to.

# DITH PRAN

Simon Wiesenthal's dilemma gets to the core of the issue of forgiveness. Can we as humans forgive people who have caused us such grief?

As a witness to and survivor of the Cambodian killing fields, I could never forgive or forget what the top leadership of the Khmer Rouge has done to me, my family, or friends. It's impossible. I blame the dozen leaders, the brains behind a sadistic plot, who ordered the deaths of millions of people, including the disabled, children, religious people, the educated, and anyone who they thought was a threat to their ideas. My father died of starvation, my three brothers and sister were killed, along with many nieces, nephews, and cousins. Friends I had known all my life and who worked beside me in the fields were taken away and killed. We lived in constant fear in the labor camps. There was no sympathy for us. We were in a cage with tigers and there was no way out. All we could do was pray to God.

When I talk about not forgiving the dozen leaders of the Khmer Rouge, I include Pol Pot, Khieu Samphan, Leng Sary, and their entourage. They are the ones who had the plan of ridding the Khmer population of unwanted elements like people who were unable to work, people with ideas, or anyone who would get in the way of transforming Cambodia into an agrarian society. Not only did they kill a massive number of people, but they destroyed all institutions including the family, religion, and education. We had to pledge allegiance only to Angka, the Khmer Rouge politburo.

Pulling away from the Khmer Rouge leadership, I can forgive the soldiers of the Khmer Rouge, those who actually did the killing, although I can never forget what they did. Placed in Simon Wiesenthal's position, I would have forgiven the soldier. Why? I have always felt that the soldiers were trapped. Most of them came from the jungle, were uneducated and very poor. They were taught to kill. They were brainwashed. More importantly, they were forced to kill. If they didn't follow the orders of the Khmer Rouge leadership, not only would they have been killed, but their entire families would have been killed. They feared death.

I'm not saying what the soldiers did was right and I'm not offering them excuses, but at least I understand why they did what they did. I think the key to forgiveness is understanding. I just will never understand why the Khmer Rouge top leaders did what they did. What was the purpose? Where was their humanity? They had the option to stop the killing, to give people more than a spoonful of rice to eat, to end the fourteen to sixteen hours a day, seven days a week forced labor. It took an invasion by the Vietnamese army to stop their atrocities.

I could never forgive or forget what the Khmer Rouge leadership has done to my family. Would my siblings have been ruthlessly killed if it weren't for them? No. Cambodia had many years of peace before the civil war and eventual Khmer Rouge victory. Would my father have died from starvation if it weren't for the Khmer Rouge leaders? No. There was plenty of food in Cambodia. The Khmer Rouge leadership decided to withhold it from the people.

We need to learn to separate the true culprits from the pawns, the evil masterminds from the brainwashed. We cannot label everyone the same. There is a world of difference between the leadership of the Khmer Rouge and the individuals who followed their orders. Yes, none of them are moral beings, but there is a chasm between someone who intentionally plots to destroy the very souls of people and someone who is not only stupid and brainwashed, but fears death enough (which is very human) to be forced to do wrong.

I cannot morally judge Simon Wiesenthal for silently walking out of the room after the soldier asked for forgiveness. But I feel this action has nagged at him because he has asked others what they would have done in his place. I feel that forgiveness is a very personal thing. I know some people won't understand my thoughts on this. But ultimately we all have to answer to God for our actions and we have to live with ourselves.

## TERENCE PRITTIE

Men who are dying expect special consideration. Often enough, they are badly frightened and deeply unhappy. To ask absolution for one's sins when near death is a perfectly normal human reflex. What is completely unusual about Simon Wiesenthal's book *The Sunflower* is that a dying SS man should have sought absolution from people whom he had helped to persecute. This, obviously, poses a problem of immense complexity.

First, there is the problem of the SS man's conscience. If he wished merely to "confess," he could have done so to a priest of his own religion. He could have asked God's forgiveness and he would, presumably, have received the standard answer that God's compassion is infinite, whenever repentance is real. Anyone who has fought on the battlefield knows that repentance, in the face of danger, seems real enough. Men under fire who have never prayed before, pray and promise "to be good" in the future—if God will oblige by rescuing them from impending death. The certainty rather than the mere possibility of death can only reinforce the plea for mercy. This is what Wiesenthal's SS man was after.

For the Jew to whom he made his plea the problem was totally different. The Jew was facing death every day that he remained alive. He knew that the very most that he could achieve for himself would be to face death bravely and to maintain his faith in his own identity up to the end. Had I been such a Jew I would have been affronted by the SS man's plea. I would have regarded it as an attempt to seek a cheap and easy "way out," and the gift of a few belongings as a histrionic, mock-sentimental gesture.

A persecuted Jew could only forgive wrongs done to him personally; he could not possibly forgive genocide. I find the idea of a mock-forgiveness of a man who had helped to burn women and children alive repellent, and I cannot see how it could be other than mock-forgiveness, granted simply because a man happened to be dying. To forgive this one SS man would mean, by implication, to forgive every other SS man who murdered, on his deathbed.

The SS man should have been asking forgiveness of God, and not of man. He had sinned against the principles of humanity far more than he had sinned against a handful of doomed human beings. This was a matter between him and his Creator, not between him and a single, stray Jew picked out of a random working-party and forced to listen to his "confession."

Should the Jew have told him this? It would be too much to expect of a badgered, brutalized concentration camp inmate to play the role of a philosopher. Nor could he possibly act as father confessor. He showed, in any case, remarkable restraint in listening to the SS man's terrible story without expressing his horror and hatred of such bestial cruelty. By walking out of the room without a word, he did the most sensible, the most logical, basically the most decent thing possible.

# JOSHUA RUBENSTEIN

As we near the close of the most violent century in human history, it seems pointless to consider the case of a mortally wounded Nazi officer who is determined to acknowledge his murder of Jews to a Jew in order to die in peace. By now, the incident he describes to Simon has been outpaced by thousands of similar massacres, from Cambodia to Rwanda, from Indonesia to Bosnia. There have been trials of some perpetrators of official terror and torture, and even more Truth Commissions to document the misdeeds of previous governments, but the number of voluntary, heartfelt confessions is small. In fact, such confessions are so rare that a recent, dramatic example— that of an Argentine naval officer who described his own involvement years before in throwing unconscious political prisoners from airplanes into the sea—reminds us that thousands of his murderous counterparts in Latin America have gotten away with their crimes and today rest soundly in their beds, not unlike so many Nazi perpetrators who grew old in the comfort of their families.

Simon's encounter with a wounded Nazi brings to mind an incident from the war involving Heinrich Himmler, the Reichsführer SS and chief of the German police. Speaking to a group of Nazi officers in Poznań in 1943, Himmler acknowledged how difficult it must be to commit mass murder and remain a normal human being.

> Most of you will know what it means when 100 corpses are lying side by side, when 500 are lying there or when 1000 are lying there. To have stuck this out and at the same time—apart from exceptions due to human weaknesses—to have remained decent, that is what has made us hard.

Himmler's claim reflects the cheap sentimentality about human emotions that so enthralls totalitarian regimes. Hitler was a vegetarian. The Nazis were not senseless brutes. They were good to their mothers, generous to their children, loving to their wives. Historical necessity required them to kill millions of people. The trick was to remain a normal, decent human being, as Himmler proudly explained to his underlings.

I cannot help but think of Himmler's speech when I consider Simon's dilemma. I find myself indifferent to the wounded Nazi's plea for forgiveness. He seems to have been moved more by his approaching death and the severity of his wounds than the enormity of his crimes. According to the story, the Nazi portrays himself as having been genuinely horrified by the massacre, even as he participated in the killing. On top of that, he recalls feeling startled by his unease, as if his years in the Hitler Youth and the SS—an overabundant feast of demagogic hatred and violence—had not prepared him adequately for this vivid, gruesome test of Aryan manhood. Himmler, at least, was clever enough to acknowledge how difficult it must be to murder a thousand people. He would not have been disturbed by the young Nazi's initial misgivings in front of the burning house. They would only confirm for Himmler that this young SS officer was still a "decent human being" who did not allow "human weaknesses" to get in the way of committing mass murder. He succeeded in overcoming them. The misgivings confirmed he was a "civilized German." Participation in the massacre confirmed he was also a good Nazi.

We know today, if Simon did not at the time, that German soldiers were not punished for refusing to slaughter innocent people. The young Nazi did not have to obey the order to burn and shoot unarmed men, women, and children. The faith he had long abandoned could have returned before he killed rather than later on the threshold of his own death. He could have shot himself in the foot. He could have induced nausea or succumbed to uncontrollable vomiting, as numerous Allied soldiers and journalists experienced when they first came upon piles of decomposing corpses. Of course for us, in the comfort of our peaceful homes, it is useless to suggest how this Nazi could have avoided getting blood on his hands. But it is more preposterous to suggest that after ten years in the Hitler Youth and the SS, including two years of brutal fighting on the Eastern Front, he did not know what was expected of him.

This particular Nazi was brought up in a religious, Catholic home, with normal, loving parents. He was not a teenage delinquent, a natural born sadist, or a brutal, unfeeling individual.

German society was now rewarding moral deviance. Even so, individuals still had to make choices for themselves. The choices this young Nazi made betray his true commitments. No one forced him to join the Hitler Youth. In fact, he did so over the objections of his parents. And no one forced him to join the SS. Other Germans, with similar backgrounds and under similar social pressure, joined the White Rose, a clandestine anti-Nazi group, or resisted military service. They were all executed. There was the extraordinary example of Reinhard Heydrich's younger brother Heinz who had been an enthusiastic Nazi. But once he grasped the meaning of the Final Solution (which Reinhard Heydrich had helped to design), he forged one hundred passports to help German Jews escape the Reich before committing suicide himself in 1944 in fear that the Gestapo had uncovered his work. Finally, we know of one SS officer named Kurt Gerstein who used his access to information to try to alert the outside world to Hitler's plans to exterminate the Jews. These Germans experienced profound remorse for the crimes done in their names and took genuine risks on behalf of the persecuted.

Confession and remorse alone are not enough to warrant forgiveness. Even though this Nazi was dying and had neither strength nor opportunity to do some kind of righteous deed, as other remorseful Germans managed to do, his dying wish to beg forgiveness from a scared, vulnerable Jewish prisoner was as much an act of callous egotism as it was a misguided act of contrition.

A sense of humanity requires regard for justice and mercy. When Simon helps the wounded man to drink water or waves an annoying bug from his face, such spontaneous gestures reflect instincts that could well have grown extinct in the camps.

The Nazi had committed mass murder. Simon was merciful enough with him. For Simon to grant him forgiveness, as well, would have been a betrayal of his and his family's suffering, and all the suffering around him. This was the first and probably last time, after all, that he confronted an utterly helpless Nazi and could have smothered him.

# DOROTHEE SOELLE

I have two contradictory replies to that which Simon Wiesenthal asks himself and us all. This contradiction is in Wiesenthal's narrative itself—between his "No, I cannot forgive you, the nice young German man and SS murderer" and "Yes, I can believe your remorse, *absolvo te,* go in peace"—in the silent departure, in the questioning of the other prisoners, and the visit to the elderly mother. Everywhere, one senses the no, and the necessity of finding a yes.

Perhaps, as a German, I have the least right to say something other than no. As a Christian, whether I wish it or not, I am always as an heir to the Jewish tradition; I cannot separate myself from yes. I would like to tell of an encounter with a professor of German literature; perhaps this will clarify what I mean. In the late 1960s, I learned that this professor, whom I greatly respected and revered for his sensitivity and receptive spirit, had not only been a Nazi but had even participated in a book burning. I couldn't fathom this, and visited him at his apartment to learn the truth. Why did you do this, who commanded it, did you know which books were burned: were Alfred Döblin's, were Kafka's? I wanted to know exactly. It was an excruciating few hours. He didn't protect himself, but he did insist on the distinction between books and people—which, naturally, was the underlying issue during every moment of our conversation.

When I asked where he stood now, he wept. He stammered something that I didn't understand. Only the word "forgiveness" was unspoken, implicit. And then something utterly extraordinary happened, something I had never experienced, before or since. He threw himself on the floor, knelt down, wrung his hands, and then folded them. I couldn't remain seated in my chair, I didn't want to leave, so I knelt beside him and we prayed aloud the Lord's prayer: . . . and forgive us our sins.

I had never known before what remorse was. Many years later, I learned what the word *teshuvah* meant in the Jewish tradition: deliverance, changing one's ways, a new beginning. A Jewish tradition tells that *teshuvah* was created even before the Creation, together with the Torah, the name of the Messiah, and other mysteries. Supposedly, there is no person, time, or place where *teshuvah* is not possible.

This is what I thought as I read Simon Wiesenthal. Wasn't *teshuvah* at work with this dying young SS man? If so, then Wiesenthal didn't have to lie, later, to the mother. Both the murderer and his mother were not alone in this one-sided conversation. God was there; together with the mother of the youth, he had awaited the murderer.

Perhaps I would have said, No, I cannot forgive you. But perhaps the other. *Oremus.*

# ALBERT SPEER

Afflicted by unspeakable suffering, horrified by the torments of millions of human beings, I acknowledged responsibility for these crimes at the Nuremberg Trial. With the verdict of guilty, the court punished only my legal guilt. Beyond that remains the moral involvement. Even after twenty years of imprisonment in Spandau, I can never forgive myself for recklessly and unscrupulously supporting a regime that carried out the systematic murder of Jews and other groups of people. My moral guilt is not subject to the statute of limitations, it cannot be erased in my lifetime.

Should you forgive, Simon Wiesenthal, even if I cannot forgive myself? Manès Sperber assumes that you would not condemn this SS man if he had lived and remained faithful to his conviction of remorse: Well, on May 20, 1975, we sat facing one another for more than three hours at your Vienna-based Documentation Center, a meeting preceded by a six-month correspondence. It was in fact your *Sunflower* that led me to you: "You are right," I wrote you earlier, "no one is bound to forgive. But you showed empathy, undertaking the difficult trip to Stuttgart in 1946. You showed compassion by not telling the mother of her son's crimes. This human kindness also resounds in your letter to me, and I am thankful for it." You showed clemency, humanity, and goodness when we sat facing one another on this May 20th, too. You did not touch my wounds. You carefully tried to help. You didn't reproach me or confront me with your anger. I looked into your eyes, eyes that reflected all the murdered people, eyes that have witnessed the misery, degradation, fatalism, and agony of your fellow human beings.

And yet, those eyes are not filled with hatred; they remain warm and tolerant and full of sympathy for the misery of others. When we parted, you wrote for me in my copy of your book that I did not repress that ruthless time, but had recognized it responsibly in its true dimensions.

My trauma led me to you. You helped me a great deal—as you helped the SS man when you did not withdraw your hand or reproach him. Every human being has his burden to bear. No one can remove it for another, but for me, ever since that day, it has become much lighter. It is God's grace that has touched me through you.

# MANÈS SPERBER

How I, in Simon Wiesenthal's place, would have reacted to the request of the SS man, I cannot say. Perhaps I would have yielded from weakness, from a false kindness, and uttered the words of forgiveness for which the dying man longed. On the other hand, it may be that I would have acted in precisely the same way as Wiesenthal . . . Yet it is true, leaving individual psychology out of consideration, that even in such a situation the individual acts in accordance with his character. As to the question of conscience placed before every reader of the epilogue to *The Sunflower*, one must first of all establish the following principle: it is possible for us to forget a wrong, even the worst misdeed which has been committed on us. If that happens, the question of forgiveness is superfluous. Why and through what internal process we are able to reach such a state of forgetting cannot here be discussed. Apart from any forgetting which the victim is able to achieve, there is forgetting on the part of the evildoer, an incomparably more frequent phenomenon. Certainly there is a deep psychological feeling that there can be no final oblivion. In this case it is a question of a more or less lasting "disactualization."

Must one forget before one can forgive? Is it possible to retain the misdeed in one's memory and nevertheless forgive it? What are the conditions in which such a thing can happen?

The first answer may sound cynical: the surest and most lasting forgiveness and reconciliation is when the descendants of the evildoers and those of the victims bind themselves into a collective and unbreakable unity—into a family, a tribe, a people, a nation. Ernest Renan, some hundred years ago, pointed out that the existence of nations depends on forgetting. Each nation represents the amalgamation of tribes who for many years, and possibly for hundreds of years, had inflicted the worst sufferings and griefs on each other. Each new generation discovers the truth about the frightful shattering past, but that does not destroy the consciousness of a common destiny.

A second tragic possibility—it comes nearer our case because of the one-sidedness of the crime—is that of extreme humiliation and ruthless persecution. In order not to have their lives fatally imperiled, the victims or their descendants subject themselves to their wrongdoers and admit that their lies and excuses are true. Whence the at least temporary success of the totalitarian oppressor and tyrant.

In both cases a purposeful "disactualization" takes place, in order to free the present and more especially the future from the heavy burden of the past. Does the forgetting in that case precede the crime, or vice versa? In each case the answer may be different. True, the old Jewish principle frequently applies: *kulo chayav*—all are guilty. And so all are guilty, and all may go free. Punishment would be too awful, it would endanger the existence of mankind, and mankind must not perish.

Doubtless one could formulate the problem in another way: do the evildoers themselves forget, do they forget before they have repented and confessed their crime? Without confession and sincere repentance their forgetting is nothing more than a continuation of their crime. So do not grant pardon before you are certain that the guilty on their side will always remember their guilt. From this point of view the ethical problem facing both Jews and Germans is not a simple one, but it is completely clear—before we have the right to forget, we must be absolutely certain that the Germans on their side have not forgotten, and that they are willing to do everything possible so as not to forget the crimes committed in their name. The two peoples are bound together in startling fashion by the terrible events, just as the young SS man on his deathbed and the prisoner Wiesenthal were bound together. And Wiesenthal will be bound until his dying day. Though their misdeeds and their sufferings may make it enormously difficult to live together in lasting peace, yet nothing now can separate them from each other.

I always rejected, both in theory and practice, the idea of collective guilt, but I do believe that there is such a thing as national or state responsibility. In this respect the reparations made by the German Federal Republic to Israel and to the surviving victims of Nazi crimes are entirely justified and significant. They replace nothing, they cannot reverse what has happened, but for the Germans they are a psychohygienic necessity. But that is no answer to the question: how can one forgive those who make it impossible for us to forget—so far as we would dare to forget—because they on their side are determined to behave as though they no longer know what there is to forgive and forget?

If the young SS man was guilty, yet he differed from the organizers of the extermination camps and the accomplices of genocide. By his obedience to his criminal leaders he augmented the guilt which he had incurred by putting himself politically and unconditionally at their disposal. There is no question of that, but it is none less true that in the end he brought the accusation against himself. As an accused person he is condemned in our eyes and rejected, but as accuser he placed himself among the victims.

Nevertheless Simon Wiesenthal was quite right in refusing to pardon him, at any rate not in the name of the martyrs, who neither then nor now had entrusted anybody with such a mission. But if that young man had lived and remained true to the convictions which tortured the last hours of his life, and maybe even transfigured him—if he were still among us would Wiesenthal condemn him? I think not. And I feel that I too could not condemn that SS man today.

The corrupt autocrats forced upon their subjects a complicity from which only he could escape who followed the dictates of his conscience even when thereby he risked his life. Thus it was that millions of people were guilty. Let none of us refuse to forgive any one of them whose guilt became the irrepressible source of a tortured conscience. There can be no counter-argument against forgiveness in such a case, or indeed against a reconciliation based on pity.

# ANDRÉ STEIN

"In our world, nothing any longer obeyed the laws of normal everyday life, . . . The only law that was left as a reliable basis for judgment was the law of death. . . . The effect on us was a mental paralysis, and . . . the clear expression of the hopelessness of our lot" (p. 68).

These words of Simon Wiesenthal allow little room for controversy as to his own action. Daily life in extremis predetermined what was or was not within his psychological and moral means. Any a posteriori speculation as to forgiving a dying SS murderer is ethically questionable. In the absurd culture of the death camp where every moment was saturated with its own premature ending, all decisions were by necessity the consequence of planned randomization of meanings. Nothing could be taken for granted on the basis of a previous stock of knowledge. Any act, decision, compliance with an order could as easily be life-affirming as life-threatening. Nothing made sense. The victims were evicted from their own destiny. Often, the result was a trance Simon calls "mental paralysis" in which one's choices were likely to lead to destruction. Since in the concentrationary universe nothing survived intact from the previous lifeworld of the Jew, Simon's silence had to be a choiceless choice; it should not be argued in the lap of ordinary daily reality and with the distance of half a century.

For me Simon's story does raise important questions about Karl's role in this matter. Did he have the right to ask for forgiveness? Can we believe in the authenticity of his repentance? Should anyone perpetrating crimes against humanity expect forgiveness? If we forgave war criminals how would such an act of questionable generosity affect the survivors and the victims' memory?

I am dismayed about the eagerness of many to forgive child-killers, torturers, rapists by transferring the blame onto a murderous ideology and propaganda, and, in Karl's case, onto his youthful vulnerability.

The call for forgiveness reminds me of the words Arthur, Simon's comrade, uttered in the camp when Simon asked his opinion: ". . . there will be people who will never forgive you for not forgiving him . . . But anyhow nobody who has not had our experience will be able to understand fully." The quote points out two truths: First, that those who cast a stone at Simon show a greater affinity with the dying murderer than with his victims. And second, that by lobbying for forgiving the young SS, they view Nazism through spuriously humane glasses. Let's remember that Karl at twenty-one was old enough to make informed choices. He could have drawn on the teachings of his faith and on the moral values of his family. Instead, he opted for endorsing a seductive myth that gave him powers nobody should have. He participated in murder. He ended up with a guilty conscience but took no action displaying genuine remorse or repentance. Thus, his deathbed confession sounds somewhat hollow.

I am not moved by his "moral pain" any more than were Simon's comrades, or for that matter than was Simon himself. When I read his story, my heart went out to his victims, and to Simon who was coerced into this drama by the arrogance of a Nazi killer terrified of dying a dirty death.

True repentance must include empathy toward the victim

and others who share his vulnerability. Instead, Karl had the nurse bring him a Jew—any Jew—so that he could confess, get the Jew's absolution, and die in peace. The request was absurd. For a Nazi to expect that a Jew, languishing in a Nazi death camp, should muster a measure of generosity toward a comrade of those who are likely to kill him, is not a proof of repentance. What it does prove is that Karl still thought of the Jew as an object. The fact that any Jew could have performed this miraculous spiritual rescue is evidence that for Karl, Simon was not a fellow human being but an instrument of salvation. Just before he dies, he further insinuates himself into Simon's life by leaving him his belongings, as if to say, "I will reach out to you from the grave and will not let you forget that you did not grant me, a dying man, his last wish." Thus, Karl succeeded in claiming squatter's rights on his conscience. Indeed, the reissue of *The Sunflower* fifty years after the event attests to his lifelong presence in Simon's journey.

As for Simon, he did not do anything morally reprehensible by not saying "I forgive you." To utter that simple sentence would have been a lie anyway. Silence emerged as the only authentic means of communication. Simon had listened to the man's story with ears belonging to the dead and the near-dead—Eli, his mother, his comrades. And still, he listened and honored the man's story. At the end, his silence was an unequivocal statement: "I heard what you did, how you feel about it. I see how scared you are of dying with a burdened conscience. And this is all I can do. I am not telling you how much I hate you, for the flames of my hatred would burn me before they would reach you. I cannot forgive you not only because it is not in my power to speak for your victims but also because you have forced me to hear your story. For me this is a curse."

Not saying these words, Simon performed an act of charity toward Karl. And he showed solidarity with himself by not giving away more than what he had to give away. He did not treat the man as a monster who had committed monstrous deeds. Rather, he honored the humanity of a man who had lost his humaneness.

Can we, indeed, advocate forgiveness toward those who have committed crimes against humanity? Should we not warn those who contemplate evil acts that there will be no mercy even on their deathbeds should they give in to the seduction of killing? The consequences of participating in genocidal acts must include dying with a guilty conscience.

Such a warning could be meaningful to those teetering between good and evil and to those who insinuate that survivors be nobler than they can afford to be. We must stop dictating moral postures to the survivors. The opposite of not forgiving is neither cruelty, nor wallowing. It is a way of healing and honoring our pain and grief.

Simon Wiesenthal should not be troubled by those who are unable to forgive him for having acted out of a choiceless choice. It is all too easy to invoke Judeo-Christian ethics on behalf of forgiveness from the distance of mundane everyday life. Reading such moral verdicts makes me wonder how some could advocate that Simon forgive the dying Nazi in the same breath as they were judging Simon. Simon himself seemed to believe that forgiveness was an option. Is it out of his desperate effort to stay clean in a morally soiled world? Does he have to be better than human?

I am familiar with Simon's predicament. In my book *Broken Silence: Dialogues from the Edge* I chronicled how a Nazi detective bartered the sanctity of my aunt Sari's womb in exchange for our lives. When Sari realized that she was carrying his child, she told him: "You either save our lives or I'll take your unborn child to its death." Reluctantly, he hid us. Why don't I have an ounce of spiritual largesse toward this ravisher of innocence who bartered human lives for his own pleasure? His acts evoke only rage whenever I think of the price he exacted from my aunt in order to save the lives of four children and two mothers. Many upon reading this tragic instance of heroism and self-sacrifice, raised their voices against my aunt: "She had no right to buy your survival at that price." Like so many, my aunt's "judges" stayed riveted on the moral stance of the victim.

I do not know what I would have done in Simon's place. His decision to remain silent makes sense to me as a moral victory achieved by the "subhuman" victim. After all the dehumanization, he still had an operating moral stance from which he was able to exercise an option: he refused to play in this macabre game.

I am not at peace with Simon's decision to let Karl's mother believe in her son's immaculate goodness. Simon had a responsibility toward past and future victims to tell her the truth. And Karl's mother had the responsibility of rising above her personal pain and telling the world what her son had done. She could have warned parents about the need to convince their children to opt against evil. By remaining silent and scared, she must take some of the burden of a guilty collective conscience. We must not forget that millions were murdered by a nation of good sons. Every woman who doggedly holds on to a pristine moral image of her son is a collaborator in his crime.

We must, therefore, let go of emotionally based conventional morality concerning the age of perpetrators and their parents. To invoke Karl's youth and his mother's advanced age is morally sloppy. The magnitude of the crime and the broad popular participation in it allows no consideration other than the welfare of the survivors, the sacredness of the victims' memory, and the prevention of future genocides. The voice of an honestly repentant mother of a dead SS murderer would have great credibility. Karl's parents are not guilt-free in his joining the SS. And by keeping the truth under cover, Simon enabled Karl's mother to live a nasty lie. As a child survivor of the Holocaust who lost sixty-two relatives to "nice boys who wouldn't hurt a fly," I feel indignant about this version of the conspiracy of silence.

# NECHAMA TEC

Right after I read *The Sunflower* I felt that were I in Wiesenthal's place I would not have absolved the dying SS man of his heinous crimes. I knew, almost intuitively, that for me forgiveness was not an option.

My private, emotional reaction was followed by a flood of arguments. Competing for my attention, collectively and singly, they advocated varied possibilities, different explanations, and diverse justifications. This avalanche of ideas led to the realization that I ought to move beyond my initial refusal to forgive. I recognized the complexity of the situation. I also knew that my final answer would be influenced both by my own past and present social settings. Could I, a Holocaust survivor, who during the Nazi occupation spent several years in a ghetto and who for about three years was passing for a Catholic, put myself in

Wiesenthal's position? To what extent can I anticipate how I would have acted in his place? Without experiencing the concentration camp's horrors, can I truly imagine myself in a concentration camp where life and death were so precariously intertwined?

I have been exposed to the issue of forgiveness. When lecturing about the Holocaust I am sometimes asked how I feel about the Germans. Occasionally, among these queries, a question slips in about forgiveness. Some of my listeners, particularly the younger ones, ask if I have forgiven those who had committed the crimes against Jews.

Recently a BBC reporter, who had interviewed me for a radio and television program, wanted to know if I thought that Jews in general and the British courts in particular should give up prosecuting those who have committed crimes against the Jewish people. After all, he argued, these crimes had happened so long ago. Besides, now those who had committed these crimes are old and in poor health. Shouldn't the authorities stop bothering these fragile, old people and forgive them their past transgressions? The reporter raised these questions with a specific man in mind. The man, now eighty-four, lives in Great Britain. During World War II, as a Belorussian chief of police, he willingly participated in the mass murder of Jews. Only recently did he come to the attention of the English authorities, who decided to try him in court. The BBC man wanted to know if I would support the release of the man; after all, the man was old and weak and had only a few years to live.

My clear-cut no was followed by an explanation. First, as human beings we ought to anticipate the consequences of our actions and take personal responsibility for them. Second, and more importantly, I have no right to forgive crimes committed against others. Only those who were harmed, in this case the murdered Jews, have a right to forgive, not I.

In line with this reasoning, I would not have forgiven the dying SS man for his crimes. I would not have forgiven because I have no right to forgive.

By no means original, my sentiments are echoed by several concentration camp inmates whom Wiesenthal consulted at the time. One of them, Josek, said: ". . . what he [the SS man] has done to other people you are in no position to forgive" (p. 65). Another friend, Arthur, elaborates on the theme: "A superman has asked a subhuman to do something which is superhuman. If you had forgiven him, you would never have forgiven yourself all your life" (p. 66). Another friend, a Catholic Pole, independently came to the same conclusion when he says: "you can only forgive a wrong that has been done to yourself" (p. 81). Finally, despite his many doubts, Wiesenthal thinks that "forgiveness is an act of volition, and only the sufferer is qualified to make the decision" (p. 98). And yet, after Wiesenthal had made this statement, he again seems to question his decision when he asks the reader to reconsider the situation and come up with his or her own decision.

Having repeated what I think I would have done, I am reluctant to let the issue rest. I am eager to know more and understand better the context of Wiesenthal's reactions, reactions which go beyond the act of not forgiving. How did this strange encounter proceed? How should we now from a distance of time, place, and experience evaluate Wiesenthal's reaction?

The request for forgiveness was delivered by a man who was guilty of horrible crimes. On his deathbed, the man was suffering both physically and emotionally and thought that his suffering would be alleviated by forgiveness. There is no evidence that, after the man had committed the crimes which bothered his conscience, he had stopped committing other crimes or would have done so in the future. Wiesenthal seems to suggest that the SS man's guilt feelings were brought on only by his approaching death. The guilt that he had experienced about the murder of a Jewish family does not seem to include the Jews in general. Nor does he show any compassion for the Jewish prisoner who stands before him. In itself the fact that the SS man wanted a Jew to absolve him from his past crimes shows an insensitivity to the Jewish plight. The dying man burdens the Jew with a request that he knows is unreasonable.

Selfish, self-centered, the dying Nazi dwells on his own personal suffering. Feeling utterly sorry for himself, he says: "... those Jews died quickly, they did not suffer as I do— though they were not as guilty as I am" (p. 52). He does not even see that the Jews he murdered were innocent victims, guilty of no transgression at all. Even on his deathbed he seems to be denying to the Jews their humanity. And it is the man's self-indulgence which propels him to impose an additional burden on a concentration camp inmate who is sentenced to death. The Nazi knows that his request causes pain to his helpless listener. He says: "I know that what I am asking is almost too much for you but without your answer I cannot die in peace" (p. 54).

Wiesenthal knows that the dying man feels sorry for himself and that he was filled with self-pity. He remarks: "He sought my pity, but had he any right to pity? Did a man of his kind deserve anybody's pity? Did he think he would find pity if he pitied himself ..." (p. 52).

The SS man's self-pity might have blinded him to the needs of others. He fails to consider the needs of the Jew who is in front of him and with whom he wants to share his most intimate longings. Indeed, he does not even want to know who the Jew is. The Nazi is well aware of this fact, when he says: "I do not know who you are, I only know that you are a Jew and that is enough" (p. 54). But why should only Simon's Jewishness matter? Because the SS man does not see his listener as an individual, as a person. He only sees him as a Jew, a representative of all the Jews, of a mass, of a race, but not as a human being. Perhaps for this Nazi all Jews are the same, their individuality is of no consequence. This attitude fits the Nazi ideology which defines all Jews as inferior beings, as nonhumans.

Wiesenthal was reluctant to remain with this dying man. He wanted to get away soon after he had come. But he stayed on. He explains: "All my instincts were against continuing to listen to this deathbed disavowal. I wanted to get away. The dying man must have felt this . . . for he groped for my arm. The movement was so pathetically helpless that all of a sudden I felt sorry for him. I would stay, although I wanted to go" (p. 35).

Although the dying man knew that the prisoner wanted to leave he insisted that he stay. But not once did the German apologize for this imposition. Insensitive to the needs of others, the Nazi was engrossed in his own wants. Perhaps were the SS man not as dominated by self-pity, he might have considered other options. He might have truly repented by trying to do something for others. If he were less self-centered he might have considered calling to his bedside a high-ranking SS officer. To this superior he might have pointed out how reprehensible the murder of the Jews was. He might have pleaded with other Germans, who were healthy and active, to desist from slaughtering innocent people. In short, instead of burdening the Jewish prisoner with tales about his cruel crimes he might have used the time for making an effort to prevent some future crimes. But he did none of this. Instead, he seemed to be competing with Jewish suffering when he insisted that they suffered less while dying than he did.

The fact that the suffering of the Jews was inflicted by him and people like him the Nazi chose to ignore. He ignored the plight of the Jews because he was trained to treat them a certain way. Even on his deathbed he did not give up the racial ideologies which became a part of his very being. To the exclusion of everything else, the SS man was concerned with his own suffering, with his soul, with his peace of mind, and with his possible salvation. But what of his possible salvation? Would his confession to an anonymous Jew, divorced from the context of his crime, be more effective than true heartfelt remorse expressed to his own God?

And how did the Jewish prisoner behave? Although Wiesenthal wanted to leave, he stayed. I am amazed at his moral strength, which he seemed to retain even though he was surrounded by physical and moral deterioration. It is to Wiesenthal's credit that he was able to consider forgiveness as an option.

Forgiveness is not a simple, discrete act. Forgiveness is a variable with many gradations. It may be attached to different degrees of approval. Just as forgiveness, non-forgiveness may come in a variety of shadings. In Wiesenthal's case his refusal to forgive came with silence.

Wiesenthal thinks that silence may mean different things. I agree. I also agree that silence can be more eloquent than words. Having commented on the different attributes of silence Wiesenthal asks: "Was my silence at the bedside of the dying Nazi right or wrong?" (p. 97). But Wiesenthal does not say what a right or wrong silence means. We are told only indirectly that Wiesenthal's silence at the bed of the dying SS man conveyed a lack of forgiveness. This is a negative definition. What other message might his silence have carried? What besides lack of forgiveness did Wiesenthal want to convey? Did his silence contain a measure of compassion? Perhaps, for the injured SS man had the opportunity to be heard.

Yet, by refusing to forgive, he thought that he failed to give comfort to a dying man. And because Wiesenthal seems to interpret his silence this way this was his subjective reality. As far as he was concerned this is what had happened.

I believe that under the circumstances, Wiesenthal's reaction was charitable. He continued to stay and listen to the dying man even though he found it repugnant. He felt sorry for the SS man though he was confronted by this man's hideous crimes. It is to Wiesenthal's credit and to the credit of his friends who, in the devastating surroundings of the concentration camp, were able to consider the moral implications of forgiveness. Instead of ridiculing Wiesenthal's concerns they listened to him patiently.

Wiesenthal was bothered that without a word he left the dying man. Personally I see his quiet exit and his prolonged stay with the SS man as benevolent acts. Wiesenthal does not seem to realize that by staying and listening he gave comfort to the dying man. Moreover, the fact that Wiesenthal was ambivalent about his actions and continues to doubt their appropriateness only underlines his decency, pointing equally to his moral superiority. In sharp contrast, the dying German was indifferent to issues that did not bear directly on him.

# JOSEPH TELUSHKIN

Was this young Nazi's repentance sincere? It certainly seems so. Then again, he was dying. Had a doctor entered the room with a miracle drug that would have restored this young man to full vigor, would he have remained weighed down with guilt? And had the German army then offered him whatever was the Nazi equivalent of the Purple Heart for bravery in battle, would he have scorned the award? I wonder.

True, this young murderer speaks with regret, but mixed in with regret is self-pity, the unembarrassed complaint that he, who has murdered others, is himself too young to die, and the statement that ". . . those Jews [who he helped burn] died quickly, they did not suffer as I do" (p. 52). Then, remembering that he is speaking to a Jew, that the purpose of this confession is to elicit this Jew's forgiveness, the young Nazi adds on: "though they were not as guilty as I am."

"They were not as guilty as I am." A stunning sentence! Is not the clear, indeed the only, implication of these words that the murdered Jews were guilty, and that he, one of their murderers, was also guilty, only their guilt was not as great as his. Suddenly, a confession that seemed so sincere, seems to be acquiring a decidedly slippery quality. A more honest, more righteous man—indeed, the sort of person who likely would never have committed such murders—would have said: "But, then again, don't I deserve to suffer for what I have done, while those Jews didn't deserve such sufferings; they were innocent victims of my comrades and myself."

Moses Maimonides teaches that we can only know the full

truth of a person's repentance if the penitent encounters the same situation in which he first sinned, and then refrains from sinning. But, of course, no such opportunity could be granted this young man. We know that he *voiced* regret over his murderous deeds; unfortunately, that is all we know.

What do I think, therefore, of Wiesenthal's silent response to the Nazi's request for forgiveness? I agree with him. How could Wiesenthal forgive crimes committed against others? Perhaps, perhaps, if this young man had been taught from the earliest of ages that irrevocable acts such as murder cannot be undone by words, he would have been less prone to murder innocent people. (Indeed, what damns this Nazi even more is the knowledge we now have that, in general, German soldiers who refrained from participating in such actions were not punished.) Of course, the large majority of evil committed by people should be forgiven, *provided* that the evildoer's repentance is sincere and that he or she makes a real effort to undo the evil. But the difference between forgiving 97 percent of evil acts that are atoned for, versus forgiving them all, is significant. The killing and torture of innocent people is an ultimate evil, and the only ones who can grant forgiveness are, by virtue of their deaths, incapable of doing so. This Nazi wanted to die with a clean, or at least a cleaner, conscience. But what had he done to entitle himself to so distinct a privilege?

If a human being should not forgive this Nazi, will God? As a medieval Jewish philosopher taught, "If I knew God, I'd be God." Nonetheless, some Jewish teachings suggest that God would not forgive such a man; a well-known talmudic text teaches that Yom Kippur, the Day of Atonement, atones only for sins committed against God; as regards offenses committed against one's fellow human beings, atonement can be achieved only through pacifying the injured party. On the other hand, there are Jewish teachings that hold that if a murderer accepts his punishment and is truly penitent, that his death may win him some measure of atonement in the next world.

How then will God regard this killer? There are limits to my presumptuousness; I know not God's will. However, in recent years, I have found myself drawn, because of unusual encounters, to the notion of *gilgul,* reincarnation. Perhaps God will send this man back to this world, and he will live a life in which he resists evil and does much good. I would like to believe that lifetimes of much good can perhaps undo a lifetime of great evil.

But such calculations must be made by God. In this world, I would feel far more sanguine to learn that the various world religions could agree on the desirability of teaching their followers, from childhood on, the significance of moral distinctions; to teach them that forgiveness is almost always a virtue, but to teach them that cruelty is evil and the murder of innocent people an unforgivable evil. In other words, to teach people the harder, more morally worthy path—to repent of irrevocable evil *before,* not *after,* they commit it.

## TZVETAN TODOROV

What should Simon have done? What would I have done if I had found myself in his place? Let me first answer the question as it stands. The only one who can forgive is the one who has experienced the injury. Every extension by analogy, from the individual to the group, seems to me illegitimate: one cannot forgive by proxy any more than one can be a victim by association or uphold the existence of a collective guilt. Therefore, murder, by definition, cannot be forgiven: the injured party is no longer there to do it. I should add that, since I was not raised as a believing Christian, I have never considered absolution as an essential element of life; justice and morality are far more important to me.

I will therefore try to go a little further to reformulate the question in my own terms: how shall we judge the SS man described by Wiesenthal, and what should we think of him? His guilt is indisputable; what poses a problem is whether we should take account of his regrets and repentance. Experience shows that the great majority of Nazi criminals felt no regret for their actions. At Nuremberg, Speer was the only one who considered himself (partially) guilty. At the Auschwitz trial in 1963, only the former victims felt anguish; the former executioners did not seem to be troubled by pangs of conscience. The same is true for the perpetrators of other atrocities, in other totalitarian countries, or even today, in former Yugoslavia: concentration camp guards, like their superiors, judge themselves not guilty. In this respect, Wiesenthal's SS man is different, and if only to emphasize the exception, he deserves different treatment: not absolution, of course, but recognition for embarking on that specifically human activity which consists of changing for the better (what Rousseau called our perfectibility).

Neither can I ignore the fact that we are raising these questions today, more than fifty years after the event. We are not contemplating an action in the present, but the place of a past action in our memory. What can we do with evil in the past, how can we put it to use in the service of our moral education?

Nazi crimes are the sort that render it impossible to confuse values: that evil really did exist and is in no way relative. For that reason alone, we must preserve a living memory of it. The second step in this education would then consist of rejecting the tendency to identify evil pure and simple with the Other, and good with ourselves, and recognizing, as Romain Gary said, that inhumanity is part of being human. Rejecting relativism does not mean embracing a Manichean split between good and evil. It is the complementary interplay of these two aspects of moral judgment, it seems to me, that alone permits us to make judicious use of the past in the present in order to fight today's evils, and not only yesterday's.

# ARTHUR WASKOW

I need to address not Simon Wiesenthal but the Nazi he addressed: What would it mean for me to "forgive" you?

First, someone has—you have—shattered the Ultimate Unity by breaking the connections that hold it together—those connections through which human beings and the earth share the world. You have shattered the Four Worlds that are the One World—the Four Worlds our great mystics the Kabbalists used as a profound and convenient map of God's Reality: the Worlds of Doing, Relating, Knowing, and Being. When these are healthy, there is physical wholeness and material sharing; emotional love; intellectual communication; and the spiritual sense of shared presence within the Divine Presence. For me and for my people, you have shattered each of these Four Worlds.

What you ask of me is to join with you to restore this Unity in each of the Four Worlds. To join *with you* in reconnecting the fragments of the shattered Unity, perhaps into a wholly/holy new pattern of Unity. To make this restoration *with you* is "forgiveness." Through it, *you and I* would give away the physical damage, the emotional upset, the intellectual disjunction, and the spiritual dislocation of my self and my people's self. *You and I* would return to a place of equilibrium and equanimity.

I cannot do it. This is why: There is no way for you to repair the physical damage to the Jews you yourself murdered, let alone those whose murder and torture you helped organize and celebrate. There is no way for you to repair the rips and tears in relationship that have left the Jewish people still struggling to be able to trust, connect, make peace, to govern itself responsibly with its newfound power in the world. And, in terms of Spirit, there is no way for you to repair our sense of God in hiding.

I may be able to make these repairs for myself (at least the ones in Relationship and Spirit); we Jews may be able together to do these for ourselves; but not with you. You can take no part in these three repairs. So I cannot "forgive" you.

There is only one of the Four Worlds in which I can even come close to being *with you*—the World of Knowing: Idea, Intellect.

You are a teacher of what is now possible. From you I learn that the H-bombs can devour the world, that every single one of them is an instant portable Auschwitz waiting for its blaze to be turned on. From you I learn that sadism can be technologized and mass-produced. From you I learn that the careless use of new technology can poison earth's air and soil and water, can murder many species, even when there is no hatred—only envy of each other. From you I learn what the mass media can do to the child of loving, gentle parents.

From you I learn the raw, ravaging Power—one aspect of God—that has come roaring into the world, into human hands.

And therefore, from you, with you, I learn the need to do all the other *tikkunim* (repairs):

- The need to shape a deeper and broader sense of community among the peoples and species of the earth.
- The need to create a form of intellect that is connective, in which knowledge is indeed like making love, as it is in the Hebrew word *yodaya.*
- The need to relocate God not Up There on a kingly throne but In Here, among us, between us, within us.
- Even the need to redo the physical boundaries of the People Israel, to reawaken our bodies through sacred dance and gesture, to reenliven our physical relationship with the Land and the Earth, to reopen the Song of Songs as a joyful flowering of earthy passion.

I can learn from you the need to do these things, but I cannot do them with you. I can talk with you, but I cannot touch you, love you, or pray with you. So I thank you for being my teacher, and I leave you alone in the three Worlds of Body, Heart, and Spirit—alone, cut off, an alien in the alien corner of the world that you yourself have cut off from the Flow of Life.

# HARRY WU

Reading Simon Wiesenthal's autobiographical story brought back a flood of memories about my own experience in China's prison labor camps. I was instantly transported back to my nineteen years in those camps, and I allowed myself to remember some of my experiences with those who were responsible for my imprisonment and with the camp prison guards.

In 1957, everyone at my university, the Geology Institute in Beijing, was forced to participate in "struggle sessions" in which we were to talk about our "capitalist" tendencies and backgrounds. A woman named Comrade Ma led these sessions with a vengeance. In April of 1959, she became insistent that everyone in our class speak out to contribute to the Party's efforts to "rectify" its previous errors. She held a series of meetings for us to air our views in the spirit of the One Hundred Flowers Campaign. During the first meeting, I managed to avoid speaking out my personal opinions.

For the second meeting, I asked to be excused to attend a baseball game as at that time I was the captain of the university's baseball team. When I tried to get out of the third meeting, Comrade Ma became angry and refused to grant me a leave. From that point on, my fate was out of my hands. Comrade Ma had singled me out and repeatedly accused me of "anti-rightist" tendencies.

On April 27, 1960, I was called to attend another struggle session. My heart stopped in fear when I saw on the blackboard the words: "Meeting to Criticize Rightist Wu Hongda." The person in charge of political education in my department got up and announced: "I now denounce, separate, and expel the rightist Hongda who has consistently refused to mold himself into a good socialist student and has chosen to remain an enemy of the revolution." That night, I was taken to a local detention center and began my nineteen years of imprisonment.

It was much later when I learned that over one hundred teachers and four hundred students from the Geology Institute had been arrested as rightists. Comrade Ma had been the one chiefly responsible for my imprisonment and those of many others.

During my nineteen years in prison, I often experienced harsh treatment at the hands of guards and prison officials. I was beaten and degraded and to this day, I suffer injuries from the abuses that I suffered. In 1962, I was transferred to Tuanhe Farm labor camp. The conditions were so bleak and horrible that two friends and I attempted to escape. Our failure resulted in harsh punishments for all of us. I was thrown into solitary confinement, a cell that was six feet long, three feet wide, and three feet high, slightly larger than a coffin. I was not given any food or water for three days. When the captain in charge came on the seventh day to hear my "confession" to my crime, he kicked me in the side of my body and left. On the ninth day, when I became too weak to eat any food, the captain ordered the guards to force a tube down my throat to feed me. Finally, I was released back to my barracks.

There were, however, several instances when I was shown kindness by prison guards, which helped me survive such brutality. I remember one winter in 1962—the coldest winter I have ever experienced—where I was imprisoned in Section 585 of Qinghe Farm. We were all huddled in our barracks trying to seek warmth from our thin quilts. All of a sudden, we heard the voice of a new guard, Captain Cao, calling us from outside. We dragged ourselves out of the barracks and braced ourselves against the outside walls. We expected to hear some new form of hardship to add to our horrible situation. But instead, Captain Cao announced that we would be receiving an extra ounce of food rations. He also encouraged us to walk outside in the sun every day to regain our strength. As I would take my short walks, Captain Cao would often encourage me: "You're doing very well. You'll be fine. That's enough for today. Go back to rest."

I don't know why Captain Cao showed us such kindness. In reality, his acts were small ones, but to us prisoners, who had not been shown any human kindness for months and even years, his acts were enormous. How could someone like Captain and Comrade Ma exist in the same society?

When I was released in 1979, I felt compelled to look up Comrade Ma in Beijing. She had been promoted for her faithful service to the head position of the Political Work Section of the Beijing Geology Bureau. When I met her in person, I realized that I had nothing to say to her. I did not feel the need to reproach her or accuse her of her wrongdoing toward me. I just wanted her to see that I had survived and had not given in to despair and suicide. She never apologized to me or asked for my forgiveness. "It's over, it's over," she said to me. "All that happened is in the past. The whole country has suffered, our Party has suffered. There have been terrible mistakes. I'm very happy you have come back. We can do something together in the future."

I looked at her and concluded in those few moments that Comrade Ma was so typical of the kind of people that the Communist society had produced. She believed in everything that the Party had done in the name of its people. As I looked at her that day, I felt a brief moment of triumph. You could not destroy all of us, I said to her silently.

In regard to Mr. Wiesenthal's story and in comparing his story to my own, I must first state that it is inconceivable for me to believe that anyone in the People's Republic of China would ask for such forgiveness as the Nazi soldier did to the Jewish prisoner. In China, there was no understanding that what the Communists did to their own people was in any way morally wrong. People like Comrade Ma were so typical. They had no regard for an individual's well-being. There was no value put on a human's life because, quite simply, the leaders of the country placed no value on human life. In order to survive in China during these times, one had to give up one's own conscience and humanity.

Captain Cao was an aberration of that time. To this day, I do not know how he could have existed and acted in such a way without being caught and punished.

Instead, the society that the Communists founded was designed to drain any remnants of humanity out of a person. Like Mr. Wiesenthal, I would not have forgiven the Nazi soldier on his deathbed, but I would have been able to say to him: "I understand why you were a part of a horrible and vicious society. You are responsible for your own actions but everyone else in this society shares that same responsibility with you."

# CONTRIBUTORS

SVEN ALKALAJ is the ambassador of the Republic of Bosnia and Herzegovina to the United States, the first to serve in this position. He was formerly a prominent businessman with "Energoinvest" Sarajevo, the largest company in Bosnia and Herzegovina. Born in 1948, he is a descendant of a well-known Jewish family in Sarajevo which traces its ancestry to Spain's "Golden Age" of Sephardic Jewry.

JEAN AMÉRY was one of Europe's most profound critics and essayists. Fleeing his native Vienna after the proclamation of the Nuremberg Laws, he joined the Resistance in Belgium, where he was subsequently captured by the Gestapo and sent to a series of concentration camps. After the war, he made his home in Belgium until his death in 1978. *At the Mind's Limits: Contemplations by a Survivor on Auschwitz and its Realities* is his unflinching analysis of his own inner world as a Holocaust victim and survivor.

SMAIL BALIĆ, a leading expert on oriental languages, Arab-Islamic history, and Bosnian culture, was born in Mostar in 1920 and earned his doctorate at the University of Vienna. He lived in Vienna for many years, where he lectured on the Turkish language at the Superior School of Commerce. Currently he is a professor in the Department of Islamic-Theological Studies at the University of Sarajevo. Through his scholarly work he seeks to strengthen the cultural and national identity of his people, the Muslim-Bosnians. He is the author of *Das unbekannte Bosnien* (The unknown Bosnia).

MOSHE BEJSKI was born in Poland and was interned in several concentration camps during World War II. He immigrated to Palestine in 1945 where he subsequently served as director of the Youth Aliyah Department in Europe and North Africa. After earning an LL.D. from the Sorbonne, he became a justice of the Supreme Court of Israel. For more than three decades he chaired the Commission for Recognition of Righteous Gentiles at Yad Vashem.

ALAN L. BERGER is the Raddock Eminent Scholar and chairman of Holocaust Studies at Florida Atlantic University in Boca Raton. He was formerly professor in the Department of Religion at Syracuse University where he founded the Jewish Studies Program. Among his books are *Crisis and Covenant* and *Judaism in the Modern World.*

ROBERT McAFEE BROWN is Professor Emeritus of Theology and Ethics at the Pacific School of Religion. He also taught at Union Theological Seminary, Macalester College, and Stanford University. He is the author of *Theology in a New Key; Elie Wiesel, Messenger to All Humanity;* and *Spirituality and Religion and Violence: A Primer for White America.*

HARRY JAMES CARGAS is the author of thirty-one books, including *A Christian Response to the Holocaust; Conversations with Elie Wiesel; Voices from the Holocaust;* and *Reflections of a Post-Auschwitz Christian.* He is the only Catholic ever appointed to the International Advisory Board of Yad Vashem. He serves as vice president of the Annual Scholars Conference on the Holocaust, and on the executive board of the Catholic Center for Holocaust Studies. He is Professor Emeritus of Literature and Language at Webster University, St. Louis, Missouri.

ROBERT COLES is Professor of Psychiatry and Medical Humanities at Harvard Medical School, and James Agee Professor of Social Ethics at Harvard University. He has published studies on children of poverty, for which he received a Pulitzer Prize, and numerous books on the "inner life" of children. He is the author of *Children of Crisis* (five volumes); *The Moral Life of Children; The Spiritual Life of Children; The Call of Stories: Teaching and the Moral Imagination;* and *The Call of Service: A Witness to Idealism.*

THE DALAI LAMA, Tenzin Gyatso, His Holiness the 14th Dalai Lama of Tibet, is spiritual leader of Buddhists around the world and revered as a teacher and man of peace. In 1959 he escaped to India, following China's invasion and occupation of Tibet. As spiritual and political leader of the Tibetan people, he has consistently advocated policies of nonviolence and compassion in the face of aggression. He was awarded the Nobel Peace Prize in 1989.

EUGENE J. FISHER is associate director of the Secretariat for Ecumenical and Interreligious Affairs of the National Conference of Catholic Bishops. He holds a doctorate in Hebrew Studies from New York University and has authored or edited over a dozen books in the field of Jewish-Christian studies, including *Spiritual Pilgrimage: Pope John Paul II on the Jews and Judaism*, coedited with Leon Klenicki, which won the National Jewish Book Award in 1995.

EDWARD H. FLANNERY is a Roman Catholic priest living near Providence, Rhode Island. He served as a member of the National Conference of Catholic Bishops' Secretariat for Catholic-Jewish Relations and on the executive committee of the National Christian Leadership Conference for Israel. Father Flannery is the author of *The Anguish of the Jews*.

EVA FLEISCHNER is Professor Emerita of Religion at Montclair State University. A member of the Church Relations Committee of the U.S. Holocaust Memorial Council and of the Advisory Board of the U.S. Catholic Conference, Office of Catholic-Jewish Relations, she is the author of *The View of Judaism in German Christian Theology* and *Auschwitz: Beginning a New Era?*

MATTHEW FOX is president of the new University of Creation Spirituality in Oakland, California. He is the author of numerous books on spirituality and culture, including *The Reinvention of Work; Original Blessing;* and *The Physics of Angels* with scientist Rupert Sheldrake. He was a Roman Catholic priest of the Dominican Order for twenty-eight years. He is now an Episcopal priest.

MARK GOULDEN, a British journalist and publisher, began his career as a reporter and editor for several newspapers and periodicals. Chairman of the British publishing firm of W. H. Allen and Co. for thirty-six years, he received numerous citations and awards for his work in humanitarian causes. He was also a pioneer in British civil aviation. He died in 1980.

HANS HABE, born in Hungary, began his literary career as a reporter and newspaper editor in Vienna. His most noted book, *The Mission*, is a documentary novel on the Evian Conference in 1938, which sought to deal with the refugee problem resulting from Nazi persecutions. After World War II, he was editor-in-chief of *Die Neue Zeitung* (Munich). A recipient of the Herzl Prize, his works include *Poisoned Stream* and *Proud Zion*. He died in 1977.

YOSSI KLEIN HALEVI grew up in New York, the son of a Holocaust survivor. He makes his home in Israel, where he is a senior writer for *The Jerusalem Report* magazine. He has written *Memoirs of a Jewish Extremist*, an autobiography.

ARTHUR HERTZBERG is the Bronfman Visiting Professor of the Humanities at New York University and Professor Emeritus of Religion at Dartmouth College. Rabbi Hertzberg is the author of many books, including *The Zionist Idea; The French Enlightenment and the Jews; The Jews in America;* and *Judaism.* He is also a frequent contributor to *The New York Times* and *The New York Review of Books.*

THEODORE M. HESBURGH, C.S.C., became president emeritus of Notre Dame in 1987, after heading the institution for thirty-five years. Paralleling his career in higher education, Dr. Hesburgh's life in public service includes fifteen presidential appointments as well as service to the Church under four popes. He is a recipient of the Medal of Freedom for his long-standing interest in peace and development issues and a board member of the U.S. Institute for Peace.

ABRAHAM JOSHUA HESCHEL, the noted theologian and philosopher, was born in Warsaw and taught extensively in Europe before coming to the United States in 1940. He was chosen as Martin Buber's successor at the Frankfort Lehrhaus, an institute for adult Jewish education. He taught Jewish philosophy, ethics, and mysticism at the Jewish Theological Seminary of America until his death in 1972. Rabbi Heschel was active in the civil rights movement, marching with the Reverend Martin Luther King, Jr., and in the Jewish-Christian dialogue preceding Vatican Council II. His original philosophy of religion is reflected in his numerous books: *Man Is Not Alone; God in Search of Man; The Prophets; The Sabbath;* and *Israel: An Echo of Eternity.*

CHRISTOPHER HOLLIS, a British journalist and author, was a former member of Parliament. He served in the R.A.F. during World War II. Among his published books are *Church and Economics; The Papacy;* and *Holy Places: Jewish, Christian and Muslim Monuments in the Holy Land.* He died in 1977.

RODGER KAMENETZ is a poet and author of *The Jew in the Lotus,* an account of Jewish Buddhist dialogue. He directs the Jewish Studies minor at Louisiana State University in Baton Rouge.

CARDINAL FRANZ KÖNIG, appointed cardinal in 1958, was formerly archbishop of Vienna. A theologian and scholar, he is the author of *The Bible in View of World History* and the three-volume *Christ and World Religions.*

HAROLD S. KUSHNER is Rabbi Laureate of Temple Israel in Natick, Massachusetts. He is the author of such influential works as *When Bad Things Happen to Good People; When Children Ask About God;* and *To Life! A Celebration of Jewish Being and Thinking.* He has taught at the Jewish Theological Seminary and Clark University.

LAWRENCE L. LANGER is Professor Emeritus of English at Simmons College in Boston. Among his books are *The Holocaust and the Literary Imagination; Holocaust Testimonies: The Ruins of Memory; Art from the Ashes: A Holocaust Anthology;* and *Admitting the Holocaust: Collected Essays.*

PRIMO LEVI, born in Turin, was both a working chemist and a distinguished writer who won almost every major literary award in his native Italy. Arrested as a member of the anti-Fascist resistance, he was deported to Auschwitz in 1944, where he remained until the camp was liberated. Levi's experience in the death camp is the subject of his two memoirs, *Survival in Auschwitz* and *The Reawakening.* He is also the author of *The Periodic Table; The Drowned and the Saved; Moments of Reprieve;* and *If Not Now, When?* He died in 1987.

DEBORAH E. LIPSTADT is Dorot Professor of Modern Jewish and Holocaust Studies at Emory University in Atlanta, Georgia, and author of *Beyond Belief: The American Press and the Coming of the Holocaust 1933–1945* and *Denying the Holocaust: The Growing Assault on Truth and Memory.*

FRANKLIN H. LITTELL studied history with Clair Francis Littell, theology with Reinhold Niebuhr, and church history with Roland Bainton and Kenneth Scott Latourette. He is

Professor Emeritus of Religion at Temple University, and has served as Distinguished Visiting Professor in several schools since 1986, most recently at Richard Stockton College of New Jersey. He has written over two dozen books, including *The Crucifixion of the Jews,* and several hundred articles.

HUBERT G. LOCKE recently retired as dean and professor of the Graduate School of Public Affairs at the University of Washington in Seattle. He is cofounder (with Franklin Littell) and vice president of the Annual Scholars Conference on the Holocaust. Among his books are *Exile in the Fatherland: Martin Niemoeller's Letters from Moabit Prison* and *The Church Confronts the Nazis.*

ERICH H. LOEWY, M.D., is Professor and Alumni Chair of Bioethics at the University of California at Davis. He is the author of *Ethical Dilemmas in Modern Medicine: A Physician's Viewpoint* and *Suffering and the Beneficent Community.*

HERBERT MARCUSE, who taught philosophy at Columbia University, Harvard, Brandeis, and the University of California at San Diego, was one of the most perceptive analysts of advanced industrial society and a leading influence on the New Left. Born in Berlin, he left Germany for the United States in 1934 and served with the U.S. Office of Strategic Services and the State Department during World War II. His major works are *Eros and Civilization; One-Dimensional Man; Soviet Marxism;* and *Reason and Revolution.* He died in 1979.

MARTIN E. MARTY has taught American religious history at the University of Chicago since 1963 and made comparative studies of worldwide movements such as fundamentalisms and ethnonationalisms. He is also senior editor of *The Christian Century* and author of many books, including the three-volume *Modern American Religion.*

CYNTHIA OZICK has won numerous prizes and awards for her novels, short stories, and essays. She is the author most recently of *Fame & Folly: Essays* and *The Puttermesser Papers,* a novel. She is a member of the American Academy of Arts and Letters, and her work has been translated into most major languages.

JOHN T. PAWLIKOWSKI, a priest of the Servite Order, is Professor of Social Ethics at the Catholic Theological Union in Chicago. He has served on the U.S. Holocaust memorial council since its inception in 1980. He is a member of the Catholic Bishops' Commission for Relations with Jews and is the author of *The Challenge of the Holocaust for Christian Theology* and *Jesus and the Theology of Israel.*

DENNIS PRAGER has been a radio talk show host in Los Angeles since 1982, and has lectured widely on moral, personal, and religious issues. Since 1985, he has been writing his own quarterly journal, *Ultimate Issues.* His books include *The Nine Questions People Ask About Judaism* coauthored with Joseph Telushkin, *Why the Jews? The Reason for Antisemitism,* and *Think a Second Time: 43 Essays on 43 Subjects.*

DITH PRAN's wartime life was portrayed in the award-winning movie *The Killing Fields.* He served as a war correspondent, together with Sydney Schanberg of *The New York Times,* covering the civil war in Cambodia from 1972 to 1975. He was arrested by the Khmer Rouge and exiled to the forced labor camps where he endured four years of starvation and torture before escaping to Thailand, and later, the United States. In 1976, Schanberg accepted the Pulitzer Prize on behalf of himself and Pran. Pran is a photojournalist for *The New York Times* and continues his efforts to publicize the plight of the Cambodian people and bring the Khmer Rouge leaders to the World Court.

TERENCE PRITTIE, a noted British journalist and author, reported from West Germany for the *Manchester Guardian* from 1946 to 1963. Subsequently, he served as a political consultant on Middle East affairs for the BBC and other news agencies. He is the author of *Germans Against Hitler* and *Willy Brandt: Portrait of a Statesman.* He died in 1985.

JOSHUA RUBENSTEIN is the northeast regional director of Amnesty International USA and a Fellow at the Kathryn W. and Shelby Cullom Davis Center for Russian Studies at Harvard University. He is the author of *Soviet Dissidents: Their Struggle for Human Rights* and *Tangled Loyalties: The Life and Times of Ilya Ehrenburg.*

DOROTHEE SOELLE is a theologian who teaches in her native Germany as well as at Union Theological Seminary in New York. Among her publications are *Choosing Life; Of War and Love; Political Theology;* and *Beyond Mere Obedience.* She was the first theologian to be awarded the Theodore Heuss Medal for "civil courage and democracy."

ALBERT SPEER was a high-ranking Nazi, one of the planners of the Third Reich and Hitler's minister of armaments from 1942 to 1945. At the Nuremberg trials, he admitted responsibility for actions of the Nazis and was sentenced to twenty years' imprisonment. In prison he wrote two books: *Inside the Third Reich* and *Spandau: The Secret Diaries.* He died in 1981.

MANÈS SPERBER, French author and editor, was born in Galicia and educated in Vienna, where he studied psychology with Alfred Adler. He escaped to France when the Nazis came to power. He worked for the French publishing house Calmann-Levy, and later turned to literature, writing in German and in French. His works include *The Burned Bramble; The Abyss; Journey Without End; The Achilles Heel;* and *Man and His Deeds.* He died in 1984.

ANDRÉ STEIN is Professor of Human Communications at the University of Toronto. He is also a practicing psychotherapist with Holocaust survivors. He is the author of *Broken Silence: Dialogues from the Edge; Quiet Heroes: True Stories of the Rescue of Jews in Nazi-Occupied Holland;* and *Hidden Children: Forgotten Survivors of the Holocaust.*

NECHAMA TEC is Professor of Sociology at the University of Connecticut. She is the author of six books, including *Defiance: The Bielski Partisans* (winner of the International Anne Frank Special Recognition Prize); *Dry Tears: The Story of a Lost Childhood;* and *When Light Pierced the Darkness: Christian Rescue of Jews in Nazi-Occupied Poland.*

JOSEPH TELUSHKIN is rabbi of the Synagogue of the Performing Arts in Los Angeles, and the author of *Jewish Literacy* and most recently of *Words That Hurt, Words That Heal.* He is co-author with Dennis Prager of *The Nine Questions People Ask About*

*Judaism* and *Why the Jews? The Reason for Antisemitism.* He lives in New York City.

TZVETAN TODOROV, born in Bulgaria in 1939, has lived in France since 1963. He is director of research at the Centre National de Recherches in Paris and has published many books on literature and society, among them *Facing the Extreme: Moral Life in the Concentration Camps.* An internationally renowned writer and critic, he has been a visiting professor at Columbia, Yale, and Berkeley.

ARTHUR WASKOW is a rabbi and a Pathfinder of ALEPH: Alliance for Jewish Renewal. He is the author of *Godwrestling—Round 2, Seasons of Our Joy,* and *Down-to-Earth Judaism: Food, Money, Sex, and the Rest of Life,* and coauthor of *Tales of Tikkun.*

HARRY WU was imprisoned by the Chinese Communist government for nineteen years in a labor camp in Laogai. He now writes and lectures worldwide on slave labor camps from his headquarters in Oakland, California. His books, *Laogai, Bitter Winds,* and *Troublemaker,* expose the harsh conditions in his native China. Among the honors he has received are the China Democracy Honor Award, the Lawyers Committee for Human Rights Award, the Peace Abbey Award, and the Hungary Freedom Fighter Federation Award.

# A NOTE ABOUT THE AUTHOR

SIMON WIESENTHAL was born in 1908 in Buczacz, Galicia, then part of the Austro-Hungarian Empire. A recent graduate of the Czech Technical University in Prague and the Polytechnic Institute in Lvov, he had just begun to work in an architectural office in Lvov when Poland was invaded by the Nazis. From 1941 to 1945, Mr. Wiesenthal was a prisoner in several ghettos and concentration camps, including Buchenwald and Mauthausen. By the war's end, he and his wife had lost eighty-nine family members to the Nazi murderers.

After the war, Mr. Wiesenthal joined the American Commission for War Crimes and was later transferred to the O.S.S. at Linz. In 1946, with thirty other concentration camp survivors, he founded the Jewish Historical Documentation Center, which functioned in the American Zone until 1954, and reopened in Vienna in 1961. Its task is to identify and locate Nazi war criminals. The center's work was instrumental in bringing over 1,100 Nazi criminals to justice.

Mr. Wiesenthal has been honored with numerous awards for his work, including "Commander of the Order of Orange" in the Netherlands, "Commendatore de la Republica Italiana" in Italy, a gold medal for humanitarian work by the United States Congress, the Jerusalem Medal in Israel, and sixteen honorary doctorates. The Simon Wiesenthal Center in Los Angeles, which has branches in New York, Miami, Toronto, and abroad, is named in his honor. Among his best-known books are *The Murderers Among Us; Justice, Not Vengeance; Sails of Hope;* and *Every Day Remembrance Day,* all of which have been translated into many languages.